T0231684

Security
in an IPv6
Environment

Security
in an IPv6
Environment

Daniel Minoli • Jake Kouns

CRC Press
Taylor & Francis Group
Boca Raton   London   New York

CRC Press is an imprint of the
Taylor & Francis Group, an **informa** business
AN AUERBACH BOOK

Auerbach Publications
Taylor & Francis Group
6000 Broken Sound Parkway NW, Suite 300
Boca Raton, FL 33487-2742

© 2009 by Taylor & Francis Group, LLC
Auerbach is an imprint of Taylor & Francis Group, an Informa business

International Standard Book Number-13: 978-1-4200-9229-5 (Hardcover)

Library of Congress Cataloging-in-Publication Data

Minoli, Daniel, 1952-
    Security in an IPv6 environment / authors, Daniel Minoli, Jake Kouns.
        p. cm.
    Includes bibliographical references and index.
    ISBN 978-1-4200-9229-5 (alk. paper)
    1. Computer networks--Security measures. 2. Wireless communication systems--Security measures. 3. TCP/IP (Computer network protocol) I. Kouns, Jake. II. Title.

TK5105.59.M56 2009
005.8--dc22   2008044401

Visit the Taylor & Francis Web site at
http://www.taylorandfrancis.com

and the Auerbach Web site at
http://www.auerbach-publications.com

Dedication

For Anna (Dan)
and
For Jill, Elora, and my family (Jake)

Contents

Chapter 3
More Advanced IPv6 Protocol Mechanisms

Chapter 4

Preface

Internet Protocol Version 6 (IPv6) is a technology now being deployed in various parts of the world that will allow truly explicit end-to-end device addressability. As the number of intelligent systems that need direct access expands to the multiple billions (e.g., including cell phones, PDAs, appliances, sensors/actuators/ Smart Dust, and even body-worn bio-metric devices), IPv6 becomes an institutional imperative in the final analysis. The expectation is that by 2010 and beyond there will be increased use of IPv6. IPv6 is already gaining momentum globally, with major interest and activity in Europe and Asia, and there also is some traction in the United States. For example, in 2005 the U.S. Government Accountability Office (GAO) recommended that all agencies become proactive in planning a coherent transition to IPv6. Specifically, OMB Memorandum M-05-22 directed that agencies must transition from IPv4 Agency infrastructures to IPv6 Agency infrastructures (network backbones) by June 2008. Where specific agency task orders required connectivity and compliance with IPv6 networks, service providers needed to ensure that services delivered support federal agencies as required to comply with OMB IPv6 directives. All agency infrastructures had to be using IPv6 by June 30, 2008 (meaning that the network backbone was either operating a dual stack network core or it was operating in a pure IPv6 mode, i.e., IPv6-compliant and configured to carry operational IPv6 traffic) and agency networks must have interface with this infrastructure. This goal was actually met, implying that broader deployment is now likely.

Corporations and institutions need to start planning at this time how to kick off the transition planning process and determining how best coexistence can be maintained during the 3- to 6-year window that will likely be required to achieve the global worldwide transition, and this book addresses the migration and macro-level scalability requirements for this transition.

Security considerations continue to be critically important. With the increased number of mission-critical commercial and military operations being supported via distributed, mobile, always-connected, hybrid public–private networks, and with the increased number of attackers or inimical agents, it is mandatory that high-assurance security mechanisms be in place in all computing environments and in various layered modes.

Key questions are being asked about the security aspects and subtending apparatuses of IPv6. While there is a reasonably extensive open literature on the topic, there is currently no book that covers the topic in a systematic manner. This text pulls together and organizes this pool of knowledge in a logically organized manner. The basic material is based on or drawn from industry sources and RFCs. Some of the pragmatic considerations are based on the authors' own security experience. This text is *not* intended to be an exhaustive treatment of all topics related to IPv6 or IPv6 security, but a point of departure for a treatment of the topic. This text can be used by corporate and government professionals, developers, security stakeholders, and college instructors.

Even network/security administrators who operate in a pure IPv4 environment need to be aware of IPv6-related security issues, because there could be a compromise of security in these traditional networks if the administrators do not at least have a rudimentary understanding of IPv6 security principles, as we discuss in the text.

Consistent with the goal of providing a systematic treatment, this book covers the field in a terse and pragmatic manner. After an overview and introduction in Chapter 1, Chapters 2 and 3 provide a primer on IPv6. Chapter 4 discusses general security mechanisms and approaches. Chapter 5 discusses other IPv6 security features. Chapter 6 covers the fundamental topic of IPsec and its use in IPv6 environments. Chapter 7 looks at firewall use in IPv6 environments. Finally, Chapter 8 addresses security considerations for migration environments that may consist of mixed IPv4-IPv6 networks.

About the Authors

Daniel Minoli has many years of technical hands-on and managerial experience in networking, telecom, wireless, video, Enterprise Architecture, and security for global Best-In-Class carriers and financial companies. He has done extensive work in IPv6, including leading-edge topics such as Voice-over-IPv6 (work documented in the first text on the topic of *Voice Over IPv6—Architecting the Next-Generation VoIP*, Elsevier, 2006), satellite communications in an IPv6 environment (work documented in the first text on the topic of *Satellite Systems Engineering in an IPv6 Environment*, Auerbach Publications, Taylor & Francis Group, 2009), IPv4 to IPv6 migration of commercial and institutional networks (work documented in the *Handbook of IPv4 to IPv6 Transition Methodologies for Institutional & Corporate Networks*, Taylor & Francis, 2008) (coauthored)), and, security in general (work documented in the *Minoli–Cordovana Authoritative Computer and Network Security Dictionary*, Wiley, 2006 (coauthored)).

Mr. Minoli has worked at financial firms such as AIG, Prudential Securities, Capital One Financial, and service provider firms such as Network Analysis Corporation, Bell Telephone Laboratories, ITT, Bell Communications Research (now Telcordia), AT&T, Leading Edge Networks, Inc., and SES Americom, where he is director of Terrestrial Systems Engineering. SES is the largest satellite company in the world. He also played a founding role in the launching of two companies through the high-tech incubator Leading Edge Networks, Inc., which he ran in the early 2000s: Global Wireless Services, a provider of secure broadband hotspot mobile Internet and hotspot VoIP services; and InfoPort Communications Group, an optical and Gigabit Ethernet metropolitan carrier supporting Data Center/SAN/channel extension and Grid Computing network access services. For several years he has been Session-, Tutorial-, and now overall technical program chair for the IEEE ENTNET (Enterprise Networking) conference. ENTNET focuses on enterprise networking requirements for large financial firms and other corporate institutions.

Mr. Minoli has also written columns for *ComputerWorld, NetworkWorld,* and *Network Computing* (1985–2006). He has taught at New York University (Information Technology Institute), Rutgers University, and Stevens Institute of Technology (1984–2006). Also, he was a technology analyst at large for

Gartner/DataPro (1985–2001); based on extensive hands-on work at financial firms and carriers, he tracked technologies and wrote CTO/CIO-level technical scans in the area of telephony and data systems, including topics on security, disaster recovery, network management, LANs, WANs (ATM and MPLS), wireless (LAN and public hotspot), VoIP, network design/economics, carrier networks (such as metro Ethernet and CWDM/DWDM), and e-commerce. Over the years he has advised venture capitals for investments of $150M in a dozen high-tech companies. He has acted as expert witness in a (won) $11B lawsuit regarding a VoIP-based wireless air-to-ground communication system, and has been involved as a technical expert in a number of patent infringement proceedings.

Jake Kouns is a business-focused technology and information security executive with an extensive knowledge base and international experience. He focuses on the application of security concepts across a broad range on information technology areas including data communications, network design, operations, database structures, operating systems, application development, and disaster recovery. He holds numerous certifications including ISC2's CISSP, and ISACA's CISM and CISA.

Mr. Kouns is currently the director of Information Security and Network Services for Markel Corporation, a specialty insurance company. He has created and implemented a repeatable information security program from the ground up to ensure that risks are properly managed as part of normal business operations. Prior to his current role he was senior network security manager for Capital One Financial, a Fortune 200 financial institution where he provided technical management, consulting, architecture and design implementation for a wide array of security mitigating strategies. He was responsible for the day-to-day global security management of a large complex firewall environment, intrusion detection, risk assessment, and resolving incidents in a timely manner.

Mr. Kouns has twice presented for Check Point Software Technologies as an expert in global firewall management and intrusion detection. In recent years, Mr. Kouns' main focus has been spent redefining the information security vulnerability industry, and he has presented on the topic at many well-known security conferences including CanSecWest and SyScan. He has also been interviewed as an expert in the security industry by *Information Week, eWeek, Processor.com, Federal Computer Week, Government Computer News* and *SC Magazine*.

Mr. Kouns is co-founder and president of the Open Security Foundation (OSF), a 501(c)3 nonprofit organization that oversees the operations of the Open Source Vulnerability Database (OSVDB.org). OSVDB is an independent and open source database created by and for the community. The goal of the OSVDB project is to provide accurate, detailed, current, and unbiased technical information on security vulnerabilities. The project manages a master collection of computer security vulnerabilities, available for free use by the world's information security community.

Chapter 1

Introduction, Overview, and Motivations

1.1 Introduction and Motivations

IP Version 6 (IPv6), defined in the mid-1990s in Request for Comments (RFC) 2460 "Internet Protocol, Version 6 (IPv6) Specification" and a host of other more recent RFCs, is an "improved, streamlined, successor version" of IP version 4 (IPv4).* Because of market pull from the Office of Management and Budget's mandate that 24 major federal agencies in the U.S. Government (USG) be IPv6-ready by June 30, 2008, a goal that was met, and because of market pull from European and Asian institutions, IPv6 is expected to see gradual deployment from this point forward and in the coming decade. IPv6 is already gaining momentum globally, with major interest and activity in Europe and Asia and also some traction in the U.S; the expectation is that in the next few years a (slow) transition to this new protocol will occur worldwide. An IP-based infrastructure has now become the ubiquitous underlying architecture for commercial, institutional, and USG/Other (non-U.S.) Government (OG) communications and services functions. IPv6 is expected to be the next step in the industry evolution of the past 50 years from analog to digital to packet to broadband.

IPv6 offers the potential of achieving increased scalability, reachability, end-to-end interworking, Quality of Service (QoS), and commercial-grade robustness for data communication, mobile connectivity, and for Voice Over IP (VoIP)/triple-play networks. The current version of the Internet Protocol, IPv4, has been in use

---

* IPv6 was originally defined in [RFC 1883], [RFC 1884], and [RFC 1885], December 1995. [RFC 2460] obsoletes [RFC 1883].

successfully for almost 30 years and exhibits some challenges in supporting emerging demands for address space cardinality, high-density mobility, multimedia, and strong security. This is particularly true in developing domestic and defense department applications utilizing peer-to-peer networking. IPv6 is an improved version of IP that is designed to coexist with IPv4 while providing better internetworking capabilities than IPv4.

When the current version of the Internet Protocol (IPv4) was conceived in the mid-1970s and defined soon thereafter (1981), it provided just over 4 billion addresses. That is not enough to provide each person on the planet with one address without even considering the myriad of other devices and device modules needing addressability (such as, but not limited to, over 3 billion cell phones.) Additionally, 74% of IPv4 addresses have been assigned to North American organizations. The goal of developers is to be able to assign IP addresses to a new class of Internet-capable devices: mobile phones, car navigation systems, home appliances, industrial equipment, and other devices (such as sensors and Body-Area-Network medical devices). All of these devices can then be linked together, constantly communicating, even wirelessly. Projections show that the current generation of the Internet will "run out of space" in the near future (2010/2011) if IPv6 is not adopted around the world. IPv6 is an essential technology for ambient intelligence and will be a key driver for a multitude of new, innovative mobile/wireless applications and services [DIR200801].

IPv6 was initially developed in the early 1990s because of the anticipated need for more end system addresses based on anticipated Internet growth, encompassing mobile phone deployment, smart home appliances, and billions of new users in developing countries (e.g., in China and India). New technologies and applications such as VoIP, "always-on access" (e.g., Digital Subscriber Line and cable), Ethernet-to-the-home, converged networks, and evolving ubiquitous computing applications will continue to drive this need even more in the next few years [IPV200501].

IPv6 features, in comparison with IPv4, include the following [RFC0791]:

- Expanded Addressing Capabilities. IPv6 increases the IP address size from 32 bits to 128 bits, to support more levels in the addressing hierarchy, a much greater number of addressable nodes, and simpler autoconfiguration of addresses. The scalability of multicast routing is improved by adding a "scope" field to multicast addresses. A new type of address called an "anycast address" is also defined to be used to send a packet to any one of a group of nodes.
- Header Format Simplification. Some IPv4 header fields have been dropped or made optional, to reduce the common-case processing cost of packet handling and to limit the bandwidth cost of the IPv6 header.
- Authentication and Privacy Capabilities. In IPv6, security is built in as part of the protocol suite: extensions to support authentication, data integrity (encryption), and (optional) data confidentiality are specified for IPv6. The

security features of IPv6 are described in the Security Architecture for the Internet Protocol RFC 2401 [RFC2401], along with RFC 2402 [RFC2402] and RFC 2406 [RFC2406]; Internet Protocol Security (IPsec), defined in these RFCs, is required (mandatory). IPsec is a set of protocols and related mechanisms that supports confidentiality and integrity. (IPsec was originally developed as part of the IPv6 specification, but due to the need for security in the IPv4 environment, it has also been adapted for IPv4.)

■ Flow Labeling Capability. A new feature is added to enable the labeling of packets belonging to particular traffic "flows" for which the sender requests special handling, such as non-default quality of service or "real-time" service. Services such as VoIP and IP-based entertainment video delivery (known as IPTV) is becoming broadly deployed, and flow labeling, especially in the network core, can be very beneficial.

■ Improved Support for Extensions and Options. Changes in the way IP header options are encoded allows for more efficient forwarding, less stringent limits on the length of options, and greater flexibility for introducing new options in the future.

Figure 1.1 depicts the positioning of IPv6 in the overall protocol stack of typical end systems. End systems (such as PCs and servers), Network Elements (customer-owned or carrier-owned) and (perhaps) applications need to be IPv6-aware to communicate in the IPv6 environment. IPv6 has been enabled on many computing platforms. At this juncture, many operating systems come with IPv6 enabled by default; IPv6-ready Operating Systems (OS) include but are not limited to: Mac OS X, OpenBSD, NetBSD, FreeBSD, Linux, Windows Vista, Windows XP (Service Pack 2), Windows 2003 Server, and Windows 2008 Server. Java began supporting IPv6 with J2SE 1.4 (in 2002) on Solaris and Linux. Support for IPv6 on Windows was added with J2SE 1.5. Other languages, such as C and C++ also support IPv6.

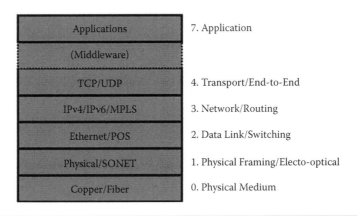

Applications	7. Application
(Middleware)	
TCP/UDP	4. Transport/End-to-End
IPv4/IPv6/MPLS	3. Network/Routing
Ethernet/POS	2. Data Link/Switching
Physical/SONET	1. Physical Framing/Electo-optical
Copper/Fiber	0. Physical Medium

Figure 1.1   Typical communications stack.

At this time, the number of applications with native IPv6 support is significant given that most important networking applications provide native IPv6 support. Hardware vendors including Apple Computer, Cisco Systems, HP, Hitachi, IBM, Microsoft, Nortel Networks, and Sun Microsystems support IPv6. Figure 1.2 depicts an example of a vendor's roadmap, to illustrate progress being made over the years in IPv6 support. One should note that IPv6 was designed with security in mind, but at the current time its implementation and deployment are (much) less mature than is the case for IPv4. When IPv4 was developed in the early 1980s, security was not a consideration; now a number of mechanisms have been added to address security considerations to IP. When IPv6 was developed in the early-to-mid 1990s, security was a consideration; hence a number of mechanisms have been built into the protocol from the get-go to furnish security capabilities to IP.*

Security considerations continue to be critically important in the networking and computing space. With the increased number of mission-critical commercial and military operations being supported via distributed, mobile, always-connected,

---

* Some purists will argue (perhaps as an exercise in semantics), that since IPsec is *available* also to IPv4, that IPv6 and IPv4 have the same level of security. We take the approach in this text that since the use of IPsec is mandated as required in IPv6 while it is optional in IPv4, that at *the practical, actual level*, "IPv6 is more secure." We know firsthand, for example, of credit card companies with extranets reaching numerous foreign locations that are supposed to be using encryption (IPsec) in their wide area IPv4 links when they do transborder transmission of sensitive personal credit card information, and in fact do not, on the excuse that their WAN routers are out of "bandwidth points" (well, just get new routers that can support such bandwidth points and protect sensitive personal credit card information). IPv6 mandates the use of IPv6, so if IPsec were used in this case, the encryption would be there by design or default.

Purists would argue philosophical points forever, but we approach the matter pragmatically: If State A mandated the use of helmets for motorcycle riders and State B does not, we believe statistics would show that riders are "safer" in State A by actual number of injuries and deaths; well, riders in State B always have the *option* of using helmets, but the question is "what do the actual accidents stats show?" If State A mandated the use of seatbelts for car riders and State B does not, we believe statistics would show that riders are "safer" in State A by actual number of injuries and deaths; well, riders in State B always have the *option* of using seatbelts, but the question is "what do the actual accidents stats show?" If State A mandated the use hardhats in construction sites and State B does not, we believe statistics would show that workers are "safer" in State A by actual number of injuries and deaths; well, workers in State B always have the *option* of using hardhats, but the question is "what do the actual accidents stats show?"

We believe that enough "ink on paper" has been spent here on this semantics issue and proceed by taking the position that, when everything else is equal, in a narrow abstract sense IPv6 is pragmatically more secure than IPv4. Naturally IPv6 is vulnerable to a multitude of attacks, infractions, compromises, and penetrations. That is precisely why these authors have written this book: because there is a need to lay out a plan, an approach, a strategy, a policy, and a set of tools to protect an IPv6-based infrastructure. The challenge is to make "everything else equal," equal firewall support, equal Intrusion Detection System (IDS) support, and so forth. Read on …

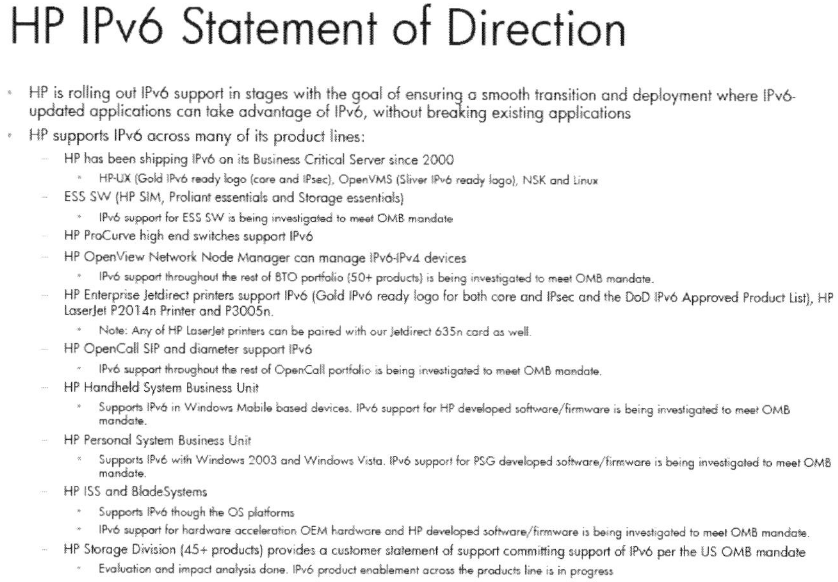

HP IPv6 Statement of Direction

- HP is rolling out IPv6 support in stages with the goal of ensuring a smooth transition and deployment where IPv6-updated applications can take advantage of IPv6, without breaking existing applications
- HP supports IPv6 across many of its product lines:
    - HP has been shipping IPv6 on its Business Critical Server since 2000
        - HP-UX (Gold IPv6 ready logo (core and IPsec), OpenVMS (Sliver IPv6 ready logo), NSK and Linux
    - ESS SW (HP SIM, Proliant essentials and Storage essentials)
        - IPv6 support for ESS SW is being investigated to meet OMB mandate
    - HP ProCurve high end switches support IPv6
    - HP OpenView Network Node Manager can manage IPv6-IPv4 devices
        - IPv6 support throughout the rest of BTO portfolio (50+ products) is being investigated to meet OMB mandate.
    - HP Enterprise Jetdirect printers support IPv6 (Gold IPv6 ready logo for both core and IPsec and the DoD IPv6 Approved Product List), HP LaserJet P2014n Printer and P3005n.
        - Note: Any of HP LaserJet printers can be paired with our Jetdirect 635n card as well.
    - HP OpenCall SIP and diameter support IPv6
        - IPv6 support throughout the rest of OpenCall portfolio is being investigated to meet OMB mandate.
    - HP Handheld System Business Unit
        - Supports IPv6 in Windows Mobile based devices. IPv6 support for HP developed software/firmware is being investigated to meet OMB mandate.
    - HP Personal System Business Unit
        - Supports IPv6 with Windows 2003 and Windows Vista. IPv6 support for PSG developed software/firmware is being investigated to meet OMB mandate.
    - HP ISS and BladeSystems
        - Supports IPv6 though the OS platforms
        - IPv6 support for hardware acceleration OEM hardware and HP developed software/firmware is being investigated to meet OMB mandate.
    - HP Storage Division (45+ products) provides a customer statement of support committing support of IPv6 per the US OMB mandate
        - Evaluation and impact analysis done. IPv6 product enablement across the products line is in progress

Figure 1.2   Illustrative roadmap.

hybrid public-private networks, and with the increased number of attackers or inimical agents, it is mandatory that high-assurance security mechanisms be in place in all computing environments and in various layered models. Given the avalanche of daily security threats being identified and directed at all sorts of corporate IT assets, ranging from PCs, midrange servers, mainframes, networks, storage systems, telecommunications and VoIP systems, and cell phones, to list just a few, the case for the effective proactive management of these IT and networking security risks does not require much motivation these days. Issues of concern include but are not limited to: interception, interruption, modification, and fabrication of corporate/institutional information. In general, infractions may entail inadvertent acts, deliberate nefarious acts, so-called Acts of God, technical failure, and management malfeasance/failure. Many agencies in USG/Department of Defense (DoD) are moving toward the introduction of next-generation systems to support collaborative architectures, geospatial application, net-centric warfare, mobility, and continuity of operations (COOP), as well as numerous other applications to better suit their mission; IPv6 security is critical to these stakeholders [JUN200801]. Attackers have already developed IPv6 Denial of Service (DoS) attacks and are exploiting weaknesses in IPv6/IPv4 tunneled networks. Tunneling is a key technique for transitioning between an IPv4 and an IPv6 environment. IPsec tunnels transit through normal firewalls or Network Address Translation (NAT) devices. It follows that tunneled IPsec traffic may contain malware, and so, new, appropriate security techniques are needed in IPv6 environments.

This recent quote is very revealing, if not alarming:

> Network administrators managing IPv4 networks often overlook or ignore IPv6. They typically do not recognize its presence or its availability, and they frequently lack the skills or expertise to manage it. So they assume it is not present on their networks. Unfortunately, this assumption is erroneous: IPv6 is available nearly anywhere IPv4 is available, because of transitional mechanisms defined by IETF [Internet Engineering Task Force]. Due to ignorance, lack of experience, and inertia, the security and administrative personnel tasked with defending IPv4 networks have not kept pace with the growth of IPv6. The underground community of black hats knows IPv6, and has developed the expertise to take advantage of it—especially given the relative lack of expertise on the part of the average network administrator. This expertise reflects a similar regional divide to the deployment of IPv6, with better IPv6 skills developing in parts of the world that are less rich in IPv4 technology [WAR200401].

Only a handful of organizations have developed principle-based security architecture frameworks intended to define the necessary elements of security. Most companies still take a fragmented, piecemeal view of security management, often even in the case of large Fortune 1000 firms. What is needed is a comprehensive framework for the uniform and organized treatment of all aspects of security facing an organization. This can be accomplished through a well-thought-out Security Architecture plan. An architecture is a blueprint for the optimal and target-conformant placement of resources in the Information Technologies (IT) environment for the ultimate support of the business function. A Security Architecture is an architecture plan that describes (a) the security services that a system is required to provide to meet the needs of its users, (b) the elements required to implement the services, and, (c) the behaviors of the elements (including the performance goals) to deal with the threat environment. Specifically, a Security Architecture includes administrative security, telecom and network security, computer security, emanations (radiation) security, personnel security, and physical security.

As part of an overall Security Architecture, organizations need security mechanisms to guard against network infractions, or breaches into a network to then use it as a vector to further compromise other IT assets. The industry has had about 20 years to develop layered approaches to network security in an IPv4 environment (the first firewall was developed in 1988). Key questions are now being posed about the security aspects and subtending apparatuses of IPv6. As the industry begins to migrate to IPv6, basic questions arise as to:

■ What vulnerabilities do IPv6 networks have?
■ What security mechanisms exist for IPv6?
■ What differences exist between securing an IPv6 versus an IPv4 network?

One challenge that institutions and USG agencies must face while transitioning to IPv6 is the context of security. "Security" has been presented by proponents as a motivating factor for transitioning to IPv6. In fact, security mechanisms and tools exist but the IETF is still working on and refining IPv6 security for Internet Control Message Protocol (ICMPv6), IPv6 firewalls, mobility, transition, and so on. In the final analysis, security approaches and issues in IPv6 are similar to security approaches and issues in IPv4. IPv6 faces many of the same risks associated with IPv4; in addition, IPv6 offers a number of new capabilities that could potentially result in additional vulnerabilities and threats to users. However, if properly implemented, IPv6 has the potential to provide a foundation for creating a secure infrastructure for an agency's enterprise as well as the Internet as a whole [JUN200801]. Prima facia security strengths of IPv6 are based on the *requirement* for IPv6 to implement IPsec [RFC2401], [RFC2402], [RFC2406], although, to date IPsec implementations are more readily available commercially in IPv4 routers and firewalls than in IPv6 devices. There are, however, some features of the protocol that reduce some specific threats (for example, fragmentation). By itself IPv6 is not a panacea for IP-level/network-level security concerns; nonetheless, IPv6 planners need to become aware of the issues, advantages, limitations, and the potential pitfalls. Corporations and institutions need to start planning the migration process and how coexistence of IPv4 and IPv6 networks can be maintained securely during the 2- to 5-year window that will likely be required to achieve the global worldwide transition.

It is critical that network and security engineers at large become IPv6-knowledgeable. There are some anecdotal indications that organizations may not be able to achieve the same security baseline for IPv6 networks as they are currently able to achieve for IPv4 networks [ICA200701]. Therefore, it is important that IPv6 planners begin to develop a baseline understanding of this space and the issues, opportunities, and challenges.

A presentation delivered during an open session at the July 2007 Internet Corporation for Assigned Names and Numbers (ICANN) Public Meeting in San Juan, Puerto Rico, made note of the accelerated depletion rate of IPv4 addresses and the growing difficulties the Regional Internet Registries (RIRs) are experiencing in allocating contiguous address blocks of sufficient size to service providers. Furthermore, the fragmentation in the IPv4 address space is taxing and stressing the global routing fabric, and the near-term expectation is that the RIRs will impose more restrictive IPv4 allocation policies and promote a rapid adoption of IPv6 addresses [ICA200701]. As of April 16, 2008, there were nominally 1,126 days before the IPv4 address space is depleted (IPv4 address space is expected to run out by 2012*). See Figure 1.3.

While there is a reasonably extensive open literature in the topic of IPv6 security, there is currently no book that covers the topic in a systematic manner. To this end, this book covers the field in a terse and pragmatic manner. After an

---

* There has been talk about reclaiming unused IPv4 space, saying that it would be a huge undertaking. A reclaiming of some portion of the IPv4 space will not help with the goal of providing an addressable IP address to appliances, cell phones, sensors (such as Smart Dust), surveillance cameras, Body Area Network devices, Unmanned Aerial Vehicle, and so forth.

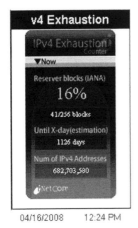

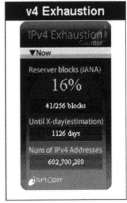

Figure 1.3 "...We have just three years until IPv4 addresses are depleted".

overview and introduction in Chapter 1, Chapters 2 and 3 provide a primer on IPv6. Chapter 4 discusses general network security mechanisms and approaches. Chapter 5 covers the fundamental topic of IPsec and its use in IPv6 environments. Chapter 6 discusses other IPv6 security features. Chapter 7 looks at firewall use in IPv6 environments. Finally, Chapter 8 addresses security considerations for migration environments that may consist of mixed IPv4-IPv6 networks.

1.2 IPv6 Overview

While the basic function of the Internet Protocol is to move information across networks, IPv6 has more capabilities built into its foundation than IPv4. A key capability is the significant increase in address space. For example, all devices could have a public IP address, so that they can be uniquely tracked.* Today inventory management of dispersed assets in a very large distributed organization such as the UAG DoD cannot be achieved with IPv4 mechanisms; during the inventory cycle someone has to manually verify the location of each desktop computer. With IPv6 one

---

* Note that this has some potential negative security issues as attackers could be able to own a machine and then exactly know how to go back to that same machine again. Therefore, reliable security mechanisms need to be understood and put in place in IPv6 environments.

can use the network to verify that such equipment is there; even non-IT equipment in the field can also be tracked by having an IP address permanently assigned. IPv6 also has extensive automatic configuration (autoconfiguration) mechanisms and reduces the IT burden by making configuration essentially plug-and-play (autoconfiguration implies that a Dynamic Host Configuration Protocol (DHCP) server is not needed or does not have to be configured). (Because IPv4 manual configuration is already a challenge in itself, one can understand that manually manipulating IPv6 addresses that are four times longer can be much more problematic). Corporations and government agencies will be able to achieve a number of improvements with IPv6. IPv6 can improve a firm's intranet, with benefits such as, but not limited to:

- Expanded addressing capabilities
- Serverless autoconfiguration (what some call plug-n-play) and reconfiguration
- Streamlined header format and flow identification
- End-to-end security, with built-in, strong IP-layer encryption and authentication (embedded security support with mandatory IPsec implementation)
- In IPv6, creating a VPN is easier and more standard than in IPv4, because of the (Authentication Header (AH) and Encapsulating Security Protocol (ESP)) Extension headers. The performance penalty is lower for the VPN implemented in IPv6 compared to those built in IPv4 [LIO199801]
- Enhanced support for multicast and QoS (more refined support for Flow Control and QoS for the near real-time delivery of data)
- More efficient and robust mobility mechanisms (enhanced support for Mobile IP and Mobile Computing Devices)
- Extensibility: improved support for feature options/extensions
- IPv6 makes it easy for nodes to have multiple IPv6 addresses on the same network interface. This can create the opportunity for users to establish overlay or Communities of Interest (COI) networks on top of other physical IPv6 networks. Department, groups, or other users and resources can belong to one or more COIs, where each can have its own specific security policy [JUN200801]
- Merging two IPv4 networks with overlapping addresses (say, if two organizations merge) is complex; it will be much easier to merge networks with IPv6
- IPv6 network architectures can easily adapt to an end-to-end security model where the end hosts have the responsibility of providing the security services necessary to protect any data traffic between them; this results in greater flexibility for creating policy-based trust domains that are based on varying parameters including node address and application [KAE200601]

IPv6 basic capabilities include the following:

- Addressing
- Anycast

- Flow labels
- ICMPv6
- Neighbor Discovery

Table 1.1 shows the core protocols that compose IPv6.

IP was designed in the 1970s for the purpose of connecting computers that were in separate geographic locations. Computers in a campus were connected by means of local networks, but these local networks were separated into essentially stand-alone islands. "Internet," as a name to designate the protocol and more recently the worldwide information network, simply means "inter network," that is, a connection between multiple networks. In the beginning, the protocol initially had only military use in mind, but computers from universities and enterprises were quickly added. The Internet as a worldwide information network is the result of the practical application of the Internet Protocol, that is, the interconnection of a large set of information networks [IPV200501]. Starting in the early 1990s, developers realized that the communication needs of the 21st century required a protocol with

Table 1.1   Key IPv6 Protocols

Protocol	Description
Internet Protocol version 6 (IPv6): RFC 2460	IPv6 is a connectionless datagram protocol used for routing packets between hosts.
Internet Control Message Protocol for IPv6 (ICMPv6): RFC 2463	A mechanism that enables hosts and routers that use IPv6 communication to report errors and send status messages.
Multicast Listener Discovery (MLD): RFC 2710, RFC 3590, RFC 3810	A mechanism that enables one to manage subnet multicast membership for IPv6. MLD uses a series of three ICMPv6 messages. MLD replaces the Internet Group Management Protocol (IGMP) v3 that is employed for IPv4.
Neighbor Discovery (ND): RFC 2461	A mechanism that is used to manage node-to-node communication on a link. ND uses a series of five ICMPv6 messages. ND replaces Address Resolution Protocol (ARP), ICMPv4 Router Discovery, and the ICMPv4 Redirect message. ND is implemented using the Neighbor Discovery Protocol (NDP).

some new features and capabilities, while at the same time retaining the useful features of the existing protocol.

While link-level communication does not generally require a node identifier (address) since the device is intrinsically identified with the link-level address, communication over a group of links (a network) does require unique node identifiers (addresses). The IP address is an identifier that is applied to each device connected to an IP network. In this setup, different elements taking part in the network (servers, routers, desktop computers, etc.) communicate among each other using their IP address as an entity identifier. In version 4 of the Internet Protocol, addresses consist of four octets. For ease of human conversation, IP addresses are represented as separated by periods, for example, 166.74.110.83, where the decimal numbers are a shorthand for (and correspond to) the binary code described by the byte in question (an 8-bit number takes a value in the 0–255 range). Since the IPv4 address has 32 bits, there are nominally 2^{32} different IP addresses (approximately 4 billion nodes if all combinations are used). (The Domain Name System (DNS) also helped the human conversation in the context of IPv4; DNS is going to be even more critical in IPv6 and will have substantial impact on security administrators that use IP addresses to define security policies (e.g., firewalls)).

IPv4 has proven, by means of its long life, to be a flexible and powerful networking mechanism. However, IPv4 is starting to exhibit limitations, not only with respect to the need for an increase of the IP address space, driven, for example, by new populations of users in countries such as China and India, and by new technologies with "always connected devices" (DSL [Digital Subscription Lines], cable, networked PDAs, 2.5G/3G mobile telephones, etc.), but also in reference to a potential global rollout of VoIP. IPv6 creates a new IP address format, so that the number of IP addresses will not exhaust for several decades or longer even though an entire new crop of devices are expected to connect to the Internet.

IPv6 also adds improvements in areas such as routing and network autoconfiguration. Specifically, new devices that connect to the Internet will be plug-and-play devices. With IPv6, one is not required to configure dynamic non-published local IP addresses, the gateway address, the subnetwork mask, or any other parameters. The equipment, when plugged into the network, automatically obtains all requisite configuration data [IPV200501].

The advantages of IPv6 can be summarized as follows:

■ Scalability: IPv6 has 128-bit addresses versus 32-bit IPv4 addresses. With IPv4, the theoretical number of available IP addresses is $2^{32} \sim 10^{10}$. IPv6 offers a 2^{128} space. Hence, the number of available unique node addressees is $2^{128} \sim 10^{39}$.

■ Security: IPv6 includes security features in its specifications such as payload encryption and authentication of the source of the communication.

■ Real-time applications: To provide better support for real-time traffic (e.g., VoIP), IPv6 includes "labeled flows" in its specifications. By means of this mechanism, routers can recognize the end-to-end flow to which transmitted packets belong. This is similar to the service offered by MultiProtocol Label Switching (MPLS), but it is intrinsic with the IP mechanism rather than an add-on. Also, it preceded this MPLS feature by a number of years.

■ Plug-and-play: IPv6 includes a plug-and-play mechanism that facilitates the connection of equipment to the network. The requisite configuration is automatic.

■ Mobility: IPv6 includes more efficient and enhanced mobility mechanisms, which are important for mobile networks.*

■ Optimized protocol: IPv6 embodies IPv4 best practices but removes unused or obsolete IPv4 characteristics. This results in a better-optimized Internet Protocol.

■ Addressing and routing: IPv6 improves the addressing and routing hierarchy.

■ Extensibility: IPv6 has been designed to be extensible and offers support for new options and extensions.

With IPv4, the 32-bit address can be represented as AdrClass|netID|hostID. The network portion can contain either a network ID or a network ID and a subnet. Every network and every host or device has a unique address, by definition. Basic NATing is a method by which IP addresses (specifically IPv4 addresses) are transparently mapped from one group to another. Specifically, private "non-registered" addresses are mapped to a small set (as small as 1) of public registered addresses; this impacts the general addressability, accessibility, and "individuality" of the device. Network Address Port Translation (NAPT), also referred to as Port Address Translation (PAT), is a method by which many network addresses and their TCP/UDP (Transmission Control Protocol/User Datagram Protocol) ports are translated into a single network address and its TCP/UDP ports. Together, these two methods, referred to as traditional NAT, provide a mechanism to connect a realm with private addresses to an external realm with globally unique registered addresses [RFC3022]. NAT is a short-term solution for the anticipated Internet growth phenomenon, and a better solution is needed for address exhaustion. There is a clear recognition that NAT techniques make the Internet, the

---

* Some of the benefits of IPv6 in the context of mobility include [YAI200001]: (i) Larger Addresses, which allow for new techniques to be used in order for the Mobile Node (MN) to obtain a care-of address; here, MNs can always get a collocated care-of address, a fact that removes the need for a Foreign Agent (FA). (ii) New Routing Header, which allows for proper use of source routing. This was not possible with IPv4. (iii) Authentication Header, which allows for the authentication of the binding messages. (iv) *Destination Options* Header, which allows for the use of options without significant performance degradation; performance degradation may have occurred in IPv4 because every router along the path had to examine the options even when they were only destined for the receiver of the packet.

applications, and even the devices more complex (especially when conducting Business-to-Business transactions) and this means a cost overhead [IPV200501]. Overlapping encryption domains have been a substantial issue for organizations to deal with when creating gateway-to-gateway Virtual Private Networks (VPNs). The expectation is that IPv6 can make IP devices less expensive, more powerful, and even consume less power; the power issue is not only important for environmental reasons, but also improves operability (e.g., longer battery life in portable devices, such as mobile phones).

IPv4 addresses can be from an officially assigned public range or from an internal intranet private (but not globally unique) block. Internal intranet addresses may be in the ranges 10.0.0.0/8, 172.16.0.0/12, and 192.168.0.0/16, as suggested in RFC 1918. In the internal intranet private address case, a NAT function is employed to map the internal addresses to an external public address when the private-to-public network boundary is crossed. This, however, imposes a number of limitations, particularly since the number of registered public addresses available to a company is almost invariably much smaller (as small as 1) than the number of internal devices requiring an address.

As noted, IPv4 theoretically allows up to 2^{32} addresses, based on a four-octet address space. Public, globally unique addresses are assigned by the Internet Assigned Numbers Authority (IANA). IP addresses are addresses of network nodes at layer 3; each device on a network (whether the Internet or an intranet) must have a unique address. In IPv4 it is a 32-bit (4-byte) binary address used to identify the device. It is represented by the nomenclature a.b.c.d (each of a, b, c, and d being from 1 to 255 (0 has a special meaning). Examples are 167.168.169.170, 232.233.229.209, and 200.100.200.100.

The problem is that during the 1980s many public, registered addresses were allocated to firms and organizations without any consistent control. As a result, some organizations have more addresses that they actually need, giving rise to the present dearth of available "registerable" Layer 3 addresses. Furthermore, not all IP addresses can be used due to the fragmentation described above.

One approach to the issue would be a renumbering and a reallocation of the IPv4 addressing space. However, this is not as simple as it appears since it requires significant worldwide coordination efforts, and it would not solve the medium-term need for a much larger address space for evolving end-user/consumer applications. Moreover, it would still be limited for the human population and the quantity of devices that will be connected to the Internet in the medium-term future [IPV200501]. At this juncture, and as a temporary and pragmatic approach to alleviate the dearth of addresses, NAT mechanisms are employed by organizations and even home users. This mechanism consists of using only a small set of public IPv4 addresses for an entire network to access to Internet. The myriad of internal devices are assigned IP addresses from a specifically designated range of Class A or Class C addresses that are locally unique but are duplicatively used and reused within various organizations.* In some cases (e.g., residential Internet access use via DSL or Cable), the legal IP address is only provided to a user on a time-lease basis, rather than permanently.

A number of protocols cannot travel through a NAT device and hence the use of NAT implies that many applications (e.g., VoIP) cannot be used effectively in all instances.† As a consequence, these applications can only be used in intranets. Examples include [IPV200501]:

- Multimedia applications such as videoconferencing, VoIP, or video-on-demand/IPTV do not work smoothly through NAT devices. Multimedia

---

* Originally IPv4 addresses were categorized into four classes:
  - Traditional Class A address. Class A uses the first bit of the 32-bit space (bit 0) to identify it as a Class A address; this bit is set to 0. Bits 1 to 7 represent the network ID, and bits 8 through 31 identify the PC, terminal device, or host/server on the network. This address space supports $2^7 - 2 = 126$ networks and approximately 16 million devices (2^{24}) on each network. By convention, the use of an "all 1s" or "all 0s" address for both the Network ID and the Host ID is prohibited (which is the reason for subtracting the 2 above.)
  - Traditional Class B address. Class B uses the first two bits (bit 0 and bit 1) of the 32-bit space to identify it as a Class B address; these bits are set to 10. Bits 2 to 15 represent the network ID, and bits 16 through 31 identify the PC, terminal device, or host/server on the network. This address space supports $2^{14} - 2 = 16,382$ networks and $2^{16} - 2 = 65,534$ devices on each network.
  - Traditional Class C address. Class C uses the first three bits (bit 0, bit 1, and bit 2) of the 32-bit space to identify it as a Class C address; these bits are set to 110. Bits 3 to 23 represent the network ID, and bits 24 through 31 identify the PC, terminal device, or host/server on the network. This address space supports about 2 million networks ($2^{21} - 2$) and $2^8 - 2 = 254$ devices on each network.
  - Traditional Class D address. This class is used for broadcasting, wherein all devices on the network receive the same packet. Class D uses the first four bits (bit 0, bit 1, bit 2, and bit 3) of the 32-bit space to identify it as a Class D address; these bits are set to 1110.
  Classless Interdomain Routing (CIDR), described in RFC 1518, RFC 1519, and RFC 2050, allows blocks of multiple addresses (for example, blocks of Class C addresses) to be combined, or aggregated, to create a larger classless set of IP addresses, with more hosts allowed. Blocks of Class C network numbers are allocated to each network service provider; organizations using the network service provider for Internet connectivity are allocated subsets of the service provider's address space as required. These multiple Class C addresses can then be summarized in routing tables, resulting in fewer route advertisements. The CIDR mechanism can also be applied to blocks of Class A and B addresses.
† The reader should be aware that we are *not* referring here to deploying corporate VoIP for an organization of 10, 1000, or 10,000 employees and then being able to pass VoIP protocols through a firewall. That is a fairly trivial exercise. We are referring here to the overreaching goal of enabling any-person-on-the-planet-to-any-other-person-on-the-planet VoIP-based communication by affording a consistent, stable, and publishable addressing scheme. The U.S. Bell System and the telecommunications world solved that problem over half a century ago, by giving the world a telephony addressing scheme that allows every person in the world to have a unique, persistent, usable telephone number (Country Code + City [if applicable] + Local number) from Antarctica (+672) to Zimbabwe (+263), from Easter Island (+56) to Tristan da Cunha (+290), and every land and island in between.

applications make use of Real-time Transport Protocol (RTP) and Real-time Control Protocol (RTCP). These in turn use UDP with dynamic allocation of ports, and NAT does not directly support this environment.

■ IPsec is used extensively for data authentication, integrity, and confidentiality. However, when NAT is used, IPsec operation is impacted, since NAT changes the address in the IP header.

■ Multicast, although possible in theory, requires complex configuration in a NAT environment and hence, in practice, is not utilized as often as could be the case.

The need for obligatory use of NAT disappears with IPv6 (but it can still be used if someone wants to).

The format of IPv6 addressing is described in RFC 2373. As noted, an IPv6 address consists of 128 bits, rather than 32 bits as with IPv4 addresses. The number of bits correlates to the address space, as follows:

IP Version	Size of Address Space
IPv6	128 bits, which allows for 2^{128} or 340,28 2,366,920,938,463,463,374,607,431,768,2 11,456 (3.4×10^{38}) possible addresses.
IPv4	32 bits, which allows for 2^{32} or 4,294,967,296 possible addresses.

The relatively large size of the IPv6 address is designed to be subdivided into hierarchical routing domains that reflect the topology of the modern-day Internet. The use of 128 bits provides multiple levels of hierarchy and flexibility in designing hierarchical addressing and routing. The IPv4-based Internet currently lacks this flexibility [MSD200401].

The IPv6 address is represented as 8 groups of 16 bits each, separated by the ":" character. Each 16-bit group is represented by 4 hexadecimal digits, that is, each digit has a value between 0 and F (0,1, 2, ... A, B, C, D, E, F with A = 10_{10}, B = 11_{10}, etc. to F = 15_{10}). What follows is an example of a hypothetical IPv6 address:

```
3223:0BA0:01E0:D001:0000:0000:D0F0:0010
```

If one or more four-digit groups is 0000, the zeros may be omitted and replaced with two colons (::). For example,

```
3223:0BA0::
```

is the abbreviated form of the following address:

```
3223:0BA0:0000:0000:0000:0000:0000:0000
```

Similarly, only one 0 is written, removing 0s in the left side, and four 0s in the middle of the address. For example, the address

```
3223:BA0::1234
```

is the abbreviated form of the following address:

```
3223:0BA0:0000:0000:0000:0000:0000:1234
```

There is also a method to designate groups of IP addresses or subnetworks that is based on specifying the number of bits that designate the subnetwork, beginning from left to right, using remaining bits to designate single devices inside the network. For example, the notation

```
3223:0BA0:01A0::/48
```

indicates that the part of the IP address used to represent the subnetwork has 48 bits. Since each hexadecimal digit has 4 bits, this points out that the part used to represent the subnetwork is formed by 12 digits, that is: "3223:0BA0:01A0." The remaining digits of the IP address would be used to represent nodes inside the network.

There are a number of special IPv6 addresses, as follows:

■ Auto-return or loopback virtual address. This address is specified in IPv4 as the 127.0.0.1 address. In IPv6 this address is represented as ::1.
■ Unspecified address (::). This address is not allocated to any node since it is used to indicate the absence of an address.
■ IPv6 over IPv4 dynamic/automatic tunnel addresses. These addresses are designated as IPv4-compatible IPv6 addresses and allow the sending of IPv6 traffic over IPv4 networks in a transparent manner. They are represented as, for example, ::156.55.23.5.
■ IPv4 over IPv6 addresses automatic representation. These addresses allow for IPv4-only-nodes to still work in IPv6 networks. They are designated as IPv4-mapped IPv6 addresses and are represented as ::FFFF: (for example, ::FFFF:156.55.43.3).

Like IPv4, IPv6 is a connectionless, unreliable datagram protocol used primarily for addressing and routing packets between hosts. Connectionless means that a session is not established before exchanging data. Unreliable means that delivery is not guaranteed. IPv6 always makes a best-effort attempt to deliver a packet. An IPv6 packet might be lost, delivered out of sequence, duplicated, or delayed. IPv6 *per se* does not attempt to recover from these types of errors. The acknowledgment of packets delivered and the recovery of lost packets is done by a higher-layer protocol, such as TCP [MSD200401]. From a packet forwarding perspective, IPv6 operates just like IPv4.

An IPv6 packet, also known as an IPv6 datagram, consists of an IPv6 header and an IPv6 payload, as shown Figure 1.4. The IPv6 header consists of two parts,

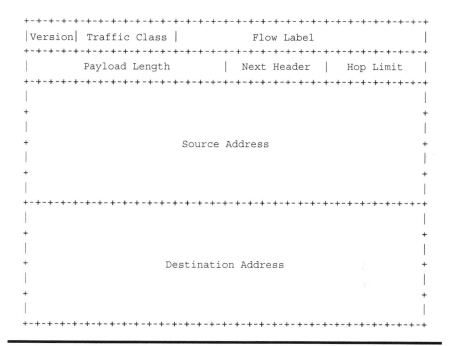

Figure 1.4   IPv6 packet.

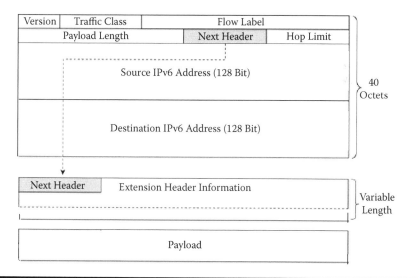

Figure 1.5   IPv6 extension headers.

the IPv6 base header, and optional extension headers. See Figure 1.5. Functionally, the optional extension headers and upper-layer protocols, for example TCP, are considered part of the IPv6 payload. Table 1.2 shows the fields in the IPv6 base header. IPv4 headers and IPv6 headers are not directly interoperable; hosts or routers must

Table 1.2   IPv6 Base Header

IPv6 Header Field	Length (bits)	Function
Version	4	Identifies the version of the protocol. For IPv6, the version is 6.
Traffic Class	8	Intended for originating nodes and forwarding routers to identify and distinguish between different classes or priorities of IPv6 packets.
Flow Label	20	Sometimes referred to as Flow ID, defines how traffic is handled and identified. A flow is a sequence of packets sent either to a unicast or a multicast destination. This field identifies packets that require special handling by the IPv6 node. The following list shows the ways the field is handled if a host or router does not support flow label field functions: ■ If the packet is being sent, the field is set to zero. ■ If the packet is being received, the field is ignored.
Payload Length	16	Identifies the length, in octets, of the payload. This field is a 16-bit unsigned integer. The payload includes the optional extension headers, as well as the upper-layer protocols, for example, TCP.
Next Header	8	Identifies the header immediately following the IPv6 header. The following shows examples of the next header: 00 = Hop-by-Hop options 01 = ICMPv4 04 = IP in IP (encapsulation) 06 = TCP 17 = UDP 43 = Routing 44 = Fragment 50 = Encapsulating security payload 51 = Authentication 58 = ICMPv6
		(Continued)

Table 1.2 IPv6 Base Header (Continued)

IPv6 Header Field	Length (bits)	Function
Hop Limit	8	Identifies the number of network segments, also known as links or subnets, on which the packet is allowed to travel before being discarded by a router. The Hop Limit is set by the sending host and is used to prevent packets from endlessly circulating on an IPv6 internetwork. When forwarding an IPv6 packet, IPv6 routers must decrease the Hop Limit by 1, and must discard the IPv6 packet when the Hop Limit is 0.
Source Address	128	Identifies the IPv6 address of the original source of the IPv6 packet.
Destination Address	128	Identifies the IPv6 address of intermediate or final destination of the IPv6 packet.

use an implementation of both IPv4 and IPv6 in order to recognize and process both header formats (see Figure 1.6). This gives rise to a number of complexities in the migration process between the IPv4 and the IPv6 environments. The IP header in IPv6 has been streamlined and defined to be of a fixed length (40 bytes). In IPv6, header fields from the IPv4 header have been removed, renamed, or moved to the new optional IPv6 Extension headers. The header length field is no longer needed since the IPv6 header is now a fixed-length entity. The IPv4 "Type of Service" is equivalent to the IPv6 "Traffic Class" field. The "Total Length" field has been replaced with the "Payload Length" field. Since IPv6 only allows for fragmentation to be performed by the IPv6 source and destination nodes, and not individual routers, the IPv4 segment control fields (Identification, Flags, and Fragment Offset fields) have been moved to similar fields within the Fragment Extension header. The functionality provided by the "Time to Live (TTL*)" field has been replaced with the "Hop Limit" field. The "Protocol" field has been replaced with the "Next Header Type" field. The "Header Checksum" field was removed, which has the main advantage of not having each relay spend time processing the checksum. The "Options" field is no longer part of the header as it was in IPv4. Options are specified in the optional IPv6 Extension headers. The removal of the Options field from the header enables more efficient routing; only the information that is required by a router needs to be processed [HER200201].

One area requiring consideration, however, is the length of the IPv6 Protocol Data Unit (PDU): the 40-octet header can be a problem for real-time IP applications

---

* TTL has been used in many attacks and Intrusion Detection System (IDS) tricks in IPv4.

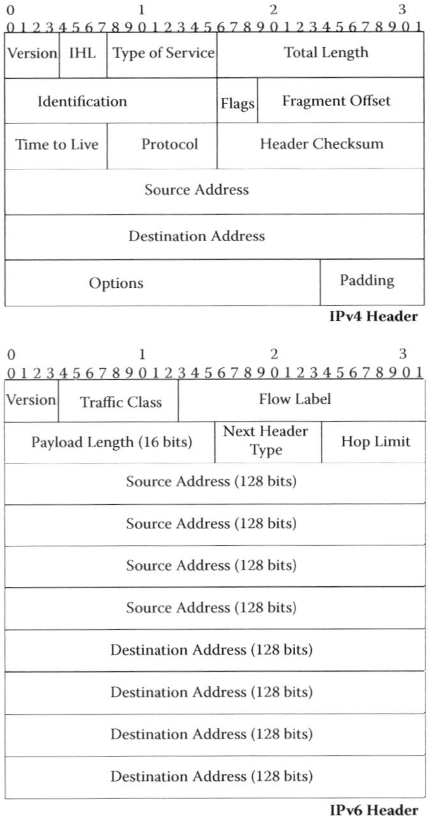

IPv4 Header	IPv6 Header	Notes
Version (4-bit)	Version (4-bit)	IPv6 header contains a new value
Header Length (4-bit)	—	Removed in IPv6, the basic IPv6 header has fixed length of 40 octets
Type of Service (8-bit)	Traffic Class (8-bit)	Same function for both headers.
—	Flow Label (20-bit)	New field added to tag a flow for IPv6 packets.
Total PDU Length (16-bit)	Payload Length (16-bit)	Same function for both headers.
Identification (16-bit)	—	Removed in IPv6 because fragmentation is no longer done by intermediate routers in the networks, but by the source node that originates the packet.
Flags (3-bit)	—	Removed in IPv6 because fragmentation is no longer done by intermediate routers in the networks, but by the source node that originates the packet.
Fragment Offset (13-bit)	—	Removed in IPv6 because fragmentation is no longer done by intermediate routers in the networks, but by the source node that originates the packet.
Time To Live (8-bit)	Hop Limit (8-bit)	Same function for both headers.
Protocol Number (8-bit)	Next Header (8-bit)	Same function for both headers.
Header checksum (16-bit)	—	Removed in IPv6; upper-layer protocols handle checksums
Source Address (32-bit)	Source Address (128-bit)	Same function, but Source address is expanded in IPv6.
Destination Address (32-bit)	Destination Address (128-bit)	Same function, but Destination address is expanded in IPv6.
Options (variable)	—	Removed in IPv6. Options handled differently.
Padding (variable)	—	Removed in IPv6. Options handled differently.
—	Extension headers	New way in IPv6 to handle Options fields, security

Figure 1.6   Comparison of IPv4 and IPv6 headers.

such as VoIP and IPTV. Header compression becomes critical.* Also, there will be some bandwidth inefficiency in general, which could be an issue in limited-bandwidth environments or applications (e.g., sensor networks.)

"Autoconfiguration" is a new characteristic of the IPv6 protocol that facilitates network management and system setup tasks by users. This characteristic is often called plug-and-play or connect-and-work. Autoconfiguration facilitates initialization of user devices; after connecting a device to an IPv6 network, one or several IPv6 globally unique addresses are automatically allocated. DHCP allows systems to obtain an IPv4 address and other required information (e.g., default router or DNS server). A similar protocol, DHCPv6, has been published for IPv6. DHCP and DHCPv6 are known as stateful protocols because they maintain tables on (specialized) servers. However, IPv6 also has a new stateless autoconfiguration protocol, which has no equivalent in IPv4. The stateless autoconfiguration protocol does not require a server component because there is no state to maintain (a DHCP server may typically run in a router or firewall). Every IPv6 system (other than routers) is able to build its own unicast global address. Stateless address autoconfiguration provides an alternative between a purely manual configuration and stateful autoconfiguration [DON200401].

The "autoconfiguration" process is flexible but it is also somewhat complex. The complexity arises from the fact that various policies are defined and implemented by the network administrator. Specifically, the administrator determines the parameters that will be assigned automatically. At a minimum (or when there is no network administrator), the allocation of a "link" local address is often included. The link local address allows communication with other nodes placed in the same physical network. Note that "link" has somewhat of a special meaning in IPv6, as follows: a communication facility or medium over which nodes can communicate at the link layer, that is, the layer immediately below IPv6. Examples are Ethernets (simple or bridged), PPP links, an X.25 packet-switched network, a Frame Relay network, a Cell Relay/Asynchronous Transfer Mode (ATM) network, and internet(working†) layer (or higher layer) "tunnels," such as tunnels over IPv4 or IPv6 itself [RFC2460].

---

* Two compression protocols emerged from the IETF in recent years [ERT200401]: (i) Internet Protocol Header Compression (IPHC), a scheme designed for low bit error rate links (compression profiles are defined in RFC 2507 and RFC 2508); it provides compression of TCP/IP, UDP/IP, RTP/UDP/IP, and ESP/IP header; "enhanced" compression of RTP/UDP/IP (ECRTP) headers is defined in RFC 3545. (ii) Robust Header Compression (ROHC) Working Group, a scheme designed for wireless links which provides greater compression compared to IPHC at the cost of greater implementation complexity (compression profiles are defined in RFC 3095and RFC 3096); this is more suitable for high Bit Error Rate (BER), long Round Trip Time (RTT) links and supports compression of Encapsulating Security Payload (ESP)/IP, UDP/IP, RTP/UDP/IP headers.

† In this text we use lower case term "internet(working)" to describe the (interconnection) of two general networks. When we refer to the Internet at large, we use the capitalized term "Internet."

As noted, two autoconfiguration basic mechanisms exist: (i) Stateful and (ii) Stateless. Both mechanisms can be used in a complementary manner or simultaneously to define parameter configurations. Stateful autoconfiguration is often employed when there is a need for rigorous control in reference to the address allocated to hosts; in stateless autoconfiguration, the only concern is that the address must be unique [IPV200501].

Stateless autoconfiguration is also described as "serverless." The acronym SLAAC is also used for *stateless address autoconfiguration.* SLAAC is defined in RFC 2462. With SLAAC, the presence of configuration servers to supply profile information is not required. The host generates its own address using a combination of the information that it possesses (in its interface or network card) and the information that is periodically supplied by the routers. Routers determine the prefix that identifies networks associated to the link under discussion. The "interface identifier" identifies an interface within a subnetwork and is often, and by default, generated from the Media Access Control (MAC) address of the network card. The IPv6 address is built combining the 64 bits of the interface identifier with the prefixes that routers determine as belonging to the subnetwork. If there is no router, the interface identifier is self-sufficient to allow the PC to generate a "link-local" address. The link-local address is sufficient to allow communication between several nodes connected to the same link (the same local network).

Stateful configuration requires a server to send the information and parameters of network connection to nodes and hosts. Servers maintain a database of all addresses allocated and a mapping of the hosts to which these addresses have been allocated, along with any information related with all requisite parameters. In general, this mechanism is based on the use of DHCPv6.

IPv6 addresses are "leased" to an interface for a fixed, established time (including an infinite time.) When this "lifetime" expires, the link between the interface and the address is invalidated and the address can be reallocated to other interfaces. For the suitable management of address expiration time, an address goes through two states (stages) while it is affiliated to an interface [IPV200501]:

a. At first, an address is in a "preferred" state, so its use in any communication is not restricted.
b. After that, an address becomes "deprecated," indicating that its affiliation with the current interface will (soon) be invalidated.

When it is in a deprecated state, the use of the address is discouraged, although it is not forbidden. However, when possible, any new communication (for example, the opening of a new TCP connection) must use a preferred address. A deprecated address should only be used by applications that have already used it before and in cases where it is difficult to change this address to another address without causing a service interruption.

To ensure that allocated addresses (granted either by manual mechanisms or by autoconfiguration) are unique in a specific link, the *link duplicated addresses detection algorithm* is used. The address to which the duplicated address detection algorithm is being applied is designated (until the end of this algorithmic session) as an "attempt address." In this case, it does not matter that such address has been allocated to an interface, and received packets are discarded.

Next, we describe how an IPv6 address is formed. The lowest 64 bits of the address identify a specific interface and these bits are designated as interface identifier. The highest 64 bits of the address identify the path or the "prefix" of the network or router in one of the links to which such interface is connected. The IPv6 address is formed by combining the prefix with the interface identifier.

It is possible for a host or device to have IPv6 and IPv4 addresses simultaneously. Most of the systems that currently support IPv6 allow the simultaneous use of both protocols. In this way, it is possible to support communication with IPv4-only networks as well as IPv6-only networks and the use of the applications developed for both protocols [IPV200501].

It is possible to transmit IPv6 traffic over IPv4 networks via tunneling methods. This approach consists of "wrapping" the IPv6 traffic as IPv4 payload data; IPv6 traffic is sent encapsulated into IPv4 traffic and at the receiving end this traffic is parsed as IPv6 traffic. Transition mechanisms are methods used for the coexistence of IPv4 or IPv6 devices and networks. For example, an "IPv6-in-IPv4 tunnel" is a transition mechanism that allows IPv6 devices to communicate through an IPv4 network. The mechanism consists of creating the IPv6 packets in a normal way and encapsulating them in an IPv4 packet. The reverse process is undertaken in the destination machine, which de-encapsulates the IPv6 packet.

There is a significant difference between the procedures to allocate IPv4 addresses, that focus on the parsimonious use of addresses (since addresses are a scarce resource and should be managed with caution), and the procedures to allocate IPv6 addresses, that focus on flexibility. Internet Service Providers (ISPs) deploying IPv6 systems follow the Regional Internet Registries (RIRs) policies relating to how to assign IPv6 addressing space among their clients. RIRs are recommending that ISPs and operators allocate to each IPv6 client a /48 subnetwork; this allows clients to manage their own subnetworks without using NAT. (The implication is that the *obligatory* need for NAT disappears in IPv6).

In order to allow its maximum scalability, the IPv6 protocol uses an approach based on a basic header, with minimum information. This differentiates it from IPv4 where different options are included in addition to the basic header. IPv6 uses a header concatenation mechanism to support supplementary capabilities. The advantages of this approach include the following:

- The size of the basic header is always the same, and is well known. The basic header has been simplified compared with IPv4, since only 8 fields are used instead of 12. The basic IPv6 header has a fixed size, hence its processing by nodes and routers is more straightforward. Also, the header's structure aligns to 64 bits, so that new and future processors (64 bits minimum) can process it in a more efficient way.

■ Routers placed between a source point and a destination point (that is, the route that a specific packet has to pass through), do not need to process or understand any following headers. In other words, in general, interior (core) points of the network (routers) only have to process the basic header, while in IPv4 all headers must be processed. This flow mechanism is similar to the operation in MPLS, yet precedes it by several years.

■ There is no limit to the number of options that the headers can support (the IPv6 basic header is 40 octets in length, while the IPv4 header varies from 20 to 60 octets, depending on the options used).

In IPv6, interior/core routers do not perform packets fragmentation, but the fragmentation is performed end-to-end. That is, source and destination nodes perform, by means of the IPv6 stack, the fragmentation of a packet and the reassembly, respectively. The fragmentation process consists of dividing the source packet into smaller packets or fragments [IPV200501].

A "jumbogram" is an option that allows an IPv6 packet to have a payload greater than 65,535 bytes. Jumbograms are identified with a 0 value in the payload length in the IPv6 header field, and include a jumbo payload option in the Hop-by-Hop Option header. It is anticipated that such packets will be used in particular for multimedia traffic.

The IPv6 specification defines a number of Extension headers [HER200201] (also see Table 1.3 [DES200301]):

■ Routing header—Similar to the source routing options in IPv4. The header is used to mandate a specific routing.
■ Authentication Header (AH)—A security header that provides authentication and integrity.
■ Encapsulating Security Payload (ESP) header—A security header that provides authentication and encryption.
■ Fragmentation Header—The Fragmentation header is similar to the fragmentation options in IPv4.
■ Destination Options header—Header that contains a set of options to be processed only by the final destination node. Mobile IPv6 is an example of an environment that uses such a header
■ Hop-by-Hop Options header—A set of options needed by routers to perform certain management or debugging functions.

As noted, IPsec provides network-level security where the application data is encapsulated within the IPv6 packet. IPsec utilizes the AH or ESP header to

Table 1.3   IPv6 Extension Headers

Header (protocol ID)	Description
Hop-by-Hop Options header (protocol 0)	The Hop-by-Hop Options header is used for jumbogram packets and the Router Alert. An example of applying the Hop-by-Hop Options header is Resource Reservation Protocol (RSVP). This field is read and processed by every node and router along the delivery path.
Destination Options header (protocol 60)	This header carries optional information that is specifically targeted to a packet's destination address. The Mobile IPv6 protocol specification makes use of the Destination Options header to exchange registration messages between mobile nodes and the home agent. Mobile IP is a protocol allowing mobile nodes to keep permanent IP addresses even if they change point of attachment.
Routing header (protocol 43)	This header can be used by an IPv6 source node to force a packet to pass through specific routers on the way to its destination. A list of intermediary routers may be specified within the Routing header when the Routing Type field is set to 0.
Fragment header (protocol 44)	In IPv6, the Path MTU Discovery (PMTUD) mechanism is recommended to all IPv6 nodes. When an IPv6 node does not support PMTUD and it must send a packet larger than the greatest MTU along the delivery path, the Fragment header is used. When this happens, the node fragments the packet and sends each fragment using Fragment headers; then the destination node reassembles the original packet by concatenating all the fragments.
Authentication Header (AH) (protocol 51)	This header is used in IPsec to provide authentication, data integrity, and replay protection. It also ensures protection of some fields of the basic IPv6 header. This header is identical in both IPv4 and IPv6.
Encapsulating Security Payload (ESP) header (protocol 50)	This header is also used in IPsec to provide authentication, data integrity, replay protection, and confidentiality of the IPv6 packet. Similar to the authentication header, this header is identical in both IPv4 and IPv6.

provide security (the AH and ESP header may be used separately or in combination). IPsec, with ESP, offers integrity and data origin authentication, confidentiality, and optional (at the discretion of the receiver) anti-replay features (using confidentiality without integrity is discouraged by the RFCs); ESP furthermore provides limited traffic flow confidentiality. Both the AH and ESP header may be employed as follows [HER200201]:

- Tunnel mode—The protocol is applied to the entire IP packet. This method is needed to ensure security over the entire packet, where a new IPv6 header and an AH or ESP header are wrapped around the original IP packet.
- Transport mode—The protocol is just applied to the transport layer (i.e., TCP, UDP, ICMP) in the form of an IPv6 header, AH or ESP header, followed by the transport protocol data (header, data). (See Figure 1.7.)

Migration to IPv6 environments is expected to be fairly complex. Initially, internetworking between the two environments will be critical. Existing IPv4-endpoints or nodes will need to run dual stack nodes or convert to IPv6 systems. Fortunately, the new protocol supports IPv4-compatible IPv6 addresses, which is an IPv6 address format that employs embedded IPv4 addresses. Tunneling, which we already described in passing, will play a major role in the beginning. There are a number of requirements that are typically applicable to an organization wishing to introduce an IPv6 service [6NE200501]:

- The existing IPv4 service should not be adversely disrupted (e.g., as it might be by router loading of encapsulating IPv6 in IPv4 for tunnels)
- The IPv6 service should perform as well as the IPv4 service (e.g., at the IPv4 line rate, and with similar network characteristics)
- The service must be manageable and be able to be monitored (thus, tools should be available for IPv6 as they are for IPv4)
- The security of the network should not be compromised, due to the additional protocol itself or a weakness of any transition mechanism used
- An IPv6 address allocation plan must be drawn up

Well-known interworking mechanisms include the following [RFC2893]:

- Dual IP layer (also known as Dual Stack): A technique for providing complete support for both Internet protocols—IPv4 and IPv6—in hosts and routers.
- Configured tunneling of IPv6 over IPv4: Point-to-point tunnels made by encapsulating IPv6 packets within IPv4 headers to carry them over IPv4 routing infrastructures.
- Automatic tunneling of IPv6 over IPv4: A mechanism for using IPv4-compatible addresses to automatically tunnel IPv6 packets over IPv4 networks.

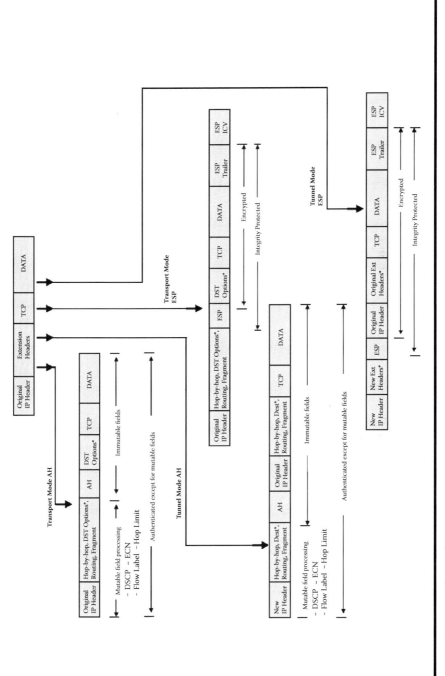

Figure 1.7 IPsec modes and types.

Tunneling techniques include the following [RFC2893]:

- IPv6-over-IPv4 tunneling: The technique of encapsulating IPv6 packets within IPv4 so that they can be carried across IPv4 routing infrastructures.
- Configured tunneling: IPv6-over-IPv4 tunneling where the IPv4 tunnel endpoint address is determined by configuration information on the encapsulating node. The tunnels can be either unidirectional or bidirectional. Bidirectionally configured tunnels behave as virtual point-to-point links.
- Automatic tunneling: IPv6-over-IPv4 tunneling where the IPv4 tunnel endpoint address is determined from the IPv4 address embedded in the IPv4-compatible destination address of the IPv6 packet being tunneled.
- IPv4 multicast tunneling: IPv6-over-IPv4 tunneling where the IPv4 tunnel endpoint address is determined using Neighbor Discovery. Unlike configured tunneling, this does not require any address configuration, and unlike automatic tunneling, it does not require the use of IPv4-compatible addresses. However, the mechanism assumes that the IPv4 infrastructure supports IPv4 multicast.

Applications (and the lower-layer protocol stack) need to be properly equipped. There are four cases [RFC4038]:

Case 1: IPv4-only applications in a dual-stack node. IPv6 protocol is introduced in a node, but applications are not yet ported to support IPv6. The protocol stack is as follows:

```
+----------------+
| appv4          |(appv4 - IPv4-only applications)
+----------------+
|TCP/UDP/others  |(transport protocols - TCP, UDP, etc.)
+----------------+
| IPv4|IPv6      |(IP protocols supported/enabled in the OS)
+----------------+
```

Case 2: IPv4-only applications and IPv6-only applications in a dual-stack node. Applications are ported for IPv6-only. Therefore, there are two similar applications, one for each protocol version (e.g., ping and ping6). The protocol stack is as follows:

```
+----------------+(appv4 - IPv4-only applications)
| appv4 | appv6  |(appv6 - IPv6-only applications)
+----------------+
|TCP/UDP/others  |(transport protocols - TCP, UDP, etc.)
+----------------+
| IPv4|IPv6      |(IP protocols supported/enabled in the OS)
+----------------+
```

Case 3: Applications supporting both IPv4 and IPv6 in a dual-stack node. Applications are ported for both IPv4 and IPv6 support. Therefore, the existing IPv4 applications can be removed. The protocol stack is as follows:

```
+---------------+
|appv4/v6       | (appv4/v6-applications supporting both IPv4
+---------------+  and IPv6)
|TCP/UDP/others | (transport protocols - TCP, UDP, etc.)
+---------------+
|IPv4|IPv6      | (IP protocols supported/enabled in the OS)
+---------------+
```

Case 4: Applications supporting both IPv4 and IPv6 in an IPv4-only node. Applications are ported for both IPv4 and IPv6 support, but the same applications may also have to work when IPv6 is not being used (e.g., disabled from the OS). The protocol stack is as follows:

```
+---------------+
|appv4/v6       | (appv4/v6-applications supporting both IPv4
+---------------+  and IPv6)
|TCP/UDP/others | (transport protocols - TCP, UDP, etc.)
+---------------+
|IPv4           | (IP protocols supported/enabled in the OS)
+---------------+
```

The first two cases are not interesting in the longer term; only a few applications are inherently IPv4- or IPv6-specific and should work with both protocols without having to care about which one is being used.

Figure 1.8 depicts some basic scenarios of carrier-based IPv6 support. Cases (a) and (b) represent traditional environments where the carrier link supports either a clear channel that is used to connect, say, two IPv4 routers, or is IP-aware. (In each case, the "cloud" on the left could also be the IPv4 Internet or the IPv6 Internet.)

In case (c) the carrier link is used to connect as a transparent link two IPv6 routers; the carrier link is not (does not need to be) aware that it is transferring IPv6 PDUs. In case (d) the carrier system is IPv4-aware, so the use of that environment to support IPv6 requires IPv6 to operate in a tunneled mode over the non-IPv6 cloud, which is a capability of IPv6.

In case (e) the carrier infrastructure needs to provide a gateway function between the IPv4 and the IPv6 world (this could entail repacking the IP PDUs from the v4 format to the v6 format.) Case (f) is the ideal long-term scenario where the "world has converted to IPv6" and "so did the carrier network."

In case (g) the carrier IP-aware network provides a conversion function to support both IPv4 (as a baseline) and IPv6 (as a new technology) handoffs. Possibly a dual-stack mechanism is utilized. In case (h) the carrier IPv6-aware network

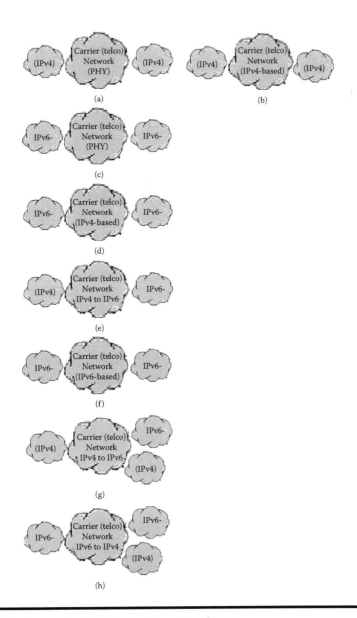

Figure 1.8 Support of IPv6 in carrier networks.

provides a support function for IPv6 (as a baseline) and also a conversion function to support legacy IPv4 islands.

Even network/security administrators that operate in a pure IPv4 environment need to be aware of IPv6-related security issues. In a standard IPv4 environment where IPv6 is not explicitly supported, any form of IPv6-based tunneling traffic must be considered abnormal, malicious traffic. For example, unconstrained 6to4-based traffic should be blocked (as noted elsewhere 6to4 is a transitional mechanism intended for individual independent nodes to connect IPv6 over the greater Internet.) Most commercial-grade IPv4 firewalls block IP protocol 41, the 6to4 and tunnel protocol, unless it has been explicitly enabled [WAR200401].

In 2008, the Cooperative Association for Internet Data Analysis (CAIDA) and the American Registry for Internet Numbers (ARIN) surveyed over 200 respondents from USG agencies, commercial organizations (including ISPs and end users), educational institutions, associations, and other profit and nonprofit entities to determine the state of affairs in the United States in reference to IPv6 plans. Between 50% and 75% of the organizations surveyed indicated that they plan to deploy IPv6 by 2010 or sooner. See Figure 1.9 for some details [CLA200801]. According to some observers, IPv6 (and IPsec) are still emerging technologies, maturing and growing as practical experience is gained [REN200701].

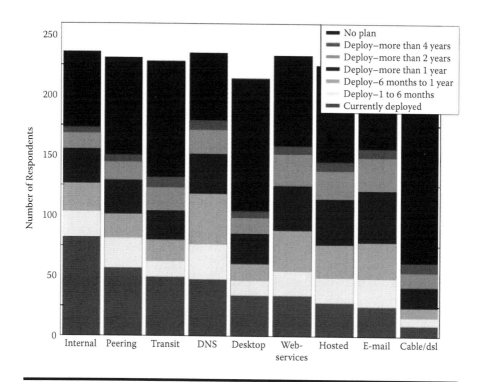

Figure 1.9 IPv6 deployment plans for U.S. institutions, 2008 CAIDA/ARIN survey.

A (near) press time summary of the IPv6 state of affairs at the worldwide level is as follows [LAD200601]:

1. IPv6 is a mature technology with significant deployment experience worldwide. The majority of deployment is in academic networks but commercial deployment is now growing, particularly in the Far East.
2. IPv6 has clear technical advantages but these need to be translated to business advantages for various sectors, with detailed but clear business models. This is a task for economists rather than standards developers and implementers.
3. IPv6 is supported fully by Microsoft; they have deployed it in their own worldwide enterprise network, and Windows Vista ships preferring use of IPv6 by default.
4. A number of companies have decided to support IPv6 as a core strategy, building products and services in advance of demand (e.g., Microsoft, NTT, KDDI).
5. A wide range of new IPv6 application scenarios is available to be exploited; many of these are green field scenarios (e.g., supply chain, sensor networks, or transport networks) that can use IPv6 from the outset.
6. IPv6 networks can enrich educational experiences, with the right support and vision.
7. IPv6 can facilitate convergence both between delivery platforms and between business sectors. This has the potential for streamlining services.
8. Commodity IPv6 devices are required for consumer (SOHO) deployment, in particular there are no IPv6 DSL routers available to the market; this hinders ISP deployment.
9. For IPv6 to be widely deployed in all commercial sectors, the immediate and realistic market needs must be addressed, in particular site multihoming and ISP independence, but also IPv6 capability in Operations Support Systems (OSS) and management tools.
10. Training and education capacity needs to be increased. Best practice, roadmap, and guidance documents are still required (e.g., defining IPv6 capable for those making public sector IT procurements).
11. While most important networking applications provide native IPv6 support, it looks like the main factor that limits the spread of IPv6 is currently shifting from a lack of applications to an apparent lack of interest among connectivity providers because only a few ISPs offer native IPv6 Internet access to their customers [BIE200801].

At press time, large U.S. carriers were offering IPv6 services targeting USG federal agencies. According to observers, U.S. carriers were in the process of *developing* IPv6 commercial services in the 2008–2009 timeframe, to be able to offer IPv6-based commercial connectivity by 2010 [MAR200801]. The globalization of multinationals is seen as a potential driver for demand to IPv6. IPv6 is now being deployed in a sustained manner in Japan and other Asian countries. Typical press time IPv6 carrier services included the following [ATT200801]:

- IPv6 Internet Connectivity Service
    - Provide connectivity to the IPv6 Internet for activities such as Web surfing and database searches
    - Support multiple access methods, Point-to-Point Protocol (PPP), Multi-Link PPP (MLPPP), Frame Relay, and ATM) for customer access, typically from large-user locations
- Remote Access Service to IPv6 Internet
    - Support IPv6 for small-user locations and individual remote users
    - Establish dynamically configurable IPv6 Tunnel Gateway through IPv4 ISPs through fractional T1, DSL, or dial-up access
    - The Tunnel Setup Protocol (TSP) can be used to create tunnels to transport IPv6 traffic over an IPv4 network to the gateway (TSP is used by the tunnel client to negotiate the tunnel with the broker. A mobile node implementing TSP can be connected to both IPv4 and IPv6 networks whether it is on IPv4 only, IPv4 behind a NAT, or on IPv6 only.) [BLA200101]
- IPv6 VPN Service
    - Use MPLS to create a VPN interconnecting a set of agency locations using the IPv6 protocol for access

Also see Table 1.4 [MAR200801].
More details on the IPv6 protocol are provided in Chapters 2 and 3.

1.3 Overview of Traditional Security Approaches and Mechanisms

As we noted, network and host security continue to be major concerns for enterprise-, institutional-, and service-provider environments. Well-documented recent studies show that cyberattacks continue to remain a substantial threat to organizations of all types. On average, companies experience several dozen attacks per week on their IT resources. About 20 percent of large companies suffer at least two severe events a year. The challenge to corporate planners just continues to get more onerous. Information security vulnerabilities are increasing at a pace that is far more than humans can understand. Carnegie Mellon University's Computer Emergency Response Team (CERT) identified just under 200 vulnerabilities in 1995 and 8,064 in 2006, showing a 4,000% increase in just 11 years (see Figure 1.10). It has been conservatively forecasted that in 2010 around 10,000 new vulnerabilities will be discovered in software applications in that year alone; this will force companies to assess and mitigate one new risk every hour each day of the year. Considering that each vulnerability instance has the potential to disrupt or bring a company's

Table 1.4   A Press-Time Snapshot of IPv6 Carrier Services/Positions in North America

Carrier	IPv6 Services
NTT America	NTT America began offering IPv6 access services in North America in 2003. NTT has been a leader in the development of new IPv6 offerings, such as an IPv6-enabled managed-firewall service in 2005. The Planet recently chose NTT America to supports its IPv6-based hosting services.
NTT Japan	NTT Japan offers a multipolicy IPv6 VPN, to provide managed security services for IPv6, to tunnel secure access over a public IPv6 infrastructure. This Multipolicy Access service (launched in August 2007), uses dedicated encryption devices that enable customers to use a secure VPN to link IPv6 systems connected to different networks. Network managers have access to an on-demand security-policy feature that allows them to set policies for different devices.
AT&T	Offers managed service for IPv6 routers but only on a custom basis, and targets a product-based approach in early 2009.
Sprint Nextel	Offers IPv6 services in a test-bed mode, and it is updating its federal telecommunications contracts to offer IPv6 services (the goal is to offer a generally available, orderable feature of IP MPLS services.) Sprint expects its IPv6 services will cost the same as its IPv4 services. The most common service will be a dual-stack solution to handle IPv4 and IPv6 traffic. For commercial customers, Sprint expects to have IPv6 over its global MPLS network and over SprintLink dedicated Internet network
Qwest Communications	Offers an IPv6 test bed. QWEST offers IPv6-related engineering support, which it plans to add to its Networx Universal and Networx Enterprise contracts.
Level 3 Communications	Has customers in North America and Europe that run IPv6 tunneled through IPv4, but it does not have commercial IPv6 services yet. As the carrier purchases new routers at the edge, it is ensuring that the equipment can support dual stack.

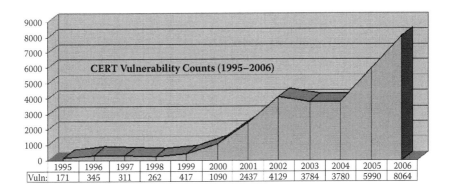

	1995	1996	1997	1998	1999	2000	2001	2002	2003	2004	2005	2006
Vuln:	171	345	311	262	417	1090	2437	4129	3784	3780	5990	8064

Figure 1.10 Documented CERT vulnerability trends.

business to a complete halt, organizations must take risk assessment seriously and determine how each risk will be handled. The increased number of vulnerabilities being discovered also drives up the number of security incidents worldwide, and it will increase to a point where 8,000 incidents a week will affect organizations that have not properly addressed and mitigated their risks. It is estimated that the worldwide financial impact of malicious code is around $100 B per year [POL200401].

If a company loses IT (computer or voice/data networking) resources for more than a day or two, the company may well find itself in financial trouble. Obviously, brokerage firms, banks, airports, medical establishments, and homeland security concerns would be impacted faster than, say, a manufacturing firm or a book publishing firm. However, the general concern is universal. If a company is unable to conduct business for more than a week, the company may well be permanently incapacitated. Therefore, there is a clear need to protect enterprises from random, negligent, malicious, or planned attacks on its IT resources. As more and more companies send their IT business abroad under the rubric of outsourcing or near-shoring, the potential IT (and, hence, corporate) risks are arguably growing at a geometric pace; these risks can have ultimately negative implications, particularly in view of cumulative exposures to risks which, in the aggregate, take on nontrivial probability.

Many companies are (now) shifting to a highly mobile work force for increased productivity and to address the generational requirement of a flexible work-life balance. To support this, mobility firms are upgrading their network architectures to support remote workforces. Mobile users need access to centrally located applications and data over the Internet; voice is also an issue. This, once again, raises the issue of system availability and, more importantly, security.

Although designed to provide better security through the mandatory use of IPsec, IPv6 also includes many enhancements, some of which can be exploited by attackers. For example, the address autoconfiguration feature can be used by attackers to announce rogue routers [BRO200801]. Some networks may already carry IPv6 traffic without the administrator's awareness. Therefore, it is critical to understand what the security issues are in the IPv6 context.

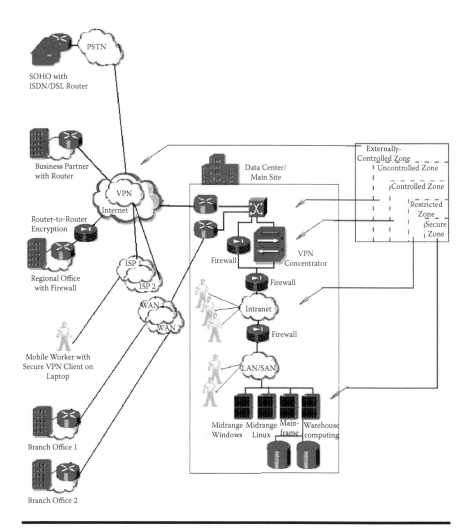

Figure 1.11   Typical firewall environment.

Firewalls are a basic mechanism to support perimeter security, even if by themselves they are only a partial solution. See Figure 1.11 for a typical environment. Firewall-based security is a method of guarding a private network by analyzing the data leaving and entering. Firewalls implement a policy-driven packet filtering function, typically used for restricting access to/from specific devices and applications. The policies are often termed Access Control Lists (ACLs) [SRI200201]. A basic firewall glossary as included in Table 1.5 (for a more extensive glossary, the reader may refer to [MIN200601].)

Firewalls are typically implemented as a network appliance (dedicated/stand-alone hardware), although it can also be just a software program (for example, for a PC client for host-based firewalls) [CSO200501]. The majority of packet-inspection

Table 1.5 Basic Security Glossary

Demilitarized Zone (DMZ)	(We prefer the expansion "demarcation zone.") An area of an intranet that is a barrier, or a buffer, between a company's internal network and resources connected to the network, and the outside public network. That portion of the intranet-to-extranet or intranet-to-Internet interface apparatus that supports a highly constrained access environment. An area between the hostile Internet and protected services; may be implemented as a Layer 2 switch that supports a number of Ethernet-attached devices sandwiched between a front- and a back-end firewall. The purpose of the DMZ is to prevent external users from getting direct access to a server or other corporate IT resources. A DMZ is usually comprised of routers, packet filters, firewalls, proxies, or mediation devices. A neutral zone, or buffer, that separates the internal and external networks. The DMZ usually exists between two firewalls. External users can access servers in the DMZ, but not the computers on the internal network. The servers in the DMZ act as intermediaries for both incoming and outgoing traffic [BRA200501]. The DMZ designates the area of protection that lies between the corporate computing environment and the Internet or publicly accessible network. The DMZ is typically where the firewalls, gateways, application proxies, and other protective computing devices are connected, and employs protective software such as filtering and intrusion detection applications.
Filter	A packet matching information mechanism that identifies a set of packets to be treated a certain way by a security mediation device. A set of terms or criteria used for the purpose of separating or categorizing. This is accomplished via single- or multifield matching of traffic header or payload data. 5-Tuple specification of packets in the case of a firewall and 5-tuple specification of a session in the case of a NAT function are examples of a filter [SRI200201].
Firewall	A method of guarding a private network by analyzing the data leaving and entering. Typically implemented as a network appliance (dedicated/standalone hardware), although it can also be just a software program (for example, for a PC client.) [CSO200501]. The majority of packet-inspection firewalls are designed to secure and
	(Continued)

Table 1.5   Basic Security Glossary (Continued)

	apply policy to the transport level. Firewalls range in functionality from basic protocol/port filtering devices to stateful session-level packet-inspection systems, to sophisticated application-layer proxy firewalls. Firewalls can also provide network address translation, so the actual IP addresses of devices inside the firewall stay hidden from public view.
	A policy based packet filtering function, typically used for restricting access to/from specific devices and applications. The policies are often termed Access Control Lists (ACLs) [SRI200201].
	Firewalls generally fall into three basic types: (1) Proxy (Application-layer) filtering firewall; (2) Stateful-inspection firewall (typically operating at the Transport or Session Layer); and, (3) Packet-filtering firewall (typically operating at the Network Layer). Firewalls form the fundamental gateway that controls (at different layers of the Open Systems Interconnection [OSI] protocol stack) traffic entering and leaving the network, and all security issues of this type (such as Denial of Service attacks) come under this heading [LIG200501].
	Packet-filtering firewalls use rules based on a packet's source, destination, port, or other basic information to determine whether or not to allow it into the network. More advanced stateful packet-filtering firewalls have access to more information from which to make their decisions. Stateful firewalls examine related inbound-outbound traffic for expected/predicted patterns.
	Proxy firewalls, that look at content and can involve authentication and encryption; they can be more flexible and secure but also tend to be slower. Although firewalls require configuration expertise, they are a critical component of network security [INF200501], [CSO200501].
Layer 2	The protocol layer below Layer 3 (that therefore offers the services used by Layer 3). Forwarding, when done by the swapping of short fixed-length labels, occurs at layer 2 regardless of whether the label being examined is an ATM (Asynchronous Transfer Mode), VPI/VCI (Virtual Path Identifier/Virtual Channel Identifier), a frame relay DLCI (Data Link Connection Identifier), or a MultiProtocol Label Switching (MPLS) label.
Layer 2 VPN (L2VPN)	Virtual Private Network (aka L2 VPN) Three types of L2VPNs are currently defined [RFC4026]: Virtual Private Wire Service (VPWS); Virtual Private LAN Service (VPLS); and IP-only LAN-like Service (IPLS).
	(Continued)

Table 1.5   Basic Security Glossary (Continued)

Layer 3	The protocol layer at which IP and its associated routing protocols operate link layer synonymous with Layer 2.
Layer 3 Security Mechanisms	Encryption mechanisms such as IPsec or Multilayer IPsec (ML-IPsec).
Layer 3 VPN (L3VPN)	(aka L3 VPN) A L3VPN interconnects sets of hosts and routers based on Layer 3 addresses; see [CAL200301].
Proxy	An intermediary program (system) that acts both as a server and as a client for the purpose of making requests on behalf of other clients. Requests are serviced internally or by passing them on, with possible translation, to other servers. A software agent that acts on behalf of a user, typical proxies accept a connection from a user, make a decision as to whether or not the user or client IP address is permitted to use the proxy, perhaps does additional authentication, and then completes a connection on behalf of the user to a remote destination [INF200501]. An intermediate relay agent between clients and servers of an application, relaying application messages between the two. Proxies use special protocol mechanisms to communicate with proxy clients and relay client data to servers and vice versa. A Proxy terminates sessions with both the client and the server, acting as server to the end-host client and as client to the end-host server. Applications such as FTP (File Transfer Protocol), SIP (Session Initiation Protocol), and RTSP (Real Time Streaming Protocol) use a control session to establish data sessions. These control and data sessions can take divergent paths. While a proxy can intercept both the control and data sessions, it might intercept only the control session. This is often the case with real-time streaming applications such as SIP and RTSP [SRI200201]. May include a function that replaces the IP address of a host on the internal (protected) network with its own IP address for all traffic passing through it.
Proxy Firewall	Unlike packet filtering, this type of firewall does more than simply block port access. Instead, it acts as a proxy server; processing access requests on behalf of the network on which it is located. This protects individual computers on the network, because they never interact directly with incoming client requests [CSO200501]. Firewalls that look at content and can involve authentication and encryption, can be more flexible and secure but may require more processing power [INF200501], [CSO200501].

(Continued)

Table 1.5 Basic Security Glossary (Continued)

Proxy Servers	Specialized application or server programs that run on a firewall host or on a dedicated appliance. Can be either a dual-homed host with an interface on the internal network and one on the external network, or some other bastion host that has access to the Internet and is accessible from the internal devices. These programs take users' requests for Internet services (such as FTP and Telnet) and forward them, as appropriate according to the site's security policy, to the actual services. The proxies provide replacement connections and act as gateways to the services. For this reason, proxies are sometimes known as *application-level gateways*. Proxy services intervene, often transparently, between a user on the inside (on the internal network) and a service on the outside (on the Internet). Instead of talking to each other directly, each talks to a proxy. Proxies handle all the communication between users and Internet services behind the scenes. To the user, a proxy server gives the appearance that the user is dealing directly with the real server. To the real server, the proxy server presents the illusion that the real server is dealing directly with a user on the proxy host (as opposed to the user's real host). Proxy servers have two main purposes: ◾ Improve Performance: Proxy servers can improve performance for groups of users by saving the results of all requests for a certain amount of time. ◾ Filter Requests: Proxy servers can also be used to filter requests. For example, a company might use a proxy server to prevent its employees from accessing a specific set of Web sites.
Proxy Services	Proxy services intervene, often transparently, between a user on the inside (on the internal network) and a service on the outside (on the Internet). Proxy services are effective only when they are used in conjunction with a mechanism that restricts direct communications between the internal and external hosts. Dual-homed hosts and packet filtering are two such mechanisms. If internal hosts are able to communicate directly with external hosts, there is no need for users to use proxy services, and so (in general) they will not; such bypass, however, is typically not in accordance with an organization's security policy.
	(Continued)

Table 1.5 Basic Security Glossary (Continued)

	A proxy service requires two components: a proxy server and a proxy client. In this situation, the *proxy server* runs on the dual-homed host. A *proxy client* is a special version of a normal client program (i.e., a Telnet or FTP client) that talks to the proxy server rather than to the real server out on the Internet; in addition, if users are taught special procedures to follow, normal client programs can often be used as proxy clients. The proxy server evaluates requests from the proxy client, and decides which to approve and which to deny. If a request is approved, the proxy server contacts the real server on behalf of the client (thus the term proxy), and proceeds to relay requests from the proxy client to the real server, and responses from the real server to the proxy client. In some proxy systems, instead of installing custom client proxy software, one employs standard software, but sets up custom user procedures for using it. A proxy service is not a firewall architecture; proxy services are used in conjunction with a firewall architecture.
Proxying	Approach that involves mediating a connection at an intermediate point. In this case the TCP connection is not between the client and the (application) host, but from the client to the intermediate proxy-server/gateway. In turn, the proxy will decide (based on some criteria) if and where a companion session to the ultimate (application) host needs to be established. Proxy servers can also be used to filter requests. Companies use proxy servers to improve performance (through caching Web pages and graphics), to filter requests to certain sites, to make sure that only certain users can get to the Internet, or as a way of accounting for Web use (logging sites that users visit). Most proxy servers can perform all of these tasks.
TCP Ports	Transport layer end-to-end protocol identifiers of traffic being carried in a network. (Long lists of well-known ports are published by the IETF.)
Extensible Markup Language (XML) Firewall	A (relatively) new type of firewall intended to secure XML messages and Web Services (WS). Traditional firewalls are not designed to understand or interpret the XML message-level security and they cannot defend against new XML message-based attacks. The majority of packet-inspection firewalls are designed to secure and apply policy to the transport level;

(Continued)

Table 1.5   Basic Security Glossary (Continued)

	therefore, they generally do not scan for content in Simple Object Access Protocol (SOAP), Universal Description, Discovery and Integration (UDDI), Security Assertion Markup Language (SAML), or other Web services protocols. The difference between an XML firewall and other firewalls is that much of the features in an XML firewall exist at the application layer and within the data payload or content, as opposed to the transport and session layer. Many modern XML firewalls act like high-performance proxies: they can approach wire speed performance by offloading crypto and XML validation functions to dedicated hardware (features such as message routing, encryption, and forwarding are somewhat of a commodity). In this role, the XML firewall performs security services such as authentication, authorization, auditing (AAA), and XML validation at a message level. The features are a separation of message-level security from transport-level security (these XML features do not act as transport-level connection security such as is done in SSL [Secure Sockets Layer]) [WRE200401].

firewalls are designed to secure and apply policy to the transport level. Firewalls generally fall into three basic types: (1) Proxy (Application-layer) filtering firewall; (2) Stateful-inspection firewall (typically operating at the Transport or Session layer); and, (3) Packet-filtering firewall (typically operating at the Network layer). Firewalls constitute the fundamental gateway (perimeter gatekeeper) that controls (at different layers of the OSI protocol stack) traffic entering and leaving the network.

As noted, firewalls range in functionality from basic protocol/port inspection, to stateful session-oriented packet inspection, to sophisticated application-layer proxy firewalls. A simple stateful edge firewall discards all traffic that is not locally destined and does not correspond to the firewall security policy or ruleset. Firewall rules are stored in a security policy table; the table is typically created manually by the security administrator. A typical firewall may support the following functions: packet filtering, object grouping, proxy services, URL filtering, stateful inspection, in-line authentication (with or without access to a RADIUS (Remote Access Dial-In User Service) server). Firewalls can also provide network address translation, so the actual IP addresses of devices inside the firewall stay hidden from public view; while many security professionals view this security through obscurity as a positive, this is precisely one of the issues of concern for end-to-end connectivity.

Most companies implement security in layers. The layering can be in terms of domains or in terms of assets categories. It is not effective to rely on a single point of protection when addressing the panoply of threats that can impact an IT environment; robust information security requires a multilayered approach. Companies typically see the environment as being comprised of the following zones (also known as domains) (see Figure 1.12 which depicts both a logical view and an example of a physical view):

■ Externally controlled Zone (ECZ) (such as a particular extranet or third-party environment with an established business relationship). Here the physical access, the IT administration, and the security authority are controlled by a third party.

■ Uncontrolled Zone (UZ) (such as the Internet and also carrier networks): no established business relationship exists where the firm can assess the security of the environment. Here the physical access, the IT administration, and the security authority are basically unknown.

■ Controlled Zone (CZ). Network point (zone) where all inbound and outbound communications are mediated (such as the firewall complex). Here the physical access, the IT administration, and the security authority are controlled by the firm in question. This domain separates the ECZ and UZ (e.g., Internet) from the Restricted Zone (typically the intranet) of the firm. This zone is used to implement a Demilitarized Zone (DMZ).

■ Restricted Zone (RZ). Here the physical access, the IT administration, and the security authority are controlled by the firm in question. Access is granted only to authorized/authenticated users or systems.

■ Secure(d) Zone (SZ). Network location (zone) that provides isolation from the RZ. This zone may contain more critical assets, such as the firm's data warehouse, the directory, or specialized applications (such as financials, payroll, etc.). Here the physical access, the IT administration, and the security authority are controlled by the firm in question.

It is also useful to look at layers from an asset category perspective. One example of this is Microsoft's Defense-in-Depth Model, as shown for illustrative purposes in Figure 1.13.

Most corporations today address security with a number of technical solutions, ranging from login/password, hardware tokens, and RADIUS servers for authentication, to VPNs for data encryption, to hardware (appliance) firewalls at corporate locations for data packet filtering, to antivirus software on remote PCs, to encrypted storage (e.g., per IEEE standard P1619). Hardware firewalls (routers or appliances), generally protect the corporate network from external attacks but cannot provide protection against attacks originating from within the corporate network (as noted above, however, the Secure Zone (Domain) is delimited by firewalls that are inside the corporate intranet itself). As noted, increasingly, enterprises make use of layered security approach. While authentication mechanisms ensure user/machine verification and VPNs ensure data privacy in transit, the conventional security tools (e.g., hardware firewalls and antivirus software) cannot fully protect the environment; malicious code, such as spyware, can use peer-to-peer file sharing, instant

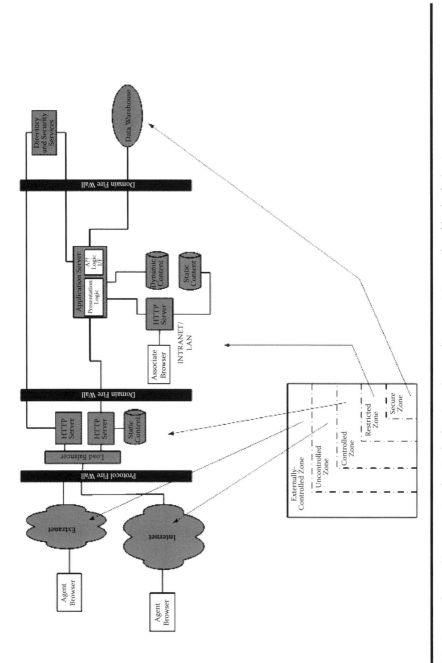

Figure 1.12 Layered security apparatus for typical enterprise environment (example of logical *view*).

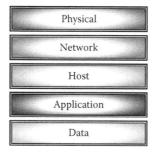

Figure 1.13   Asset category layering per Microsoft's defense-in-depth model.

messaging, and file downloading as a vehicle, and so can enter the corporate network to create damage or hog network bandwidth. These are the reasons why specific firewalls have implemented deep packet inspection and XML firewalls (which inspect deep into the headers and tags) can be useful [POL200401].

TCP/IP-based networking uses the TCP-Port apparatus to identify the protocol or applications with which a given TCP session should be associated. Firewall technology is very much dependent on this arrangement for proper functioning (other/supplementary techniques such as specifying an IP address or IP address ranges are also utilized). Two general observations are useful:

Applications using TCP are easier to manage through a firewall than applications using UDP (namely, firewalls are able to provide more security for TCP services).

Protocols/applications that have a smaller range of allowed port are easier to manage through a firewall than applications using a larger range—those using a single port are the easiest of all (namely, there is a greater level of security to reduce the number of ports that are opened up; in addition, many applications open a session on a specific port and then potentially open data on any TCP high port).

In the context of layered security, it should be mentioned that many organizations end up using the mechanism of NAT as part of the toolkit of available techniques by providing what some call security through obscurity. This entails keeping outside entities unaware of the addresses of internal devices such as servers, and so forth, so that these entities cannot then launch a direct attack (e.g., via a TELNET or a specifically targeted flow of Protocol Data Units (PDUs) and the like) against such devices. Clearly, NAT is a means to an end; hence, if every device has a globally unique address as in IPv6, then other methods will have to be put in place to provide a comparable layer of security that was provided by the previous state of obscurity.

A number of security issues on the Internet arise from the use of NAT and private IPv4 address space. It is virtually impossible to obtain a level of assurance based on IP addresses, since most users sit behind one or more NAT or similar devices that prevent the direct association of an IP address to a specific user or node. With the changes in IPv6 structure and increased address space, architectures and services can be developed to prevent address spoofing and establish the necessary association to support true network-level access control and authentication [JUN200801]. However, strong authentication is needed, because mechanisms always can be found to spoof any noncryptographically secured address. Figure 1.14 [ISL200501] depicts today's security environment compared to what is possible/desirable in an IPv6 future state. The new (NAT-free) security mechanisms facilitate end-to-end connectivity, mobility, and collaboration under a VoIP or 3G wireless environment in the coming years.

Security considerations and protection mechanisms must be a part of any IPv6 short-term (transition) and long-term (steady-state) plan for enterprises, institutions, and service providers (including traditional carriers, ISP, satellite operators, cellular operators, etc.). However, one must keep in mind that IPv6 (and the use of IPsec as part of IPv6) are still emerging technologies. Operating Systems (OS), router implementations, and firewall implementations may still be unstable, especial from 2nd tier providers; furthermore, not all the IPv6 features (e.g., mobility support, etc.) may be implemented. The 2008 CAIDA/ARIN survey mentioned earlier [CLA200801] found that vendor support for IPv6 was high on the list of obstacles according to almost a quarter of the respondents. While major router vendors support IPv6, support is lacking in security products, making IT managers wary that if they enable IPv6 they may open up security holes and not have the tools to mitigate them; even in products that support IPv6, it tended to be less robust than a product's IPv4 capabilities at press time [CAM200801]. For example, IPv6 may be supported in software rather than hardware, with concern over potential performance impact, or IPv6 may be supported at the command line interface but not be configurable from the GUI that is used to configure other product features. This text serves the purpose of both documenting what the security issues may be in IPv6, as well as serving as advocacy to equipment providers to add appropriate security mechanisms to their products.

When designing a security apparatus, one assumes an adversary may get complete access to the communications channels such that the intruder can read, write, replay, modify, reorder, rearrange, truncate, reroute, spoof headers and addresses, and so forth; that the intruder will be able to take control of routers and hosts; and that the intruder will launch new attacks from a system that has been penetrated and compromised. The security planner at an organization needs to know when

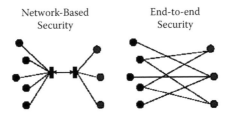

Figure 1.14   End-to-end security environment in IPv6.

and if this is happening, who is sending the attack or the malformed packets, and who is intercepting the data being transmitted by the organization. Clearly, the security planner aims at retaining network availability, data integrity, data confidentiality, and control of all the organization's IT assets. One of the weaknesses in IPv4 is the ability for malicious attackers to quickly scan and identify nodes on the Internet; once an attacker has access to an organization's subnet, it is a fairly quick and simple process to identify all of the nodes and focus on the ones with the greatest weakness. IPv6 provides a significant advantage due to the sheer number of potential addresses on a single subnet. There are 2^{64} or 18,446,744,073,709,551,616 potential IPv6 nodes on each subnet, making typical network scanning more difficult (i.e., taking much longer) [JUN200801].

It should be self-evident, but it is worth repeating, that IPv6 does not eliminate the requirements for perimeter-based/Defense-in-Depth mechanisms; organizations will continue to need application security, data security, physical security, auditing procedures, security policies, and so on. The basic approach will continue to be via perimeter defenses and firewalls; however, a definitive set of policies and profiles for IPv6 firewalls has not been developed as of press time.

Security personnel at institutions that make use of IPv6 need to be involved in order to appropriately update security policies and processes to include IPv6 technology. Vendors and tool developers need to add features to relevant products that make these products IPv6-aware (a short list of equipment or systems that need extensions include firewalls, certificates (objects distributed to businesses containing public keys), Certificate Authorities (entity that provides a way for two or more businesses to establish trust by virtue of the fact that they each trust a third party—VeriSign is an example of a public CA.)

Security experts have established that IPv6 has been found running today without administrators' knowledge, enabled intentionally by users or otherwise by intruders. This can provide a stealth network for intruders; at this time IPv6 networks are harder to scan, evading many intrusion detection systems. The problem here is that attacks on IPv6 can compromise coexisting IPv4 networks* [REN200701].

After a discussion of additional IPv6 protocol specifics in the two chapters that follow, a more detailed assessment of security-related approaches will be provided.

References

[ATT200801] AT&T, Promotional Literature on IPv6, 2008, "http://www.corp.att.com/gov/ipv6"

[BIE200801] Bieringer, P., F. Baraldi, et al. *Current status of ipv6 support for networking applications.* http://www.deepspace6.net/docs/ipv6_status_page_apps.html#security.

---

* Security administrators should block protocol 41; handle Teredo as a "dangerous UDP port" at IPv4 firewalls; and look out for Router Advertisements and for Neighbor Discovery packets (ICMPv6 over layer 2).

[BLA200101] M. Blanchet, R. Desmeules, A. Cormier, Tunnel Setup Protocol (TSP), IETF Internet-Draft, draft-vg-ngtrans-tsp-00, June 2001.

[BRA200501] Bradley, T. *Glossary.* http://netsecurity.about.com/library/glossary/bldef-appg. htm.

[BRO200801] BroadbandReports.com, dslreports.com. Does IPv6 introduce new security vulnerabilities? New York: Silver Matrix LLC, Feb, 15, 2008. http://www.broadban dreports.com/faq/ipvsix/4.0_IPv6_Security.

[CAL200301] Callon R., and M. Suzuki. A framework for layer 3 provider provisioned virtual private networks. Work in progress, July 2003.

[CAM200801] Campbell, D. *CAIDA and ARIN release IPv6 survey.* Apr. 13, 2008, CircleID (an online community hub for the Internet Infrastructure). www.circleid.com.

[CLA200801] Claffy, K.C. *ARIN & CAIDA IPv6 survey results.* ARIN XXI Public Policy Meeting in Denver, Apr. 7, 2008.

[CSO200501] CSO Online. http://www.csoonline.com/glossary/category.cfm?ID=13.

[DES200301] Desmeules, R. *Cisco self-study: Implementing Cisco IPv6 Networks (IPv6).* Cisco Press, June 6, 2003.

[DIR200801] Directorate-Generals Information Society "IPv6: Enabling the Information Society", European Commission Information Society, Europe Information Society Portal, 18 *February 2008*, http://ec.europa.eu/information_society/policy/ipv6/ index_en.htm

[DON200401] Donzé, F. IPv6 autoconfiguration, *The Internet Protocol Journal,* Volume 7, Number 2, June 2004. http://www.cisco.com/web/about/ac123/ac147/archived_ issues/ipj_7-2/ipv6_autoconfig.html.

[ERT200401] Ertekin, E., and C. Christou. IPv6 header compression, *North American IPv6 Summit.* June 2004, Booz Allen Hamilton.

[HER200201] Hermann-Seton, P. *Security features in IPv6.* SANS Institute 2002, as part of the Information Security Reading Room, 2002.

[ICA200701] ICANN Security and Stability Advisory Committee (SSAC). *Survey of IPv6 support in commercial firewalls.* Oct. 2007.

[INF200501] Infosec. http://www.infosec.uga.edu/glossary.html.

[IPV200501] IPv6 Portal, http://www.ipv6tf.org/meet/faqs.php

[ISL200501] Islam, J. IPv6 applications, *v6 Application Initiative.* IPv6 Forum, 2005.

[JUN200801] Juniper Networks. An IPv6 security guide for U.S. government agencies: Executive summary, *The IPv6 World Report Series*, Volume 4. Sunnyvale, CA:, Juniper Networks, Feb. 2008.

[KAE200601] Kaeo, M., D. Green, J. Bound, and Y. Pouffary. IPv6 security technology paper, *North American IPv6 Task Force (NAv6TF) Technology Report*, July 22, 2006.

[LAD200601] L. Ladid, "European IPv6 Roadmap 2006 Recommendations, European IPv6 Task Force, IPv6 Task Force Steering Committee, IST-2-004572-CA IPv6 TF-SC Euro-v6-Roadmap, 8/10/2006.

[LIG200501] Lightreading Online Magazine. http://www.lightreading.com.

[LIO199801] Lioy, A. Security features of IPv6, Chapter 8, *Internetworking IPv6 with Cisco routers,* Silvano Gai. New York: McGraw-Hill, 1998, also available at www.ip6.com/ us/book/Chap8.pdf.

[MAR200801] Marsan, C. D. Carriers quietly developing IPv6 services, *NetworkWorld.* Apr. 2, 2008.

[MIC200501] Microsoft Promotional Material on IPv6.

[MIN200601] Minoli, D., and J. Cordovana. *Authoritative computer and network security dictionary.* New York: Wiley, 2006.

[MSD200401] Microsoft Corporation, MSDN Library, Internet Protocol, 2004, http://msdn.microsoft.com

[POL200401] Pollock, R. Secure Networks, *Communications News*, Apr. 2004.

[REN200701] Renard, K. *Security issues in IPv6.* San Diego, CA: WareOnEarth Communications Inc., 2007.[RFC0791] Postel, J. Request for Comments: 0791, Internet Protocol, STD 5, RFC 791, Sept. 1981.

[RFC1883] Deering, S., and R. Hinden. Request for Comments: 1883, Internet Protocol, Version 6 (IPv6) Specification, Dec. 1995.

[RFC1884] Hinden, R., and S. Deering, eds. Request for Comments: 1884, IP Version 6 Addressing Architecture, RFC 1884, Dec. 1995.

[RFC1885] Conta, A., and S. Deering. Request for Comments: 1885, Internet Control Message Protocol (ICMPv6) for the Internet Protocol Version 6 (IPv6) Specification, RFC 1885, Dec. 1995.

[RFC2401] Kent, S., and R. Atkinson. Request for Comments: 2401, Security Architecture for the Internet Protocol, Nov. 1998.

[RFC2402] Kent, S., and R. Atkinson. Request for Comments: 2402, IP Authentication Header, Nov. 1998.

[RFC2406] Kent, S., and R. Atkinson. Request for Comments: 2406, IP Encapsulating Security Protocol (ESP), Nov. 1998.

[RFC2460] Deering, S., and R. Hinden. Request for Comments: 2460, Internet Protocol, Version 6 (IPv6) Specification, Dec. 1998.

[RFC2893] R. Gilligan, E. Nordmark, Transition Mechanisms for IPv6 Hosts and Routers, RFC 2893, August 2000. Copyright The Internet Society (2000). All Rights Reserved. This document and translations of it may be copied and furnished to others, and derivative works that comment on or otherwise explain it or assist in its implementation may be prepared, copied, published and distributed, in whole or in part, without restriction of any kind, provided that the above copyright notice and this paragraph are included on all such copies and derivative works.

[RFC3022] Srisuresh, P., and K. Egevang. Request for Comments: 3022, Traditional IP Network Address Translator (Traditional NAT), RFC 3022, Jan. 2001.

[RFC4026] Andersson, L., and T. Madsen. Request for Comments: 4026, Provider Provisioned Virtual Private Network (VPN) Terminology, RFC 4026, Mar. 2005.

[RFC4038] M-K. Shin, Ed., Y-G. Hong, J. Hagino, P. Savola, E. M. Castro, "Application Aspects of IPv6 Transition", RFC 4038, March 2005.

[SHI200201] P. Srisuresh, J. Kuthan, J. Rosenberg, A. Molitor, A. Rayhan, "Middlebox Communication Architecture and Framework", RFC 3303, August 2002.

[WAR200401] Warfield, M. H. *Security implications of IPv6.* X-Force, Internet Security Systems, Inc. (ISS), 16th Annual FIRST Conference on Computer Security Incident Handling, June 13–18, 2004, Budapest, Hungary. www.iss.net, http://www.first.org/conference/2004/papers/c06.pdf.

[WRE200401] Wrenn, G. *Securing Web services: A job for the XML firewall.* Mar. 8, hsecurity.techtarget.com/tip/1,289483,sid14_gci954170,00.html?Offer=SEcpwslg25.

[YAI200001] Yaiz, R. A., and O. Öztürk. *Mobility in IPv6,* The IPv6 Portal, 2000. www.ipv6tf.org.

[6NET200501] 6NET, "D2.2.4: Final IPv4 to IPv6 Transition Cookbook for Organizational/ISP (NREN) and Backbone Networks", Version: 1.0 (4th February 2005), Project Number. IST-2001-32603, CEC Deliverable Number: 32603/UOS/DS/2.2.4/A1.

Appendix A: Six-Month Listing of IPv6 Press

This appendix lists six-months' worth of IPv6 headlines and activities at press time, from the IPv6 Portal (www.ipv6tf.org), to illustrate the kind of busy activities taking place in the IPv6 context worldwide.

Apr 22, 2008	Survey: Agencies not ready for IPv6 deadline
Apr 22, 2008	Exponential Growth of Enterprise Data Causing Increased Adoption of WAN Data Compression and Acceleration Technologies—New Research From TheInfoPro
Apr 22, 2008	Fujitsu Introduces the First 802.3ap (KR) Compliant 10GbE Switch IC, Featuring the Industry's Highest Density of 26 Ports and Lowest Power Consumption
Apr 22, 2008	SMC Expands and Improves Product Offerings for Small Office, Hospitality, Broadband MSO and High-Performance Networking
Apr 22, 2008	Working to keep the Internet running
Apr 21, 2008	Is Peering Breaking Down?
Apr 21, 2008	2 Colo. firms assist with new Internet address protocol
Apr 21, 2008	Can Users Be Enticed Over to IPv6?
Apr 21, 2008	Ph-Domains: Ahead of its time
Apr 21, 2008	Wanted: 10 IT skills employers need today
Apr 21, 2008	Is the internet doomed
Apr 21, 2008	The End of The Internet: Switching to IPv6
Apr 21, 2008	Storm clouds looming for Internet, experts say
Apr 21, 2008	Western DataCom received a Phase II SBIR contract from the US Navy for $1.2 million dollars
Apr 17, 2008	Allied Telesis Shows Off New SwitchBlade(R) x908 Layer 3 Modular Switch to the Americas
Apr 17, 2008	Migrate to IPv6 vendors warn again
Apr 17, 2008	Industry execs sound IPv6 alarm—is the sky really falling?
Apr 17, 2008	Notes from the Global IPv6 Summit in China
Apr 17, 2008	Government IT Survey Shows IPv6 Confusion and Low Adoption for Virtualization Management Tools
Apr 17, 2008	Sound the Alarm, IPv6 Execs Say

Apr 17, 2008	Arch Rock Brings IP-Based Wireless Sensor Networking to Atmel Embedded Hardware
Apr 17, 2008	Progress Software Announces OpenEdge 10.1c
Apr 17, 2008	Sensinode Ltd. Joins Texas Instruments' Low-Power RF Developer Network, Offers IPv6 Wireless Network Solutions Based on 6LoWPAN Standard Technology
Apr 14, 2008	Tiscali International Network Scales High-Performance Infrastructure with Juniper Networks T1600 Core Router
Apr 14, 2008	CAIDA and ARIN Release IPv6 Survey
Apr 13, 2008	SEH Print Server Serves Up Energy Savings
Apr 13, 2008	Next generation optical broadband networks
Apr 13, 2008	The Rocky Mountain IPv6 Summit: Getting Real
Apr 11, 2008	NTT Com Named Best Wholesale Carrier at Telecom Asia Awards 2008
Apr 11, 2008	U.S. Cable—New Strategies for a Competitive World
Apr 11, 2008	Nominum Foundation ANS/CNS
Apr 11, 2008	ICANN Posts Schedule for Paris Meeting
Apr 11, 2008	ICANN Partnering to Promote Internet Education in Russia
Apr 11, 2008	Cisco reveals Australian contribution to ASR 1000 super-router
Apr 11, 2008	SEH Introduces Security Features to New Print Server
Apr 11, 2008	NTT Communications Silver Sponsor of Rocky Mountain IPv6 Summit
Apr 11, 2008	Interface Masters Technologies Introduces Internal Gigabit Secure Bypass NIC with Gigabit Rate SSL/IPsec Accelerator
Apr 11, 2008	Lumeta's IPsonar 4.1 Enables Discovery of IPv6 Devices Connected to the Network
Apr 07, 2008	Everything Over IP
Apr 07, 2008	Cisco Speaks at FOSE on IPv6 Enterprise Architecture Transition
Apr 07, 2008	Are Domain Name Registrars Ready for IPv6?
Apr 07, 2008	ARIN to Hold Meetings in Denver
Apr 07, 2008	VLC Media Player Portable 0.8.6f

Apr 07, 2008	Virtutech beefs up virtualized software dev't platform
Apr 07, 2008	Feds ready for IPv6
Apr 07, 2008	A key to IPv6 transition
Apr 07, 2008	U.S. Carriers Quietly Developing IPv6 Services
Apr 07, 2008	Product spotlight: Fose 2008
Apr 07, 2008	Axis Announces AXIS P3301 New Generation of Network Camera With H.264 Performance
Apr 07, 2008	Agencies get ready to reduce Internet gateways
Apr 02, 2008	IPv6 Deployment: Just Where Are We?
Apr 02, 2008	Ubuntu Security Notice—openssh vulnerability (USN-597-1)
Apr 02, 2008	Nigeria: Experts Give Reasons for IPv4 Decline
Apr 02, 2008	C&M industry to grow 10% this year
Apr 02, 2008	Feds: We will meet June IPv6 deadline
Apr 02, 2008	Canon U.S.A. Brings the Power of Its imageRUNNER Line to the Desktop with the Addition of New Laser Beam Printers
Apr 02, 2008	NTT Com to Offer Global Unified Threat Management Service
Apr 02, 2008	IPv6 will hit like an avalanche, NTT America CTO predicts
Apr 02, 2008	No More IP's for Web?
Apr 02, 2008	Metaaso mermaid IPv6 P2P App
Apr 02, 2008	Spirent Federal Systems Announces New Website
Apr 02, 2008	Arch Rock Builds Internet Protocol Links Into Wireless Sensors
Apr 02, 2008	Leading Online Gaming Provider Chooses A10 Networks' AX Series Advanced Traffic Manager to Boost Application Performance
Mar 30, 2008	IPv6… A Pre-Game Show in Denver and Featured at the Geneva Auto Show
Mar 30, 2008	InterNiche Technologies Releases v3.1 of its Embedded Protocol and Announces Availability of RTP/RTCP and SNTP Modules
Mar 30, 2008	IPv6: How Many IP Addresses Can Dance on the Head of a Pin?

Mar 30, 2008	Cisco patches IOS vulnerabilities
Mar 30, 2008	The five hottest skills for your networking career
Mar 30, 2008	.NET on the 'NET March 18-25: New IIS7 Goodness and MVC opens up
Mar 26, 2008	OpenSSH X11 Forwarding Information Disclosure Vulnerability
Mar 26, 2008	Admin Alert: How System i Boxes Impersonate Each Other
Mar 26, 2008	ZigBee Alliance Forms New Group To Expand Existing ZigBee IP Capabilities
Mar 26, 2008	BT to Exhibit at FOSE, April 1-3, 2008
Mar 26, 2008	NIST unveils tool to foil attacks via DNS
Mar 26, 2008	Nissin Systems Selects Lantronix Technology Platform to Support IPv6, the Next-Generation Internet Protocol
Mar 25, 2008	Configuring an L2TPv3 Ethernet Pseudowire
Mar 25, 2008	Vyatta VP: Cisco stockholders should be screaming bloody murder
Mar 25, 2008	The Planet Chooses NTT America to Deliver IPv6 Functionality to Its Network
Mar 25, 2008	CAI Networks Announces Enhancements to HTTP Compression, DDoS Attack Protection, and L7 Traffic Management in its WebMux Load Balancer
Mar 25, 2008	10 Gig access switches: Not just packet pushers anymore
Mar 25, 2008	The Planet to offer IPv6 hosting services
Mar 25, 2008	Philippines urged to start moving to IPv6
Mar 25, 2008	Kenya: Experts Caution Over Aging Internet System
Mar 25, 2008	A Peek at Snort 3.0
Mar 25, 2008	NTT America and Pulvermedia Join Forces on IPv6 Education Series
Mar 25, 2008	Windows Vista: Another Windows ME? I hope so!
Mar 25, 2008	Government Insights Examines Top IT Security Vendors in Government for 2008
Mar 25, 2008	IETF douses IPv4

Mar 25, 2008	Vista Service Pack 1 released
Mar 25, 2008	Portable MPEG recorder and player
Mar 25, 2008	Microsoft eyes a meaner, 'greener' P2P for Windows 7
Mar 17, 2008	IDT Introduces Innovative Packet Processing Solution for Delivery of Advanced Network Applications
Mar 17, 2008	Taiwan market: Farglory to launch IPv6 residential applications through cooperation with CHT and TWNIC
Mar 17, 2008	Docsis 3.0 Testing Skips a Beat
Mar 17, 2008	The Internet's Space Shortage
Mar 14, 2008	Allied Telesis Launches SwitchBlade x908 Layer 3 Modular Switch
Mar 14, 2008	Gates, Mundie Urge More Long Term U.S. Investment In Tech
Mar 14, 2008	Tenable releases Nessus 3.2 security scanner
Mar 14, 2008	Broadcom Enables Downstream Channel Bonded Services With Industry Leading Single-Chip Modem Solutions
Mar 14, 2008	Network interface card ups security for HP printers
Mar 14, 2008	The future of the 'Net, past and present
Mar 14, 2008	Network Time Protocol Updated for Improved Granularity, IPv6
Mar 14, 2008	What the U.S. is missing by ignoring IPv6
Mar 14, 2008	DigiWorld Summit 2008: The Future of the Internet
Mar 14, 2008	IPv6 faces trial by fire tonight
Mar 14, 2008	Work on IPv6 integration and migration surges
Mar 14, 2008	Red Hat Enterprise Linux 5.2 Beta Now Available
Mar 12, 2008	Is Google live with IPv6 ?
Mar 12, 2008	Ciena Uses EZchip's Network Processors for Carrier Ethernet Switching
Mar 12, 2008	Nigeria: Use of IPv4 Declines—Report
Mar 12, 2008	CIO Panel Live from FOSE
Mar 12, 2008	MIMOS launches two centres of excellence
Mar 12, 2008	The IPv6 experience: Are you experienced yet?

Mar 11, 2008	Google IPv6 Conference 2008
Mar 11, 2008	New generation internet laboratory to open in Sofia
Mar 11, 2008	Who guards the guards: Security
Mar 11, 2008	IETF Highlights Future Numbering System for the Internet – Demonstration of the IPv6-only Network
Mar 09, 2008	Research and Markets: A Brief Introduction and Refresher to the IPv6 Networking Protocol
Mar 09, 2008	WiWi Solution Offers Affordable & Wider Broadband Coverage
Mar 08, 2008	Uninterruptible power systems meet factory automation security
Mar 08, 2008	Internet Engineering Task Force to Meet in Philadelphia, March 9–14, 2008
Mar 08, 2008	AppGate Adds Kerberos, IPv6 Support
Mar 08, 2008	33 Million Domain Names Registered in 2007, Total Domains Now Over 153 Million
Mar 08, 2008	Optimize Your Windows Server 2008 Deployment
Mar 07, 2008	IPv6 allocations: The tide comes in
Mar 06, 2008	3G Americas Provides IPv6 Transition Recommendations for the Americas
Mar 06, 2008	VeriSign Publishes Domain Brief
Mar 06, 2008	A fragile experiment is under way
Mar 06, 2008	Cisco unveils compact new edge router
Mar 06, 2008	Kyocera Mita America Introduces Highly-Efficient, Compact Monochrome Desktop Printer
Mar 06, 2008	3K Computers Introduces Two New Notebooks
Mar 06, 2008	Black Sea-Area Researchers to Get Online
Mar 06, 2008	Double-Take Software Announces Support for Microsoft® Windows Server 2008 and New IPv6 and Transactional NTFS Features
Mar 03, 2008	IP routing enables net-centric warfare
Mar 03, 2008	Windows Server 2008 in the spotlight

Mar 01, 2008	Q&A: Evans says feds steaming ahead on cybersecurity plan, but with privacy in mind
Mar 01, 2008	VLC Media Player 0.8.6e
Feb 29, 2008	IPv6 Hour... One, Two, Three, IPv4 Switched Off!
Feb 29, 2008	Linksys WRVS4400N
Feb 29, 2008	Radios in Combat
Feb 29, 2008	Guidance for demonstrating IPv6 capability
Feb 29, 2008	Internet Infrastructure, Web Development & Audio-Visual Coding
Feb 29, 2008	ZigBee Alliance Continues Expanding the Internet of Things
Feb 29, 2008	IPv6 Over Satellite: Pie in the Sky?
Feb 29, 2008	Survey shows CIOs losing seat at the table
Feb 29, 2008	Microsoft touts Longhorn security
Feb 29, 2008	NTT Managed Hosted Firm, Participates in Federal Computer Week IPv6 Webcast
Feb 29, 2008	Buffalo WZR-AG300NH draft-n Wi-Fi router review
Feb 29, 2008	F5 Networks Announces Application Ready Network for Microsoft Windows Server 2008
Feb 29, 2008	Apple Mac OS X "ipcomp6_input()" Denial of Service
Feb 29, 2008	Will Microsoft Windows Server 2008's Rising Tide Lift Vista's Boat?
Feb 29, 2008	Apple's Mac OS X Vulnerable To Networking Exploit
Feb 29, 2008	YouTube's loss shows a bigger picture
Feb 29, 2008	New Teknovus EPON Optical Line Terminal Chip to Revolutionize Service Provider ROI and Subscriber Experience
Feb 26, 2008	Fortinet Completes Requirements for IPv6 Certification on FortiOS 3.0 Firmware
Feb 26, 2008	Lumeta Expands Executive Team with Industry Veterans
Feb 26, 2008	Axis Communications Announces Instant PTZ Network Camera With Vandal Resistance for Demanding Environments
Feb 26, 2008	OpenBSD Two Denial of Service Vulnerabilities

Feb 26, 2008	NTT Managed Hosted Network Platform, Chosen for Twitter Messaging Network
Feb 24, 2008	Domain Pulse 2008: Day 2 Focuses on DNS Security
Feb 24, 2008	Computer security's dubious future
Feb 24, 2008	IPv6 Hour at NANOG: A Follow-Up
Feb 24, 2008	New Software Systems From Harris Corporation Deliver Best-In-Class, Interoperable Workflow Solutions For Broadcasters
Feb 24, 2008	Mu Discovers Vulnerabilities in MPlayer
Feb 24, 2008	Motorola Unveils Full Portfolio of DOCSIS(R) 3.0 CPE
Feb 24, 2008	IPv6 and IPv4—big trouble coming, and soon
Feb 24, 2008	Some agencies must plan for TIC initiative, officials say
Feb 24, 2008	Juniper Networks Report Describes IPv6 Security Issues & Transition Strategies for U.S. Government Agencies
Feb 24, 2008	Tech Nite Set For March 5
Feb 24, 2008	HP ProCurve switches on link in space
Feb 24, 2008	IPv6 Hour at NANOG
Feb 24, 2008	The struggle to conform
Feb 24, 2008	Holistic tack to 32-bit design
Feb 24, 2008	Canon U.S.A. Adds to Its Color Line-up with the Introduction of the Canon Color imageRUNNER C2550 Multifunction Device
Feb 24, 2008	4 entrepreneurs at the forefront of IPv6
Feb 24, 2008	Express Logic Unveils NetX Duo™ IPv4/IPv6 Dual Stack for Embedded Networking
Feb 24, 2008	RAD Selects EZchip's Carrier-Ethernet Access Network Processors
Feb 24, 2008	Infraco delays Neotel
Feb 24, 2008	XAVi Technologies Launches IP-STB with Integrated 802.11n and DVB-T Functionality
Feb 24, 2008	Can an IPv4 stock market stave off address depletion, IPv6?

Feb 24, 2008	Michigan's Own bitServe Celebrates 10 Years of Service Despite Struggling Economy
Feb 24, 2008	Get Your Business SOA and Web Services Enabled
Feb 18, 2008	31st ICANN meeting at New Delhi concludes
Feb 18, 2008	HP-UX update for Apache
Feb 18, 2008	Will there be an IP address black market?
Feb 18, 2008	Ubuntu Security Notice—linux-source-2.6.15 vulnerabilities (USN-578-1)
Feb 18, 2008	FreeBSD Security Advisory—IPsec null pointer dereference panic (FreeBSD-SA-08:04.ipsec)
Feb 18, 2008	A new Internet
Feb 18, 2008	New Software Systems From Harris Deliver Best-in-Class, Interoperable Workflow Solutions For Broadcasters
Feb 14, 2008	Experts: Use a vision of the future to sell IPv6
Feb 14, 2008	Could IP address plan mean another IPv6 delay?
Feb 13, 2008	BreakingPoint Systems to Upgrade Metasploit-Inspired Tool
Feb 13, 2008	VeriSign moves closer to IPv6
Feb 13, 2008	Tests have shown military value for the latest version of the wireless standard, which offers high data throughputs while moving at high speeds.
Feb 13, 2008	You're All Going to Need IP Addresses
Feb 13, 2008	ICANN Recovers Large Block of Internet Address Space
Feb 13, 2008	ICANN meeting begins in New Delhi with call for IPv4 - IPv6 interoperability
Feb 13, 2008	Special IPv6 report|The promise of opportunities
Feb 13, 2008	American Systems Appoints Edward Ghafari to Develop New High-End Systems Engineering Practice
Feb 13, 2008	NextPoint rolls out IP Multimedia Exchange to meet growing demand for FMC applications and services
Feb 11, 2008	VeriSign Announces Key Operational Enhancements to Root Server Infrastructure
Feb 10, 2008	F5 warns organizations to plan carefully on IPv6

Feb 10, 2008	Businesses should not delay move to IPv6, caution experts
Feb 10, 2008	Extreme Networks Boosts Adoption of Internet2 With IPv6 Enabled Network for Pennsylvania Community College
Feb 10, 2008	SAIX prepares for IPv6
Feb 10, 2008	College rolls out IPv6 in full upgrade
Feb 07, 2008	Digi Launches Industry's First Flexible Ethernet Networking Module
Feb 07, 2008	SUSE Security Announcement—kernel (SUSE-SA:2008:006)
Feb 07, 2008	NetBSD "ipcomp6_input()" Remote Denial of Service Vulnerability
Feb 07, 2008	KAME Project "ipcomp6_input()" Denial of Service
Feb 07, 2008	NIST Releases a Profile for IPv6 in the U.S. Government for Comment—Comments Due Feb. 29
Feb 07, 2008	Who's afraid of IPv4 address depletion? Apparently no one.
Feb 07, 2008	Telstra Europe Selects Foundry's NetIron MLX Metro Routers for Its UK Network
Feb 07, 2008	Extreme Networks Completes US Department of Defense Joint Interoperability Test Command VoIP Assurance Testing
Feb 07, 2008	SEH Enlarges Print Server Portfolio With Gigabit Print Servers
Feb 07, 2008	Expand support for IPv6
Feb 07, 2008	ICANN flips switch on IPv6 DNS root servers
Feb 07, 2008	Alcatel-Lucent Introduces A New Appliance For IP Management
Feb 07, 2008	HP-UX has issued an update for Apache
Feb 07, 2008	IPv6 Address Added for Root Servers in the Root Zone—ICANN
Feb 07, 2008	Will the new Internet address system be a second Y2K?
Feb 07, 2008	IPv6 tries, tries again
Feb 07, 2008	IP Version 6 switches on
Feb 06, 2008	ICANN Finally Begins Updated IP Standard Rollout
Feb 06, 2008	Ubuntu Security Notice—linux-source-2.6.17/20/22 vulnerabilities (USN-574-1)

Feb 06, 2008	Internet Address Upgrade Creates More Tubes
Feb 06, 2008	Enterasys Announces New 10 Gigabit Ethernet Connectivity
Feb 06, 2008	SecureInfo RMS 5.0 Simplifies FISMA Compliance Through Comprehensive C&A Automation and Management Reporting
Feb 06, 2008	Massive internet switchover begins
Feb 06, 2008	Q&A: IP Version 6
Feb 04, 2008	Overhaul of net addresses begins
Feb 04, 2008	Taking control of IPv6
Feb 04, 2008	IP addresses: A wasted resource?
Feb 04, 2008	Internet Repotting About to Start!
Feb 04, 2008	FDCC compliance slowed by manual checks
Feb 04, 2008	NovaPower Solutions Adds Features, Reduces Maintenance/Training With Next-Generation SRNDTI UPS
Feb 04, 2008	Cyber Defence: National Security in a Borderless World
Feb 04, 2008	INPUT Expects Communications and Network Services Market to Reach $22.4 Billion By 2012
Feb 04, 2008	GSA ensuring offerings are IPv6-compliant
Feb 04, 2008	The Planet Dedicated Server Web Host, Participates in Pacific Telecom Event
Feb 04, 2008	Research and Markets: Analysis of the WiMax Forum, IPv6, and the Emergence of ENUM Is All Covered Inside the Q1 2008 'Wireless Broadband Technology Trends Report'
Feb 04, 2008	Dr.Web Enterprise Suite 4.44 — next generation of antivirus and antispam protection of corporate networks!
Jan 31, 2008	Behind the scenes of Internet2
Jan 31, 2008	UK Government fails to take IPv6 implementation seriously
Jan 31, 2008	Radiocrafts And Sensinode Announce 6LoWPAN Wireless IPv6-Network Solutions
Jan 31, 2008	Xelerated Extends Leadership in High-Performance Network Processing With Introduction of two new Products
Jan 31, 2008	About the Windows Server 2008 stack
Jan 31, 2008	Korea's NGN Technology Being Adopted as International Standard

Jan 31, 2008	IPv6 profile takes the long view
Jan 31, 2008	Nortel Ethernet Solutions Power IPTV Network For Vastar Cable TV
Jan 31, 2008	Wireless Broadband Opportunities Fuel Rapid Development of Mobile WiMAX
Jan 31, 2008	Client-based WDS: Providing Application Acceleration in Mobile and VPN Environments
Jan 31, 2008	NTT America to Demonstrate IPv6 at Largest Capitol Hill Tech Policy Exhibition
Jan 31, 2008	NetLogic Microsystems Introduces the World's First "Hybrid" Knowledge-based Processor with a Revolutionary Convergence Architecture
Jan 27, 2008	NIST Releases Requirements for IPv6-Ready Products
Jan 27, 2008	3K Computers Announces New VAR Channel Sales Program
Jan 25, 2008	Prime Time for IPv6 Ready Logo Phase II
Jan 25, 2008	Latest draft of federal IPv6 profile released for comment
Jan 25, 2008	Enterasys extends 10G Ethernet support across switch family
Jan 25, 2008	Juniper Ditches DX Line
Jan 25, 2008	What will IPv6 do for you? The applications aren't clear
Jan 25, 2008	Green Hills Software Announces Single Source Access to Advanced Layer 3 Routing Solutions
Jan 25, 2008	Cisco Extends Catalyst Switch Portfolio to Address Evolving Application and Network Requirements
Jan 25, 2008	Get IPv6 skills now rather than later
Jan 25, 2008	Google Balks at EU Take on IP Addresses
Jan 23, 2008	Test Reveals A10's AX Series Next-Generation Server Load Balancers Outperform Industry Leader
Jan 23, 2008	A10 Networks' AX Series Wins Server Load Balancer of the Year Award from China Computer World Magazine
Jan 23, 2008	A10 Networks Unveils New Capabilities for AX Series Advanced Traffic Manager Appliances
Jan 22, 2008	FBI requests spawn network forensics start-up
Jan 22, 2008	NTT's 'Killer' IPv6 App a Potential Lifesaver

Jan 22, 2008	xStack Switches It Up
Jan 18, 2008	Telematics devices built with INTEGRITY OS
Jan 16, 2008	GSA, DHS issue RFI for Trusted Internet Connections
Jan 16, 2008	ProCurve Adds IPv6 Support To Switch Software
Jan 16, 2008	NTT America Supports Further IPv6 Development and Migration
Jan 15, 2008	Gigabit switch offers flexibility
Jan 15, 2008	Ipswitch, Inc. to Host Webinar Featuring Independent Research Firm on 'Why You Need to Think About Network Management'
Jan 15, 2008	EMC Introduces Virtual Provisioning, New Management Capabilities for Symmetrix
Jan 15, 2008	The Planet's Stan Barber to Deliver Address at PTC 08
Jan 12, 2008	3K Computers Verified as IPv6 Ready by UNH-IOL Technology Consortium
Jan 12, 2008	Federal Government Adds BDNA to Premier Software Procurement Vehicles
Jan 12, 2008	Verizon Business Increases Network Speeds, Performance to Stay Ahead of Customers' IP Growth Needs
Jan 12, 2008	Critical Windows flaw affects XP, Vista
Jan 12, 2008	Feds Look To Fudge IPv6 Mandates
Jan 12, 2008	The straight story on OMB's Internet connection policy
Jan 12, 2008	Group Logic Signs Global Procurement Contract with Omnicom Group Inc.
Jan 12, 2008	Mindspeed and Jungo Introduce Carrier-Class Residential Gateway Reference Platform
Jan 11, 2008	Rapid7 Adds Web 2.0 and Web Application Security Expert to Executive Team
Jan 11, 2008	Up to 300 Megawatt Worth of Keepalive Messages to be Saved by IPv6?
Jan 11, 2008	Ikanos Featured in Major Korean Telco's First Trial Deployment of Residential Gateways
Jan 07, 2008	IPv6 Set for Root Adoption?

Jan 04, 2008	DNS Enhancements in Windows Server 2008
Jan 04, 2008	Mu Security Analyzer
Jan 03, 2008	IPv6: Six Months And Counting
Jan 03, 2008	IPv6 reality check
Jan 03, 2008	IPv6: coming to a root server near you
Jan 03, 2008	Gentoo Linux Security Advisory—Wireshark: Multiple vulnerabilities (GLSA 200712-23)
Jan 03, 2008	Perspective: Get ready for a rocking '08 in networking tech
Dec 31, 2007	Everything you need to know about Microsoft certs
Dec 31, 2007	CMTS Downstream Prices Plummet
Dec 28, 2007	The Sprint to IPv6
Dec 28, 2007	IPv4 Address Exhaustion and a Trading Market
Dec 24, 2007	The Dark Ages of Identity Management
Dec 24, 2007	CCID Consulting Forecasts Ten Trends of China's ICT Market in 2008
Dec 24, 2007	Fidelis Security Systems First to Comply with IPv6 Support in Newest Release of Fidelis Extrusion Prevention System
Dec 24, 2007	Ubuntu Security Notice—linux-source-2.6.17/20/22 vulnerabilities (USN-558-1)
Dec 19, 2007	Feds readying for 2008 IPv6 deadline, but not for actual use
Dec 19, 2007	CableLabs® Awards Industry 'First' With DOCSIS® 3.0 Qualification
Dec 19, 2007	Is the OMB IPv6 mandate faltering?
Dec 19, 2007	Sprint Readies IPv6 MPLS Trial
Dec 19, 2007	Rogue Wave Releases Next Edition of Market Leading Enterprise C++ Application Development Suite
Dec 19, 2007	Rugged new network security processor PMC card
Dec 19, 2007	Avocent First to Deliver IPv6-compatible Server Management Solution to Federal Government
Dec 17, 2007	With Internet gateways, less is more
Dec 17, 2007	The Internet Running Out of Everything?

Dec 17, 2007	Sprint's Vision of Mobility and IPv6 Expertise Bring Value and Services to Customers
Dec 17, 2007	IPv6 vs. Y2K and GOSIP
Dec 17, 2007	Juniper JUNOS BGP UPDATE Message Processing Denial of Service
Dec 17, 2007	IPv6 guru predicts last-minute switch to protocol
Dec 17, 2007	How feds are dropping the ball on IPv6
Dec 17, 2007	Traffic snags on Juniper router glitch
Dec 17, 2007	The rise and rise of the mobile machines
Dec 17, 2007	SSL versus IPsec—choosing your VPN
Dec 17, 2007	GE Fanuc Intelligent Platforms Extends Range of VMEbus Gigabit Ethernet Switches With IPv6 capability
Dec 16, 2007	QNX Releases Source Code for New Networking Stack
Dec 12, 2007	GSA seeks help with IPv6 training
Dec 12, 2007	Team mixes MPLS and IPv6 for enterprising results
Dec 12, 2007	U.S. Army NETCOM Awards NitroSecurity $3 Million Contract
Dec 12, 2007	Penetrating the Japan network-equipment market: Q&A with Toru Okubo, managing director of D-Link Japan
Dec 12, 2007	Vendors worried Vista IPv6 too slippery for managed networks
Dec 12, 2007	CWNP and Bitcricket Partner for the Next Generation IP Subnet Calculator
Dec 12, 2007	NetLogic Microsystems Extends Its Worldwide Leadership in Fourth-Generation Knowledge-Based Processors With the Introduction of the NL8256 Processor
Dec 07, 2007	pbxnsip Announces Support for IPv6
Dec 06, 2007	Microsoft Vista's IPv6 raises new security concerns
Dec 06, 2007	E-Gov Institute IPv6 Seminar
Dec 06, 2007	The Year IPv6 Made it to Major League
Dec 06, 2007	IDT Network Search Engines, Powers Mobile Radio Network Controller
Dec 06, 2007	Lockheed Martin readies for federal IPv6 transition
Dec 06, 2007	Cisco wants to spur Internet economy in RP

Dec 06, 2007	Japanese University links Juniper's network infrastructure
Dec 04, 2007	Isocore Test Validates Extreme Scalability of Ixia's Highest Density Gigabit Ethernet Solution
Dec 04, 2007	The Man in the Machine
Dec 04, 2007	Lancope Predicts Increased Adoption of NetFlow and sFlow in 2008
Dec 04, 2007	Arch Rock and Hitachi Demo 6LoWPAN Interoperability With Renesas at December IETF Meeting
Dec 04, 2007	Textechnologies Signs LOI to Acquire Innofone.com
Dec 04, 2007	3K Computers Launches Two Lines of Ready-To-Ship Computers
Dec 04, 2007	SUSE Security Announcement—kernel (SUSE-SA:2007:064)
Dec 04, 2007	Foundry Networks Helps Propel Record Traffic At the World's Largest Public Internet Exchange
Dec 04, 2007	Former WildPackets CTO Launches Bitcricket
Dec 04, 2007	Alcatel-Lucent provides Softbank Mobile with a scalable mobile backhaul solution
Dec 04, 2007	Google's spectrum play
Dec 03, 2007	Hexago Selected By Lockheed Martin for IPv6 Transition Pilot
Dec 03, 2007	PMC-Sierra Introduces MSP7160 Integrated GPON Fiber Access Gateway Device
Dec 03, 2007	Building for cable's future
Dec 03, 2007	Microsoft makes Exchange 2007 SP1 available
Dec 03, 2007	IPv6 Transition Strategies—Develop a Clear, Manageable Migration Path from IPv4 to IPv6
Dec 03, 2007	Features Managing Technology 2008
Nov 30, 2007	Shorter SANS 'Net risk list doesn't mean more security
Nov 30, 2007	Comcast Closes In on 100 Mbit/s
Nov 30, 2007	Verio Unveils Industry's First IPv6-Enabled Managed Hosting In North America
Nov 30, 2007	The Business Case for IMS
Nov 30, 2007	The Inevitability of IPv6, Part 2

Nov 30, 2007	IBM Shares Plans for New Tools to Support Tivoli System z Management Software
Nov 29, 2007	BMW brings Internet Protocol under the hood
Nov 29, 2007	Allied Telesis Launches Enhanced Ethernet Solution
Nov 29, 2007	CA Empowers Regional Clientele With New Version Of Identity And Access Management Solution
Nov 29, 2007	New Windows Operating Systems Put to the Speed Test
Nov 29, 2007	Isocore Demonstrates Leading Next Generation Networking Technologies at MPLS2007 International Conference
Nov 29, 2007	Research and Markets: Third Edition of CCNA
Nov 29, 2007	Take the 2008 IT Survey
Nov 29, 2007	Recursion Software Launches Voyager Edge 6.2 With IPv6 Support
Nov 29, 2007	Thomson Bonds With Docsis
Nov 27, 2007	NTT America Operates World's Largest IPv6 Network
Nov 27, 2007	NetLogic Microsystems and TSMC Collaborate on Industry-Leading 55nm Technology for Advanced Low-Power Knowledge-based Processors
Nov 27, 2007	Axis' new instant PTZ network camera gears up for tough situations
Nov 27, 2007	Prospects of next generation Internet application in China
Nov 27, 2007	IPv6 more secure? Forget it...
Nov 27, 2007	China University of Petroleum Deploys Nortel Ethernet Solution
Nov 27, 2007	OMB to limit number of Internet connections for agencies
Nov 27, 2007	Agencies face new foe in data storage fray
Nov 27, 2007	Internet gridlock warning gains ground
Nov 27, 2007	Radware Partners With MSPX to Bring Next Generation Technology to the Public Sector
Nov 23, 2007	Chinese seeks Internet innovations
Nov 23, 2007	Only a third of global ISPs on the way to IPv6 compliance
Nov 21, 2007	Vendors Ride First Docsis 3.0 Wave

Nov 21, 2007	Interview to Vint Cerf
Nov 21, 2007	Make IPv6 part of corporate DNA and Internet's new world order
Nov 21, 2007	Enterprises still dragging their feet on IPv6 migration
Nov 21, 2007	GE Fanuc Intelligent Platforms Announces Telum NPA 58x4 4-port Gigabit Ethernet IP Packet Processor AdvancedMC
Nov 20, 2007	Internet Technologies Handbook Volume 1—Infrastructure 2007
Nov 20, 2007	Qtel hosting network engineers' meet
Nov 20, 2007	Ubuntu Server: Good Concept, Flawed Execution
Nov 20, 2007	The myths and realities of standard configuration
Nov 20, 2007	DataPath Launches Baseband Solutions Under GSA Schedule Contract to Complement SATCOM Systems
Nov 20, 2007	Exhaustion of IP addresses, Vietnam proposes IPv6 use
Nov 20, 2007	Agnitum Outpost Firewall Pro 2008 6.0.2175
Nov 20, 2007	Streaming21 and Cool.revo Showcase IPTV Solutions at Inter BEE 2007
Nov 15, 2007	Internet exchange points should be encouraged for IPv6
Nov 15, 2007	Apple Security Update—Mac OS X v10.4.11 and Security Update 2007-008 (APPLE-SA-2007-11-14)
Nov 15, 2007	Internet Governance Forum Addresses Access, Diversity
Nov 15, 2007	Blue Coat Senior Technologist and IPv6 Expert to Address IPv6 Global Summit
Nov 15, 2007	Network Instruments Observer 12
Nov 15, 2007	Virtualization Hot, ITIL and CMDB Lukewarm, ScienceLogic Survey Finds
Nov 15, 2007	Atheros releases second-generation PCIe GbE chips
Nov 15, 2007	Group issues first-responder network requirements
Nov 13, 2007	Mandriva Linux Security Update Advisory—kernel (MDKSA-2007:216)
Nov 13, 2007	Internet growth calls for address migration

Nov 13, 2007	ISOC supports "The Internet Model" for sustainable development
Nov 13, 2007	The Low-Down on Red Hat Enterprise Linux 5.1 Enhancements
Nov 13, 2007	Use the ANEMONE testbed for your own research in the field of IPv6
Nov 13, 2007	ViaSat To Develop New High Speed Networking Modem for Military Satellite Communications with Globecomm
Nov 13, 2007	VoIPowering Your Office: Defeat the Pesky NATs of VoIP With IAX
Nov 13, 2007	Check Point's own UTM-1 2050
Nov 13, 2007	Nokia IP290 (running CheckPoint VPN-1 and Secure Platform)
Nov 13, 2007	UTM and IPv6: Do they mix?
Nov 13, 2007	CA IAM r12 Helps Secure and Streamline Business Enablement of SOA and Web Services
Nov 12, 2007	Hexago Launches Gateway6 Mobile at Mobile Asia Congress
Nov 10, 2007	Little Snitch ready for Mac OS X 10.5 ("Leopard")
Nov 10, 2007	Security Worries Leave Federal IT Personnel Sleep Deprived
Nov 10, 2007	IPv6: Will matter to the enterprise in five years
Nov 10, 2007	NetCracker Technology Ramps Up Capabilities
Nov 08, 2007	Atheros ETHOS Technology Portfolio Expands With New Gigabit Ethernet Solutions
Nov 08, 2007	Broadcom Accelerates Next Generation 'Green' Data Centers with 'Coolest' 10GbE Switch
Nov 08, 2007	Federal IT Decision Makers Report Lower Confidence in Security
Nov 08, 2007	EZchip announces new product family for Ethernet access apps
Nov 07, 2007	The Time Has Come for IPv6
Nov 07, 2007	Protocol analysis for the masses

Chapter 2

Basic IPv6 Protocol Mechanisms

Introduction

Chapter 1 introduced some basic concepts in IPv6. As we have seen, IPv6 (RFC 2460) is a connectionless datagram protocol used for routing packets between hosts. However, there are a number of ancillary functions that support the main protocol. The two chapters that follow provide additional IPv6 details that require understanding on the part of network and security planners. This chapter focuses on addressing and the next focuses on protocol structures. This chapter is in two parts: Part 1 (Sections 2.1–2.3) provides an overview and Part 2 (Sections 2.4–2.7) provides additional technical details.

2.1 IPv6 Addressing Mechanisms

From a packet-forwarding perspective IPv6 operates just like IPv4. An IPv6 packet, also known as an IPv6 datagram, consists of an IPv6 header and an IPv6 payload, as shown Figure 2.1. The IPv6 header consists of two parts, the IPv6 base header, and optional extension headers. Functionally, the optional extension headers and upper-layer protocols, for example TCP, are considered part of the IPv6 payload. IPv4 headers and IPv6 headers are not directly interoperable: hosts or routers must use an implementation of both IPv4 and IPv6 in order to recognize and process both header formats; this gives rise to a number of complexities and security concerns in the migration process between the IPv4 and the IPv6 environments.

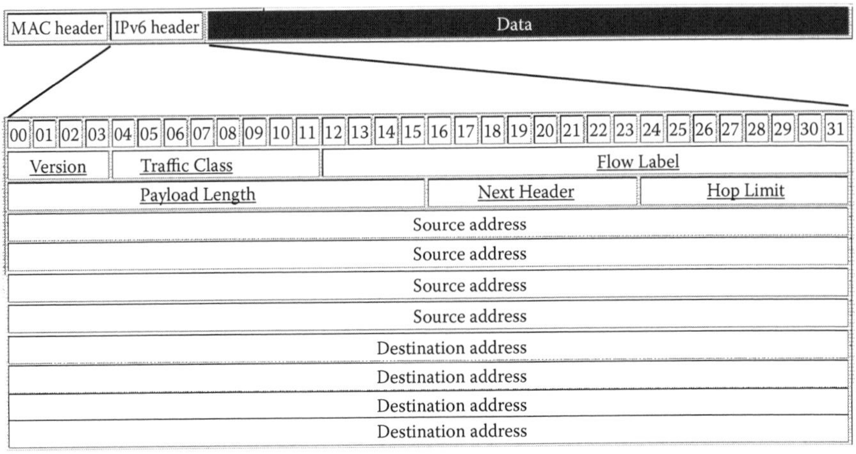

MAC header	IPv6 header	Data

00	01	02	03	04	05	06	07	08	09	10	11	12	13	14	15	16	17	18	19	20	21	22	23	24	25	26	27	28	29	30	31
Version				Traffic Class								Flow Label																			
Payload Length																Next Header								Hop Limit							
Source address																															
Source address																															
Source address																															
Source address																															
Destination address																															
Destination address																															
Destination address																															
Destination address																															

Figure 2.1   IPv6 Base Header.

The IPv6 addressing scheme is defined in RFC 3513 "The IPv6 Addressing Architecture specification" [HIN200401] (RFC 3513, April 2003, obsoletes RFC 2373). The IPv6 Addressing Architecture specification defines the address scope that can be used in an IPv6 implementation and the various configuration architecture guidelines for network designers of the IPv6 address space. Two advantages of IPv6 are that support for multicast is intrinsic (it is required by the specification) and nodes can create link-local addresses during initialization [RFC3315]. Some portions of this discussion are based on reference [MSD200401].

2.1.1 Addressing Conventions

As we saw in Chapter 1, the IPv6 128-bit address is divided along 16-bit boundaries; each 16-bit block is then converted to a 4-digit hexadecimal number, separated by colons. The resulting representation is called colon-hexadecimal. This is in contrast to the 32-bit IPv4 address represented in dotted-decimal format, divided along 8-bit boundaries, and then converted to its decimal equivalent, separated by periods. The following examples show 128-bit IPv6 address in binary form:

```
Address 1: 0010000111011010000000000110100110000000000000000000101
           1110011101100000010101010100000000001111111111111110001010001
           001110001011010
Address 2: 0010000111011010000000000110100110000000000000000000101
           1110011101100000010101010100000000001111111110000000000000001
           001110001011010
```

```
Address 3: 0010000111011010000000000110100110000000000000000010011
    1000101101000000010101010100000000011111111000000000000000001
    001110001011010
Address 4: 0010000111011010000000000110100110000000000000000010011
    1000101101000000010101010100000000011111111000000000000000000
    010111100111011
```

The following example shows these same addresses divided along 16-bit boundaries:

```
Address 1: 0010000111011010:0000000011010011:0000000000000000:0
    010111100111011:0000001010101010:0000000011111111:1111111000
    101000:1001110001011010:
Address 2: 0010000111011010:0000000011010011:0000000000000000:0
    010111100111011:0000001010101010:0000000011111111:000000000
    0000000:1001110001011010:
Address 3: 0010000111011010:0000000011010011:0000000000000000:1
    001110001011010:0000001010101010:0000000011111111:0000000000
    000000:1001110001011010:
Address 4: 0010000111011010:0000000011010011:0000000000000000:1
    001110001011010:0000001010101010:0000000011111111:0000000000
    000000:0010111100111011:
```

The following shows each 16-bit block in the address converted to hexadecimal and delimited with colons:

```
Address 1:  21DA:00D3:0000:2F3B:02AA:00FF:FE28:9C5A
Address 2:  21DA:00D3:0000:2F3B:02AA:00FF:0000:9C5A
Address 3:  21DA:00D3:0000:9C5A:02AA:00FF:0000:9C5A
Address 4:  21DA:00D3:0000:9C5A:02AA:00FF:0000:2F3B
```

IPv6 representations can be further simplified by removing the *leading* zeros (trailing zeros are not removed) within each 16-bit block. However, each block must have, in the abbreviated nomenclature, at least a single digit. The following example shows the addresses without the leading zeros:

```
Address 1:  21DA:D3:0:2F3B:2AA:FF:FE28:9C5A
Address 2:  21DA:D3:0:2F3B:2AA:FF:0:9C5A
Address 3:  21DA:D3:0:9C5A:2AA:FF:0:9C5A
Address 4:  21DA:D3:0:9C5A:2AA:FF:0:2F3B
```

Some types of addresses contain long sequences of zeros. In IPv6 addressing, a contiguous sequence of 16-bit blocks set to 0 in the colon-hexadecimal format can be compressed to :: (known as *double-colon*).

The following list shows examples of compressing zeros:

- The address 21DA:0:0:0:2AA:FF:9C5A:2F3B can be compressed to 21DA:: 2AA:FF:9C5A:2F3B.
- The multicast address of FF02:0:0:0:0:0:0:2 can be compressed to FF02::2.

Note:

Zero-compression can only be used to compress a single contiguous series of 16-bit blocks expressed in colon-hexadecimal notation—one cannot use zero-compression to include part of a 16-bit block; e.g., one *cannot* abbreviate FF01:30:0:0:0:0:0:8 as FF01:3::8.) Also, zero-compression can be used only once in an address, which enables one to determine the number of 0 bits represented by each instance of a double-colon (::). To determine how many 0 bits are represented by the ::, simply count the number of blocks in the compressed address, subtract this number from 8, and then multiply the result by 16. For example, in the address FF02::2, there are two blocks (the FF02 block and the 2 block); the number of bits expressed by the :: is 96 (= (8 − 2) × 16) [MSD200401].

2.1.2 Addressing Issues/Reachability

Every IPv6 address has a defined reachability scope. Table 2.1 shows the address and associated reachability scopes. The reachability of *Node-local addresses* is "the same node"; the reachability of *Link-local addresses* is "the local link"; and the reachability of *Global addresses* is "the IPv6-enabled Internet." Packets with a link-local destination must stay on the link where they have been generated. By design, routers are not allowed to forward them to other links to do so because there is no guarantee of uniqueness outside the context of the origin link. IPv6 interfaces can have multiple addresses that have different reachability scopes; for example, a node may have a link-local address and a global address.

Similar to the IPv4 address space, the IPv6 address space is partitioned according to the value of high-order bits (known as a Format Prefix) in the address. Table 2.2 depicts the IPv6 address space allocation by Format Prefixes. The (current) set of unicast addresses that can be employed by IPv6 nodes consists of aggregatable global unicast addresses, and link-local unicast addresses, and site-local unicast addresses (now deprecated) (these addresses represent about 12.6% of the entire IPv6 address space, but it is still ~3.4 × 10^{37}). The prefix is the portion of the address that indicates the bits that have fixed values or are the bits of the network identifier. Prefixes for IPv6 routes and subnet identifiers are expressed in the same way as Classless Inter-Domain Routing notation for IPv4. An IPv6 prefix is written in address/prefix-length notation (IPv4 environments use a dotted decimal representation known as the subnet mask in order to establish the network prefix of a given IP address; the subnet mask approach is *not used* in IPv6, rather, only the prefix-length notation is used.)

Table 2.1   IPv6 Address and Associated Reachability Scopes

Address Scope/ Reachability	Description
Node-local addresses to reach same node	Used to send Protocol Data Units (PDUs) to the same node: ■ Loopback address (PDUs addressed to the loopback address are never sent on a link or forwarded by an IPv6 router—this is equivalent to the IPv4 loopback address) ■ Node-local multicast address
Link-local addresses to reach local link (*)	Used to communicate between hosts devices (e.g., servers, VoIP devices, etc.) on the link; these addresses are always configured automatically: ■ Unspecified address. It indicates the absence of an address, and is typically used as a source address for PDUs that are attempting to verify the uniqueness of a tentative address (it is equivalent to the IPv4 unspecified address.) The unspecified address is never assigned to an interface or used as a destination address. ■ Link-local Unicast address ■ Link-local Multicast address
Site-local addresses to reach the private intranet (internetwork) (*)	Used between nodes that communicate with other nodes in the same site; site-local addresses are configured by router advertisement: ■ Site-local Unicast address—these addresses are not reachable from other sites, and routers must not forward site-local traffic outside of the site. Site-local addresses can be used in addition to aggregatable global unicast addresses. ■ Site-local Multicast address **Note: Site-local addresses were deprecated in September 2004 by RFC 3879 ("Deprecating Site Local Addresses"); see additional details in the text**

(Continued)

Table 2.1   IPv6 Address and Associated Reachability Scopes (Continued)

Address Scope/ Reachability	Description
Global addresses to reach the Internet (IPv6-enabled); also known as aggregatable global unicast addresses	Globally routable and reachable addresses on the IPv6 portion of the Internet (they are equivalent to public IPv4 addresses); global addresses are configured by router advertisement: ■ Global Unicast address ■ Other scope Multicast address Global addresses are designed to be aggregated or summarized to produce an efficient, hierarchical addressing and routing structure.

(*) *When one specifies a link-local address, one needs to also specify a scope ID, which further defines the reachability scope for these (nonglobal) addresses*

Table 2.2   IPv6 Address Space Allocation

Address Space Allocation	Format Prefix	Percentage of the Address Space	Hex Notation	Fraction of the Address Space
Reserved	0000 0000	0.391%	0x00	1/256
Reserved for NSAP allocation	0000 001	0.781%	0x0001	1/128
Aggregatable global unicast addresses	001	12.500%	001	1/8
Link-local unicast addresses	1111 1110 10	0.098%	0xFE10	1/1024
Site-local unicast addresses (now deprecated)	1111 1110 11	0.098%	0xFE11	1/1024
Multicast addresses	1111 1111	0.391%	0xFF	1/256
The remainder of the IPv6 address	Unassigned	85.742%		

Note: 0xY is the hexadecimal notation for digit "Y"

Note: Site-local addresses are deprecated in RFC 3879, September 2004

As noted earlier, the prefix is the part of the address that indicates the bits that have fixed values or are the bits of the network identifier. For example, 21DA:D3::/48 is a 48-bit route prefix

21DA	00D3	0000	16 bits	16 bits	16 bits	16 bits	16 bits
<- route prefix ->							

and
21DA:D3:0:2F3B::/64 is a 64-bit subnet prefix (a 48-bit route prefix plus a site topology identifier for the next 16 bits)

21DA	00D3	0000	2F3B	16 bits	16 bits	16 bits	16 bits
<- route prefix ->			<- subnet prefix ->	16 bits	16 bits	16 bits	16 bits

Note:

RFC 3879, September 2004, formally deprecated the IPv6 site-local unicast prefix defined in RFC 3513, that is, 1111111011 binary or FEC0::/10. The special behavior of this prefix is no longer to be supported in new implementations. The prefix has not been reassigned for other use except by a future IETF standards action. A brief discussion follows below, based directly on the RFC [RFC3879].

Studies in IETF outlined several defects of the site local addressing scope originally included in the IPv6 specification. These defects fall in two broad categories: ambiguity of addresses, and fuzzy definition of sites. As originally defined, site local addresses are ambiguous: an address such as FEC0::1 can be present in multiple sites, and the address itself does not contain any indication of the site to which it belongs. This creates "pain" for developers of applications, for the designers of routers and for the network managers. This issue is compounded by the fuzzy nature of the site concept.

Early feedback from developers indicates that site-local addresses were hard to use correctly in an application. This is particularly true for multihomed hosts, which can be simultaneously connected to multiple sites, and for mobile hosts, and can be successively connected to multiple sites. Applications would learn or remember that the address of some correspondent was "FEC0::1234:5678:9ABC," they would try to feed the address in a socket address structure and issue a connect, and the call will fail because they did not fill up the "site identifier" variable, as in "FEC0::1234:5678:9ABC%1." (The % character is used as a delimiter for zone identifiers) The problem is compounded by the fact that the site identifier varies with the host instantiation, for example, sometimes %1 and sometimes %2, and thus that the host identifier cannot be remembered in memory, or learned from a name server.

The issue is caused by the ambiguity of site-local addresses. Since site-local addresses are ambiguous, application developers have to manage the "site identifiers" that qualify the addresses of the hosts. This management of identifiers has proven hard for developers to understand, and, therefore, difficult to execute even by those developers who do understand the concept.

The management of IPv6 site-local addresses is in many ways similar to the management of RFC 1918 addresses in some IPv4 networks. In theory, the private addresses defined in RFC 1918 should only be used locally, and should never appear in the Internet. In practice, these addresses "leak." The conjunction of leaks and ambiguity ends up causing management problems. Names and literal addresses of "private" hosts leak in mail messages, Web pages, or files. Private addresses end up being used as source or destination of TCP requests or UDP messages, for example, in DNS or trace-route requests, causing the request to fail, or the response to arrive at unsuspecting hosts.

Having nonambiguous addresses solves a large part of the developers' 'pain,' as it removes the need to manage site identifiers. The application can use the addresses as if they were regular global addresses, and the stack will be able to use standard techniques to discover which interface should be used. Some level of pain will remain, as these addresses will not always be reachable; however, applications can deal with the un-reachability issues by trying connections at a different time, or with a different address. Having nonambiguous addresses will not eliminate the leaks that cause management 'pain'; however, since the addresses are not ambiguous, debugging these leaks will be simpler.

Having nonambiguous addresses will solve a large part of the router issues: since addresses are not ambiguous, routers will be able to use standard routing techniques, and will not need different routing tables for each interface. Some of the 'pain' will remain at border routers, which will need to filter packets from some ranges of source addresses; this is however a fairly common function.

Avoiding the explicit declaration of scope will remove the issues linked to the ambiguity of the site concept. Non-reachability can be obtained by using firewalls where appropriate. The firewall rules can explicitly accommodate various network configurations, by accepting or refusing traffic to and from ranges of the new non-ambiguous addresses.

2.2 Address Types

This section looks at some more detailed information related to address types. We discuss a number of unicast addresses, multicast addresses, and anycast addresses.

2.2.1 Unicast IPv6 Addresses

A unicast address identifies a single interface within the scope of the unicast address type. This could be a VoIP handset in a VoIPv6 environment, a PC on a LAN and so on. Utilizing an up-to-date unicast routing topology, Protocol Data Units (PDUs) addressed to a unicast address are delivered to a single interface. A unicast address refers to a unique interface. A packet sent to such an address is (legally) accepted only by the corresponding interface. Unicast addresses fall into the following categories:

- Aggregatable global unicast addresses (e.g., used to reach an Internet-connected VoIP phone);
- Link-local addresses (e.g., used to reach a VoIP phone on the same LAN segment);
- Special addresses, including unspecified and loopback addresses; and,
- Compatibility addresses, including 6to4 addresses.

These are discussed next.

Aggregatable Global Unicast Addresses

The IPv6-based Internet has been designed to support efficient, hierarchical addressing and routing (this is in contrast to IPv4-based Internet which has a mixture of both flat and hierarchical routing.) Aggregatable global unicast addresses are globally-routable and globally-reachable on the IPv6 portion of the (IPv6) Internet. The region of the Internet over which the aggregatable global unicast address is unique (the scope) is the entire IPv6 Internet. As we saw earlier, aggregatable global unicast addresses (aka global addresses), are identified by the Format Prefix of 001. This type of addressing can be used, for example, to reach an Internet-connected VoIP (SIP [Session Initiation Protocol]) phone (say, the author's phone given to him by his company and utilized by him while traveling on business and using the Internet for connectivity), from any origination point, be such origination point on the firm's intranet or on any other-company's intranet, or even at another Internet point. This enables end-to-end connectivity.

Link-Local (Unicast) Addresses

Link-local addresses are utilized by nodes when communicating with neighboring nodes on the same link. For example, Link-local addresses are used to communicate between hosts on the link on a single link IPv6 network without the intervention/utilization of a router (e.g., in a LAN segment, a VLAN, etc.). This type of addressing can be used to reach a company colleague on a LAN-connected VoIP phone (say, for colleagues working in the same building—assuming that both are on the same LAN.)

The scope of a Link-local address is the local link. An IPv6 router does not forward link-local traffic beyond the link. A Link-local address is required for Neighbor Discovery processes and is always automatically configured, even in the absence of all other unicast addresses. As seen earlier, Link-local addresses are identified by the Format Prefix of 1111 1110 10. The address starts with FE (for example 1111 1110 1000 is 0xFE8; 1111 1110 1001 is 0xFE9; 1111 1110 1010 is 0xFEA; and, 1111 1110 1011 is 0xFEB.) With the 64-bit interface identifier, the prefix for link-local addresses is, by convention, always FE80::/64.

Unspecified (Unicast) Address

The unspecified address, 0:0:0:0:0:0:0:0 (that is, ::) indicates the absence of an address, and is typically used as a source address for PDUs that are attempting to verify the uniqueness of a tentative address. It is equivalent to the IPv4 unspecified address of 0.0.0.0. The unspecified address is never assigned to an interface or used as a destination address.

Loopback (Unicast) Address

The loopback address, 0:0:0:0:0:0:0:1 or ::1, identifies a loopback interface, enabling a node to send PDUs to itself. It is equivalent to the IPv4 loopback address of 127.0.0.1. PDUs addressed to the loopback address are never sent on a link or forwarded by an IPv6 router.

Compatibility (Unicast) Addresses

IPv6 provides what are called *6to4 addresses* to facilitate the coexistence of IPv4-to-IPv6 environments and the migration from the IPv4 to the IPv6 environment. The 6to4 address is used for communicating between two nodes operating both IPv4 stacks and IPv6 stacks (also known as dual stack) over an IPv4 routing infrastructure (more on this in Chapter 8). The 6to4 address is formed by combining the prefix 2002::/16 with the 32 bits of the public IPv4 address of the node, forming a 48-bit prefix.

2.2.2 Multicast IPv6 Addresses

A useful feature supported in IPv6 is multicasting. The use of multicasting in IP networks is defined in RFC 1112 which describes addresses and host extensions for the way IP hosts support multicasting—the concepts originally developed for IPv4 also apply to IPv6. Besides a variety of protocol-level functionality supported by multicasting (e.g., MLD and ND), one also can use this mechanism to support VoIP/IPTV functionality (e.g., audioconferencing/bridging and program distribution). Multicast traffic is promulgated by utilizing a single destination address in the IPv6 header, but the IPv6 datagram is received and processed by multiple hosts. Hosts and devices listening on a specific multicast address comprise a multicast group; these devices receive and process traffic sent to the group address. As seen earlier, IPv6 multicast addresses have the Format Prefix of 1111 1111; namely, the multicast address always begins with 0xFF.

Group membership in multicast is dynamic, allowing hosts to join and leave the group at any time. Groups can be from multiple network segments (links or subnets) if the connecting routers support forwarding of multicast traffic and group membership information [MSD200401]. A host (e.g., a VoIP SIP proxy or a H.323 gatekeeper) can send traffic to a group address without belonging to the group. In fact, to join a group, a host sends a group membership message. Each multicast group is identified by one IPv6 multicast address. All group members who listen and receive IPv6 messages sent to the group address share the group address. Multicast routers periodically poll membership status.

Some of the reserved IPv6 multicast addresses (RFC 2375) are shown in Table 2.3.

A multicast address is an addressing mechanism that identifies multiple interfaces; it is used for one-to-many communication. With the appropriate multicast routing topology, PDUs addressed to a multicast address are delivered to all interfaces that are identified by the address. Multicast addresses cannot be utilized as source addresses. Multicast address flags, Scope, and Group, are shown in Figure 2.2.

To identify all nodes for the node-local and link-local scopes, the following multicast addresses are defined:

- FF01::1 (node-local scope all-nodes address)
- FF02::1 (link-local scope all-nodes address)

Table 2.3   Reserved Multicast IPv6 Addresses

IPv6 Multicast Address	Description
FF02::1	The all-nodes address used to reach all nodes on the same link.
FF02::2	The all-routers address used to reach all routers on the same link.
FF02::4	The address used to reach all Distance Vector Multicast Routing Protocol (DVMRP) multicast routers on the same link.
FF02::5	The address used to reach all Open Shortest Path First (OSPF) routers on the same link.
FF02::1:FF*XX:XXXX*	The solicited-node address used in the address resolution process to resolve the IPv6 address of a link-local node to its link-layer address. The rightmost 24 bits (*XX:XXXX*) of the solicited-node address are the rightmost 24 bits of an IPv6 unicast address.

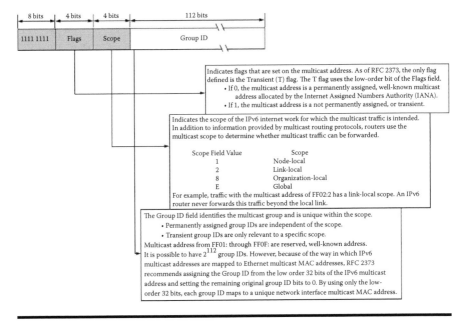

Figure 2.2   Multicast Address.

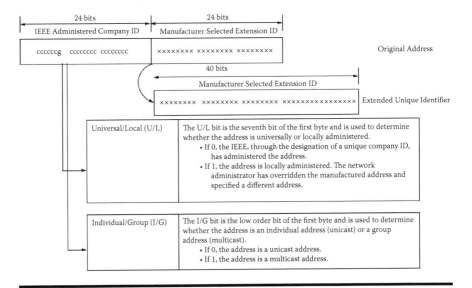

Figure 2.3   IEEE Address along with the Extended Unique Identifier.

To identify all routers for the node-local and link-local scopes, the following multicast addresses are defined:

- FF01::2 (node-local scope all-routers address)
- FF02::2 (link-local scope all-routers address)

Next, we briefly look at solicited-node addresses. The solicited-node address supports efficient querying of network nodes for the purpose of address resolution. IPv6 uses the Neighbor Solicitation message to perform address resolution. This multicast address consists of the prefix FF02::1:FF00:0/104 along with the last 24 bits of the IPv6 address that is being resolved. In contrast to IPv4 where the ARP Request frame is sent via a Media Access Control (MAC)-level broadcast, and in doing so imposing on all nodes on the network segment, in IPv6 the solicited-node multicast address is used as the Neighbor Solicitation message destination. This avoids imposing on all IPv6 nodes on the local link by using the local-link scope all-nodes address.

2.2.3 Anycast IPv6 Addresses

An anycast address identifies multiple interfaces (typically belonging to different nodes), but not an entire broadcast universe. This could be used, for example, to support VoIP Voice Mail group distribution. With the appropriate routing topology, PDUs addressed to an anycast address are delivered to a single interface for further appropriate handling (a PDU addressed to an anycast address is delivered to the nearest interface identified by the address.) To make possible the delivery to the nearest anycast group member, the routing infrastructure must be aware of the interfaces that are assigned anycast addresses and must know their distances in terms of routing metrics. At present, anycast addresses are used only as destination addresses and are assigned only to routers. Note that an anycast address is syntactically indistinguishable from a unicast address. Thus, nodes sending packets to anycast addresses are not explicitly aware that an anycast address is being used.

2.3 Addresses for Hosts and Routers

In contrast to IPv4 where a host with a single network adapter has a single IPv4 address assigned to that adapter, an IPv6 host (e.g., a SIP proxy) typically has multiple IPv6 addresses (even in the case of a single interface.) (When a computer is configured with more than one IP address, it is referred to as a *multihomed* system.) IPv6 host and router address usage is as follows [MSD200401]:

Host: Typical IPv6 hosts are logically multihomed because they have at least two addresses with which they can receive PDUs. Each host is assigned the following unicast addresses:

- A link-local address for each interface. This address is used for local traffic.
- An address for each interface. This could be one or more global addresses.
- The loopback address (::1) for the loopback interface.

Additionally, each host is listening for traffic on the following multicast addresses:

- The node-local scope all-nodes address (FF01::1)
- The link-local scope all-nodes address (FF02::1)
- The solicited-node address for each unicast address on each interface
- The multicast addresses of joined groups on each interface

Router: An IPv6 router is assigned the following unicast addresses:

- A link-local address for each interface. This address is used for local traffic.
- An address for each interface. This could be one or more global addresses.
- The loopback address (::1) for the loopback interface.

An IPv6 router is assigned the following anycast addresses:

- A subnet-router anycast address for each subnet
- Additional anycast addresses (optional)

Each router is listening for traffic on the following multicast addresses:

- The node-local scope all-nodes address (FF01::1)
- The node-local scope all-routers address (FF01::2)
- The link-local scope all-nodes address (FF02::1)
- The link-local scope all-routers address (FF02::2)
- The solicited-node address for each unicast address on each interface
- The addresses of joined groups on each interface

2.3.1 Interface Determination

The last 64 bits of an IPv6 address are the interface identifier that is unique to the 64-bit prefix of the IPv6 address. There are two ways for interface identifier determination: (1) derived from the Electrical and Electronic Engineers (IEEE) Extended Unique Identifier (EUI)-64 address; and, (2) randomly generated and randomly changed over time. IETF RFC 2373 stipulates that unicast addresses that use format prefixes 001 through 111 must use a 64-bit interface identifier that is derived from the EUI-64 address. Related to the second approach, RFC 3041 states that to provide a level of anonymity, the identifier can be randomly generated, and changed over time.

EUI-64 addresses are either *assigned* to a network adapter or *derived* from IEEE 802 addresses. LAN Network Interface Cards (NICs) that (at this point in the development of hardware) typically comprise the physical interface (network adapters) of hosts and devices identifiers use the 48-bit IEEE 802 address. This address (also called the physical, hardware, or MAC address) consists of two parts: (i) Company ID; and (ii) Extension ID. The Company ID is a 24-bit ID uniquely assigned to each manufacturer of network adapters; this is also known as the manufacturer ID. The Extension ID (also known as the board ID) is a 24-bit uniquely assigned to each network adapter at the time of assembly. The IEEE 802 address is thus a globally unique 48-bit address. The IEEE EUI-64 address is a newly defined standard for network interface addressing. The company ID is 24-bits in length, but the extension ID is 40 bits, supporting a larger address space for a network adapter manufacturer. See Figure 2.3.

To generate an EUI-64 address from an IEEE 802 address, 16 bits of 11111111 11111110 (0xFFFE) are inserted into the IEEE 802 address between the company ID and the extension ID. See Figure 2.4.

2.3.2 Mapping EUI-64 Addresses to Ipv6 Interface Identifiers

An IPv6 unicast address utilizes a 64-bit interface identifier. To obtain this identifier from an EUI-64 address, the U/L bit in the EUI-64 address is complemented (if it is a 1, it is set to 0; if it is a 0, it is set to 1). The resulting bitstream is used as a universally administered unicast EUI-64 address.

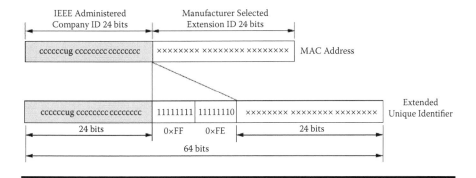

Figure 2.4   IEEE Address along with the Extended Unique Identifier.

2.3.3 Mapping IEEE 802 Addresses to IPv6 Interface Identifiers

To obtain an IPv6 interface identifier from an IEEE 802 address, one must first map the IEEE 802 address to an EUI-64 address, as discussed previously; then complement (flip) the U/L bit. The resulting bitstream is used as a universally administered unicast IEEE 802 address.

2.3.4 Randomly Generated Interface Identifiers

IPv6 interface identifiers remain static over time, hence, for security reasons, a capability is needed to generate temporary addresses. (Because of NAT/DHCP, in an IPv4 environment it is difficult to track a user's traffic on the basis of IP address.) However, it should be noted that many—if not most—attack techniques do not rely on knowing the IP address of a *specific* device on a network; instead, such techniques simply look for *any* available entry point. IPv6 will change this approach as once a host is compromised, attackers will now have the ability to specifically revisit a host. Due to limited address space in IPv4, once a host was compromised, in most cases, an attacker would only have the ability to control the endpoint for a small period of time since the IP address would change at some point. Attackers began to adapt to this issue by developing sophisticated command and control botnets. A botnet (also known as zombies) is a term for a collection of Internet computers that have been configured to participate in malicious acts (including sending spam or even attacking Websites without the knowledge of their owners).

In IPv6, after the connection is made through router discovery and stateless address autoconfiguration, the end-user device is assigned a 64-bit prefix. If the interface identifier is based on an EUI-64 address (which, as we saw earlier, is derived from the static IEEE 802 address), the traffic of a specific node can be identified which opens up the possibility of tracking a specific user, should that be of interest to an intruder. To address this issue, an alternative IPv6 interface identifier can be randomly generated and changed over time, as described in RFC 3041. For IPv6 systems that have storage capabilities, a history value is stored. When the IPv6 protocol is initialized, a new interface identifier is created through the following process (the IPv6 address based on this random interface identifier is known as a temporary address):

a. Retrieve the history value from storage and append the interface identifier based on the EUI-64 address of the adapter.
b. Compute the Message Digest-5 (MD5) one-way encryption hash over the quantity in step a.
c. Save the last 64 bits of the MD5 hash computed in step b as the history value for the next interface identifier computation.
d. Take the first 64 bits of the MD5 hash computed in step b and set the seventh bit to zero. The seventh bit corresponds to the U/L bit which, when set to 0, indicates a locally administered interface identifier. The result is the interface identifier.

Temporary addresses are generated for public address prefixes that use stateless address autoconfiguration.

The sections that follow provide additional details.

2.4 IPv6 Addressing (Details)

This section defines the addressing architecture of the IPv6 protocol in some details (RFC 3513). The RFC includes the basic formats for the various types of IPv6 addresses (unicast, anycast, and multicast). This section covers the IPv6 addressing model, text representations of IPv6 addresses, and the definition of IPv6 unicast addresses, anycast addresses, and multicast addresses, based on the RFC [RFC3513]. The discussion is for pedagogical purposes and developers should refer to the latest IETF documentation.

By now we know that IPv6 addresses are 128-bit identifiers for interfaces and sets of interfaces (where "interface" is as defined earlier.) There are three types of addresses:

- Unicast: An identifier for a single interface. A packet sent to a unicast address is delivered to the interface identified by that address.
- Anycast: An identifier for a set of interfaces (typically belonging to different nodes). A packet sent to an anycast address is delivered to one of the interfaces identified by that address (the "nearest" one, according to the routing protocols' measure of distance).
- Multicast: An identifier for a set of interfaces (typically belonging to different nodes). A packet sent to a multicast address is delivered to all interfaces identified by that address.

There are no broadcast addresses in IPv6, their function being superseded by multicast addresses. In RFC 3513, fields in addresses are given a specific name, for example "subnet." When this name is used with the term "ID" for identifier after the name (e.g., "subnet ID"), it refers to the contents of the named field. When it is used with the term "prefix" (e.g., "subnet prefix"), it refers to all of the address from the left up to and including this field. In IPv6, all zeros and all ones are legal values for any field, unless specifically excluded. Specifically, prefixes may contain, or end with, zero-valued fields.

2.4.1 Addressing Model

IPv6 addresses of all types are assigned to interfaces, not nodes. An IPv6 unicast address refers to a single interface. Since each interface belongs to a single node, any of that node's interfaces' unicast addresses may be used as an identifier for the node. All interfaces are required to have at least one link-local unicast address. A single interface may also have multiple IPv6 addresses of any type (unicast, anycast, and multicast) or scope. Unicast addresses with scope greater than link-scope are not needed for interfaces that are not used as the origin or destination of any IPv6 packets to or from non-neighbors. This is sometimes convenient for point-to-point interfaces. There is one exception to this addressing model:

> A unicast address or a set of unicast addresses may be assigned to multiple physical interfaces if the implementation treats the multiple physical interfaces as one interface when presenting it to the Internet layer. This is useful for load sharing over multiple physical interfaces.

Currently, IPv6 continues the IPv4 model that a subnet prefix is associated with one link. Multiple subnet prefixes may be assigned to the same link.

2.4.2 Text Representation of Addresses

There are three conventional forms for representing IPv6 addresses as text strings:

1. The preferred form is x:x:x:x:x:x:x:x, where the x's are the hexadecimal values of the eight 16-bit pieces of the address.
   Examples:
   ```
   FEDC:BA98:7654:3210:FEDC:BA98:7654:3210
   1080:0:0:0:8:800:200C:417A
   ```
   Note that it is not necessary to write the leading zeros in an individual field, but there must be at least one numeral in every field (except for the case described in 2.).
2. Due to some methods of allocating certain styles of IPv6 addresses, it will be common for addresses to contain long strings of zero bits. In order to make writing addresses containing zero bits easier, a special syntax is available to compress the zeros. The use of "::" indicates one or more groups of 16 bits of zeros. The "::" can only appear once in an address. The "::" can also be used to compress leading or trailing zeros in an address.
   For example, the following addresses:
   ```
   1080:0:0:0:8:800:200C:417A a unicast address
   FF01:0:0:0:0:0:0:101 a multicast address
   0:0:0:0:0:0:0:1 the loopback address
   0:0:0:0:0:0:0:0 the unspecified addresses
   ```
   may be represented as:
   ```
   1080::8:800:200C:417A a unicast address
   FF01::101 a multicast address
   ::1 the loopback address
   :: the unspecified addresses
   ```
3. An alternative form that is sometimes more convenient when dealing with a mixed environment of IPv4 and IPv6 nodes is x:x:x:x:x:x:d.d.d.d, where

the x's are the hexadecimal values of the six high-order 16-bit pieces of the address, and the d's are the decimal values of the four low-order 8-bit pieces of the address (standard IPv4 representation).

Examples:

```
0:0:0:0:0:0:13.1.68.3
0:0:0:0:0:FFFF:129.144.52.38
```

or in compressed form:

```
::13.1.68.3
::FFFF:129.144.52.38
```

2.4.3 Text Representation of Address Prefixes

The text representation of IPv6 address prefixes is similar to the way IPv4 address prefixes are written in Classless Interdomain Routing (CIDR) notation. An IPv6 address prefix is represented by the notation:

```
ipv6-address/prefix-length
```

where

- ipv6-address is an IPv6 address in any of the notations listed earlier.
- prefix-length is a decimal value specifying how many of the left-most contiguous bits of the address comprise the prefix.

For example, the following are legal representations of the 60-bit prefix 12AB00000000CD3 (hexadecimal):

```
12AB:0000:0000:CD30:0000:0000:0000:0000/60
12AB::CD30:0:0:0:0/60
12AB:0:0:CD30::/60
```

The following are not legal representations of the above prefix:

```
12AB:0:0:CD3/60 may drop leading zeros, but not trailing zeros,
within any 16-bit chunk of the address
12AB::CD30/60 address to left of "/" expands to
12AB:0000:0000:0000:0000:000:0000:CD30
12AB::CD3/60 address to left of "/" expands to
12AB:0000:0000:0000:0000:000:0000:0CD3
```

When writing both a node address and a prefix of that node address (e.g., the node's subnet prefix), the two can combined as follows:

```
the node address 12AB:0:0:CD30:123:4567:89AB:CDEF
and its subnet number 12AB:0:0:CD30::/60
can be abbreviated as 12AB:0:0:CD30:123:4567:89AB:CDEF/60
```

2.4.4 Address Type Identification

The type of an IPv6 address is identified by the high-order bits of the address, as follows:

```
Address type          Binary prefix         IPv6 notation
------------          -------------         -------------
Unspecified           00...0 (128 bits)     ::/128
Loopback              00...1 (128 bits)     ::1/128
Multicast             11111111              FF00::/8
Link-local unicast    1111111010            FE80::/10
[Site-local unicast   1111111011            FEC0::/10] deprecated
Global unicast        (everything else)
```

Anycast addresses are taken from the unicast address spaces (of any scope) and are not syntactically distinguishable from unicast addresses.

2.4.5 Unicast Addresses

IPv6 unicast addresses are aggregable with prefixes of arbitrary bit-length similar to IPv4 addresses under CIDR.

There are several types of unicast addresses in IPv6, in particular global unicast, site-local unicast, and link-local unicast. There are also some special-purpose subtypes of global unicast, such as IPv6 addresses with embedded IPv4 addresses or encoded Network Service Access Point (NSAP) addresses.

IPv6 nodes may have considerable or little knowledge of the internal structure of the IPv6 address, depending on the role the node plays (for instance, host versus router). At a minimum, a node may consider that unicast addresses (including its own) have no internal structure:

```
|                           128 bits                           |
+--------------------------------------------------------------+
|                         node address                         |
+--------------------------------------------------------------+
```

A slightly sophisticated host (but still rather simple) may additionally be aware of subnet prefix(es) for the link(s) it is attached to, where different addresses may have different values for n:

```
|                     n bits                 |    128-n bits    |
+--------------------------------------------+------------------+
|                 subnet prefix              |   interface ID   |
+--------------------------------------------+------------------+
```

Though a very simple router may have no knowledge of the internal structure of IPv6 unicast addresses, routers will more generally have knowledge of one or more of the hierarchical boundaries for the operation of routing protocols. The known boundaries will differ from router to router, depending on what positions the router holds in the routing hierarchy.

Interface Identifiers

Interface identifiers in IPv6 unicast addresses are used to identify interfaces on a link. They are required to be unique within a subnet prefix. It is recommended that the same interface identifier not be assigned to different nodes on a link. They may also be unique over a broader scope. In some cases, an interface's identifier will be derived directly from that interface's link-layer address. The same interface identifier may be used on multiple interfaces on a single node, as long as they are attached to different subnets.

Note that the uniqueness of interface identifiers is independent of the uniqueness of IPv6 addresses. For example, a global unicast address may be created with a nonglobal scope interface identifier, and a site-local address may be created with a global scope interface identifier.

For all unicast addresses, except those that start with binary value 000, Interface IDs are required to be 64 bits long and to be constructed in Modified EUI-64 format.

Modified EUI-64 format-based Interface identifiers may have global scope when derived from a global token (e.g., IEEE 802 48-bit MAC or IEEE EUI-64 identifiers) or may have local scope where a global token is not available (e.g., serial links, tunnel end-points, etc.) or where global tokens are undesirable (e.g., temporary tokens for privacy).

Modified EUI-64 format interface identifiers are formed by inverting the "u" bit (universal/local bit in IEEE EUI-64 terminology) when forming the interface identifier from IEEE EUI-64 identifiers. In the resulting Modified EUI-64 format, the "u" bit is set to one (1) to indicate global scope, and it is set to zero (0) to indicate local scope. The first three octets in binary of an IEEE EUI-64 identifier are as follows:

```
0          0 0         1 1         2
|0         7 8         5 6         3|
+----+----+----+----+----+----+
|cccc|ccug|cccc|cccc|cccc|cccc|
+----+----+----+----+----+----+
```

written in Internet standard bit-order, where "u" is the universal/local bit, "g" is the individual/group bit, and "c" are the bits of the company_ID. The motivation for inverting the "u" bit when forming an interface identifier is to make it easy for system administrators to manually configure nonglobal identifiers when hardware tokens are not available. This is expected to be the case for serial links, tunnel end-points, and so forth. The alternative would have been for these to be of the form 0200:0:0:1, 0200:0:0:2, and so forth, instead of the much simpler 1, 2, and so forth.

The use of the universal/local bit in the Modified EUI-64 format identifier is to allow development of future technology that can take advantage of interface identifiers with global scope.

The Unspecified Address

The address 0:0:0:0:0:0:0:0 is called the unspecified address. It must never be assigned to any node. It indicates the absence of an address. One example of its use is in the Source Address field of any IPv6 packets sent by an initializing host before it has learned its own address. The unspecified address must not be used as the destination address of IPv6 packets or in IPv6 Routing Headers. An IPv6 packet with a source address of unspecified must never be forwarded by an IPv6 router.

The Loopback Address

The unicast address 0:0:0:0:0:0:0:1 is called the loopback address. It may be used by a node to send an IPv6 packet to itself. It may never be assigned to any physical interface. It is treated as having link-local scope, and may be thought of as the link-local unicast address of a virtual interface (typically called "the loopback interface") to an imaginary link that goes nowhere. The loopback address must not be used as the source address in IPv6 packets that are sent outside a single node. An IPv6 packet with a destination address of loopback must never be sent outside a single node and must never be forwarded by an IPv6 router. A packet received on an interface with destination address of loopback must be dropped.

Global Unicast Addresses

The general format for IPv6 global unicast addresses is as follows:

```
|          n bits         | m bits |      128-n-m bits      |
+-------------------------+--------+-----------------------+
| global routing prefix | subnet ID |      interface ID     |
+-------------------------+--------+-----------------------+
```

where the global routing prefix is a (typically hierarchically structured) value assigned to a site (a cluster of subnets/links), the subnet ID is an identifier of a link within the site, and the interface ID is as defined earlier. All global unicast addresses other than those that start with binary 000 have a 64-bit interface ID field (i.e., $n + m = 64$). Global unicast addresses that start with binary 000 have no such constraint on the size or structure of the interface ID field. Examples of global unicast addresses that start with binary 000 are the IPv6 address with embedded IPv4 addresses and the IPv6 address containing encoded NSAP addresses.

IPv6 Addresses with Embedded IPv4 Addresses

The IPv6 transition mechanisms include a technique for hosts and routers to dynamically tunnel IPv6 packets over IPv4 routing infrastructure. IPv6 nodes that use this technique are assigned special IPv6 unicast addresses that carry a global IPv4 address in the low-order 32 bits. This type of address is termed an "IPv4-compatible IPv6 address" and has the format:

```
|            80 bits            | 16 |      32 bits      |
+------------------------------+----+-------------------+
|0000........................0000|0000|   IPv4 address    |
+------------------------------+----+-------------------+
```

Note:

The IPv4 address used in the "IPv4-compatible IPv6 address" must be a globally unique IPv4 unicast address.

A second type of IPv6 address which holds an embedded IPv4 address is also defined. This address type is used to represent the addresses of IPv4 nodes as IPv6 addresses. This type of address is termed an "IPv4-mapped IPv6 address" and has the format:

```
|            80 bits            | 16 |      32 bits      |
+------------------------------+----+-------------------+
|0000........................0000|FFFF|   IPv4 address    |
+------------------------------+----+-------------------+
```

Local-Use IPv6 Unicast Addresses

There are two types of local-use unicast addresses defined. These are link-local and site-local. The link-local is for use on a single link and the site-local is for use in a single site (recall that site-local addresses have been deprecated). Link-local addresses have the following format:

```
|   10    |                   |                           |
|  bits   |      54bits        |        64 bits            |
+---------+-------------------+---------------------------+
|1111111010|         0         |       interface ID        |
+---------+-------------------+---------------------------+
```

Link-local addresses are designed to be used for addressing on a single link for purposes such as automatic address configuration, neighbor discovery, or when no routers are present.

Routers must not forward any packets with link-local source or destination addresses to other links.

2.4.6 Anycast Addresses

An IPv6 anycast address is an address that is assigned to more than one interface (typically belonging to different nodes), with the property that a packet sent to an anycast address is routed to the "nearest" interface having that address, according to the routing protocols' measure of distance.

Anycast addresses are allocated from the unicast address space, using any of the defined unicast address formats. Thus, anycast addresses are syntactically indistinguishable from unicast addresses. When a unicast address is assigned to more than one interface, thus turning it into an anycast address, the nodes to which the address is assigned must be explicitly configured to know that it is an anycast address.

For any assigned anycast address, there is a longest prefix P of that address that identifies the topological region in which all interfaces belonging to that anycast address reside. Within the region identified by P, the anycast address must be maintained as a separate entry in the routing system (commonly referred to as a "host route"); outside the region identified by P, the anycast address may be aggregated into the routing entry for prefix P. Note that in the worst case, the prefix P of an anycast set may be the null prefix, that is, the members of the set may have no topological locality. In that case, the anycast address must be maintained as a separate routing entry throughout the entire Internet, which presents a severe scaling limit on how many such "global" anycast sets may be supported. Therefore, it is expected that support for global anycast sets may be unavailable or very restricted.

One expected use of anycast addresses is to identify the set of routers belonging to an organization providing Internet service. Such addresses could be used as intermediate addresses in an IPv6 Routing header to cause a packet to be delivered via a particular service provider or sequence of service providers.

Some other possible uses are to identify the set of routers attached to a particular subnet, or the set of routers providing entry into a particular routing domain.

There is little experience with widespread use of Internet anycast addresses, and some known complications and hazards when using them in their full generality. Until more experience has been gained and solutions are specified, the following restrictions should be imposed on IPv6 anycast addresses:

- An anycast address must not be used as the source address of an IPv6 packet;
- An anycast address must not be assigned to an IPv6 host, that is, it may be assigned to an IPv6 router only.

Required Anycast Address

The Subnet-Router anycast address is predefined. Its format is as follows:

```
|                   n bits                  |    128-n bits    |
+-------------------------------------------+------------------+
|               subnet prefix               | 0000000000000000 |
+-------------------------------------------+------------------+
```

The "subnet prefix" in an anycast address is the prefix which identifies a specific link. This anycast address is syntactically the same as a unicast address for an interface on the link with the interface identifier set to zero. Packets sent to the Subnet-Router anycast address will be delivered to one router on the subnet. All routers are required to support the Subnet-Router anycast addresses for the subnets to which they have interfaces. The Subnet-Router anycast address is intended to be used for applications where a node needs to communicate with any one of the sets of routers.

2.4.7 Multicast Addresses

An IPv6 multicast address is an identifier for a group of interfaces (typically on different nodes). An interface may belong to any number of multicast groups. Multicast addresses have the following format:

```
|   8    | 4  | 4  |                   112 bits                     |
+------- -+----+----+------------------------------------------------+
|11111111|flgs|scop|                   group ID                     |
+--------+----+----+------------------------------------------------+
```

- binary 11111111 at the start of the address identifies the address as being a multicast address.
- flgs is a set of 4 flags: |0|0|0|T|
  - The high-order 3 flags are reserved, and must be initialized to 0.
  - T = 0 indicates a permanently assigned ("well-known") multicast address, assigned by the Internet Assigned Number Authority (IANA).
  - T = 1 indicates a nonpermanently assigned ("transient") multicast address.
- scop is a 4-bit multicast scope value used to limit the scope of the multicast group. The values are:
  ```
  0 reserved
  1 interface-local scope
  2 link-local scope
  3 reserved
  4 admin-local scope
  5 site-local scope (deprecated)
  6 (unassigned)
  7 (unassigned)
  8 organization-local scope
  ```

```
9 (unassigned)
A (unassigned)
B (unassigned)
C (unassigned)
D (unassigned)
E global scope
F reserved
```

 − interface-local scope spans only a single interface on a node, and is useful only for loopback transmission of multicast.
 − link-local multicast scopes span the same topological regions as the corresponding unicast scopes.
 − admin-local scope is the smallest scope that must be administratively configured, that is, not automatically derived from physical connectivity or other, non-multicast-related configuration.
 − organization-local scope is intended to span multiple sites belonging to a single organization.
 − scopes labeled "(unassigned)" are available for administrators to define additional multicast regions.
■ group ID identifies the multicast group, either permanent or transient, within the given scope.

The "meaning" of a permanently assigned multicast address is independent of the scope value. For example, if the "NTP servers group" is assigned a permanent multicast address with a group ID of 101 (hex), then:

FF01:0:0:0:0:0:0:101 means all NTP servers on the same interface (i.e., the same node) as the sender.
FF02:0:0:0:0:0:0:101 means all NTP servers on the same link as the sender.
FF05:0:0:0:0:0:0:101 means all NTP servers in the same site as the sender.
FF0E:0:0:0:0:0:0:101 means all NTP servers in the Internet.
Nonpermanently-assigned multicast addresses are meaningful only within a given scope.

Multicast addresses must not be used as source addresses in IPv6 packets or appear in any Routing header. Routers must not forward any multicast packets beyond the scope indicated by the scop field in the destination multicast address.

Nodes must not originate a packet to a multicast address whose scop field contains the reserved value 0; if such a packet is received, it must be silently dropped. Nodes should not originate a packet to a multicast address whose scop field contains the reserved value F; if such a packet is sent or received, it must be treated the same as packets destined to a global (scop E) multicast address.

Predefined Multicast Addresses

The following well-known multicast addresses are predefined. The group IDs defined in this section are defined for explicit scope values.

Use of these group IDs for any other scope values, with the T flag equal to 0, is not allowed.

```
Reserved Multicast Addresses:   FF00:0:0:0:0:0:0:0
                                FF01:0:0:0:0:0:0:0
                                FF02:0:0:0:0:0:0:0
                                FF03:0:0:0:0:0:0:0
                                FF04:0:0:0:0:0:0:0
                                FF05:0:0:0:0:0:0:0
                                FF06:0:0:0:0:0:0:0
                                FF07:0:0:0:0:0:0:0
                                FF08:0:0:0:0:0:0:0
                                FF09:0:0:0:0:0:0:0
                                FF0A:0:0:0:0:0:0:0
                                FF0B:0:0:0:0:0:0:0
                                FF0C:0:0:0:0:0:0:0
                                FF0D:0:0:0:0:0:0:0
                                FF0E:0:0:0:0:0:0:0
                                FF0F:0:0:0:0:0:0:0
```

The above multicast addresses are reserved and shall never be assigned to any multicast group.

```
All Nodes Addresses:   FF01:0:0:0:0:0:0:1
                       FF02:0:0:0:0:0:0:1
```

The above multicast addresses identify the group of all IPv6 nodes, within scope 1 (interface-local) or 2 (link-local).

```
All Routers Addresses:   FF01:0:0:0:0:0:0:2
                         FF02:0:0:0:0:0:0:2
                         FF05:0:0:0:0:0:0:2
```

The above multicast addresses identify the group of all IPv6 routers, within scope 1 (interface-local), 2 (link-local), or 5 (site-local).

```
Solicited-Node Address:   FF02:0:0:0:0:1:FFXX:XXXX
```

Solicited-node multicast addresses are computed as a function of a node's unicast and anycast addresses. A solicited-node multicast address is formed by taking the low-order 24 bits of an address (unicast or anycast) and appending those bits to the prefix FF02:0:0:0:0:1:FF00::/104, resulting in a multicast address in the range

```
FF02:0:0:0:0:1:FF00:0000
to
FF02:0:0:0:0:1:FFFF:FFFF
```

For example, the solicited-node multicast address corresponding to the IPv6 address 4037::01:800:200E:8C6C is FF02::1:FF0E:8C6C. IPv6 addresses that differ only in the high-order bits, for example, due to multiple high-order prefixes associated with different aggregations, will map to the same solicited-node address, thereby reducing the number of multicast addresses a node must join.

A node is required to compute and join (on the appropriate interface) the associated solicited-node multicast addresses for every unicast and anycast address it is assigned.

2.4.8 A Node's Required Addresses

A host is required to recognize the following addresses as identifying itself:

- Its required link-local address for each interface.
- Any additional unicast and anycast addresses that have been configured for the node's interfaces (manually or automatically).
- The loopback address.
- The all-nodes multicast addresses.
- The solicited-node multicast address for each of its unicast and anycast addresses.
- Multicast addresses of all other groups to which the node belongs.

A router is required to recognize all addresses that a host is required to recognize, plus the following addresses as identifying itself:

- The subnet-router anycast addresses for all interfaces for which it is configured to act as a router.
- All other anycast addresses with which the router has been configured.
- The all-routers multicast addresses.

2.5 IANA Considerations

The initial assignment of IPv6 address space is as follows:

```
Allocation                       Prefix      Fraction of
                                 (binary)    Address Space

----------------------------     --------    ------------
Unassigned (see Note 1 below)    0000 0000   1/256
Unassigned                       0000 0001   1/256
Reserved for NSAP allocation     0000 001    1/128 (RFC 1888)
Unassigned                       0000 01     1/64
Unassigned                       0000 1      1/32
Unassigned                       0001        1/16
Global Unicast                   001         1/8 (per RFC 2374)
Unassigned                       010         1/8
Unassigned                       011         1/8
                                                   (Continued)
```

```
Allocation                      Prefix          Fraction of
                                (binary)        Address Space
------------------------------  --------        -------------
Unassigned                      100             1/8
Unassigned                      101             1/8
Unassigned                      110             1/8
Unassigned                      1110            1/16
Unassigned                      1111 0          1/32
Unassigned                      1111 10         1/64
Unassigned                      1111 110        1/128
Unassigned                      1111 1110 0     1/512
Link-local unicast addresses    1111 1110 10    1/1024
[Site-local unicast addresses   1111 1110 11    1/1024]
Multicast addresses             1111 1111       1/256
```

Notes:

1. The "unspecified address," the "loopback address," and the IPv6 addresses with embedded IPv4 addresses are assigned out of the 0000 0000 binary prefix space.
2. For now, IANA should limit its allocation of IPv6 unicast address space to the range of addresses that start with binary value 001. The rest of the global unicast address space (approximately 85% of the IPv6 address space) is reserved for future definition and use, and is not to be assigned by IANA at this time.
3. Site-local addresses are deprecated (no longer supported for new implementations.)

2.6 Creating Modified EUI-64 Format Interface Identifiers

Depending on the characteristics of a specific link or node, there are a number of approaches for creating Modified EUI-64 format interface identifiers. This section describes some of these approaches.

EUI is defined in IEEE, "Guidelines for 64-bit Global Identifier (EUI-64) Registration Authority," March 1997.

Links or Nodes with IEEE EUI-64 Identifiers

The only change needed to transform an IEEE EUI-64 identifier to an interface identifier is to invert the "u" (universal/local) bit. For example, a globally unique IEEE EUI-64 identifier of the form:

```
|0                 1|1                 3|3                 4|4                 6|
|0                 5|6                 1|2                 7|8                 3|
+------------------+------------------+------------------+------------------+
|cccccc0gcccccccc|ccccccccmmmmmmmm|mmmmmmmmmmmmmmmm|mmmmmmmmmmmmmmmm|
+------------------+------------------+------------------+------------------+
```

where "c" are the bits of the assigned company_ID, "0" is the value of the universal/
local bit to indicate global scope, "g" is individual/group bit, and "m" are the bits of
the manufacturer-selected extension identifier. The IPv6 interface identifier would
be of the form:

```
|0                 1|1               3|3               4|4               6|
|0                 5|6               1|2               7|8               3|
+----------------+----------------+----------------+----------------+
|cccccc1gcccccccc|ccccccccmmmmmmmm|mmmmmmmmmmmmmmmm|mmmmmmmmmmmmmmmm|
+----------------+----------------+----------------+----------------+
```

The only change is inverting the value of the universal/local bit.

Links or Nodes with IEEE 802 48-bit MACs

EUI-64 defines a method to create an IEEE EUI-64 identifier from an IEEE
48-bit MAC identifier. This is to insert two octets, with hexadecimal values of
0xFF and 0xFE, in the middle of the 48-bit MAC (between the company_ID
and vendor supplied ID). For example, the 48-bit IEEE MAC with global scope:

```
|0                 1|1               3|3               4|
|0                 5|6               1|2               7|
+----------------+----------------+----------------+
|cccccc0gcccccccc|ccccccccmmmmmmmm|mmmmmmmmmmmmmmmm|
+----------------+----------------+----------------+
```

where "c" are the bits of the assigned company_ID, "0" is the value of the universal/
local bit to indicate global scope, "g" is individual/group bit, and "m" are the bits
of the manufacturer-selected extension identifier. The interface identifier would be
of the form:

```
|0                 1|1               3|3               4|4               6|
|0                 5|6               1|2               7|8               3|
+----------------+----------------+----------------+----------------+
|cccccc1gcccccccc|cccccccc11111111|11111110mmmmmmmm|mmmmmmmmmmmmmmmm|
+----------------+----------------+----------------+----------------+
```

When IEEE 802 48-bit MAC addresses are available (on an interface or a node),
an implementation may use them to create interface identifiers due to their availability and uniqueness properties.

Links with Other Kinds of Identifiers

Originally, there were a number of types of links that have link-layer interface
identifiers other than IEEE EIU-64 or IEEE 802 48-bit MACs. Examples include
LocalTalk and Arcnet. These are now mostly of historical interest. The method to
create a Modified EUI-64 format identifier is to take the link identifier (e.g., the

LocalTalk 8-bit node identifier) and zero fill it to the left. For example, a LocalTalk 8-bit node identifier of hexadecimal value 0x4F results in the following interface identifier:

```
|0               1|1               3|3               4|4               6|
|0               5|6               1|2               7|8               3|
+----------------+----------------+----------------+----------------+
|0000000000000000|0000000000000000|0000000000000000|0000000001001111|
+----------------+----------------+----------------+----------------+
```

Note that this results in the universal/local bit set to zero ("0") to indicate local scope.

Links without Identifiers

There are a number of links that do not have any type of built-in identifier. The most common of these are serial links and configured tunnels. Interface identifiers must be chosen that are unique within a subnet prefix.

When no built-in identifier is available on a link, the preferred approach is to use a global interface identifier from another interface or one that is assigned to the node itself. When using this approach, no other interface connecting the same node to the same subnet prefix may use the same identifier.

If there is no global interface identifier available for use on the link, the implementation needs to create a local-scope interface identifier. The only requirement is that it be unique within a subnet prefix. There are many possible approaches to select a subnet-prefix-unique interface identifier. These include:

- Manual configuration
- Node serial number
- Other node-specific token

The subnet-prefix-unique interface identifier should be generated in a manner such that it does not change after a reboot of a node or if interfaces are added or deleted from the node.

The selection of the appropriate algorithm is link and implementation dependent. It is strongly recommended that a collision detection algorithm be implemented as part of any automatic algorithm.

2.7 64-Bit Global Identifier (EUI-64) Registration Authority

The IEEE defined 64-bit extended unique identifier (EUI-64) is a concatenation of the 24-bit company ID value by the IEEE Registration Authority Committee (RAC) and a 40-bit extension identifier assigned by the organization with that companyID assignment. The IEEE administers the assignment of 24-bit *company_ID* values. The assignments of these values are public, so that a user of an EUI-64 value can identify the manufacturer that provided any value. The IEEE RAC has no control over the assignments of 40-bit extension identifiers and assumes no liability for assignments of duplicate EUI-64 identifiers assigned by manufacturers.

Application Restrictions

Given the minimal probability of consuming all the EUI-64 identifiers, the IEEE/RAC places minimal restrictions on their use within standards. However, if used within the context of an IEEE standard, the documentation shall be reviewed by the IEEE/RAC for correctness and clarity. The IEEE/RAC shall not otherwise restrict the use of EUI-64 identifiers within standards. If the EUI-64 is referenced within non-IEEE standards, there shall not be any reference to IEEE unless approved by the IEEE/RAC.

Distribution Restrictions

Given the minimal probability of consuming all the EUI-64 identifiers, the IEEE/RAC places minimal restrictions on their redistribution through third parties, as follows:

1. Allocation. The EUI-64 values shall be sold within electronically readable parts; no more than one EUI-64 value shall be contained within each component that is manufactured.
2. Packaging. A component containing the EUI-64 value shall have a distinguishing characteristic (such as color or shape) to distinguish it from other commonly used identifier components.
3. Documentation. Readily available documentation.
4. Legal indemnification. Any organization producing EUI-64 values shall indemnify the IEEE for damages arising from duplicate number assignments.

The term EUI-64 is trademarked by the IEEE. Companies are allowed to use this term for commercial purposes, but only if their use of this term has been reviewed by the IEEE/RAC and the proposed products using the EUI-64 conform to these restrictions.

Application Documentation

As a condition for receiving a *company_ID* assignment, a manufacturer of EUI-64 values accepts the following responsibilities:

1. This documentation shall be readily available (at no cost) to any purchaser of EUI-64 values.
2. The manufacturer's part specification should include an unambiguous description of how the EUI-64 value is accessed (pin or address descriptions).

Manufacturer-Assigned Identifiers

The manufacturer identifier assignment allows the assignee to generate approximately 1 trillion (10^{12}) unique EUI-64 values by varying the last 40 bits. The IEEE intends not to assign another OUI/*company_ID* value to a manufacturer of EUI-64 values until the manufacturer has consumed, in product, the preponderance (more than 90%) of this block of potential unique words. It is incumbent upon the manufacturer to ensure that large portions of the unique word block are not left unused in manufacturing.

References

[6NE200501] 6NET. *D2.2.4: Final IPv4 to IPv6 transition cookbook for organizational/ISP (NREN) and backbone networks*, Version: 1.0. Project Number: IST-2001-32603, CEC Deliverable Number: 32603/UOS/DS/2.2.4/A1. Feb. 4, 2005.

[ATT200801] AT&T. *Promotional literature on IPv6*. 2008. http://www.corp.att.com/gov/ipv6/.

[DAV200201] Davies, J. *Understanding IPv6*. Microsoft Press, 2002.

[DES200301] Desmeules, R. *Cisco self-study: Implementing IPv6 networks (IPV6)*. Pearson Education, CiscoPress, May 2003.

[DIR200801] Directorate-Generals Information Society. *IPv6: Enabling the information society*. European Commission Information Society, Europe Information Society Portal, Feb. 18, 2008. http://ec.europa.eu/information_society/policy/ipv6/index_en.htm.

[GON199801] Goncalves, M., and K. Niles. *IPv6 networks*. New York: McGraw-Hill Osborne, 1998.

[GOS200301] Goswami, S. *Internet protocols: Advances, technologies, and applications*. Dordrecht: Kluwer, May 2003.

[GRA200001] Graham, B. *TCP/IP addressing: Designing and optimizing your IP addressing scheme* (2nd edition). Morgan Kaufmann, 2000.

[HAG200201] Hagen, S. *IPv6 essentials*. O'Reilly, 2002.

[HUI199701] Huitema, C. *IPv6 the new Internet protocol* (2nd edition). Englewood Cliffs, NJ: Prentice Hall, 1997.

[IPV200401] IPv6Forum. IPv6 vendors test voice, wireless and firewalls on Moonv6, Nov. 15, 2004. http://www.ipv6forum.com/modules.php?op=modload&name=News&file=article&sid=15& mode=thread&order =0&thold=0.

[IPV200501] IPv6 Portal. http://www.ipv6tf.org/meet/faqs.php.

[ITO200401] Itojun Hagino, J. *IPv6 network programming*. Oxford: Butterworth-Heinemann, 2004.

[LAD200601] Ladid, L. *European IPv6 roadmap 2006 recommendations.* European IPv6 Task Force, IPv6 Task Force Steering Committee, IST-2-004572-CA IPv6 TF-SC Euro-v6-Roadmap, Aug. 10, 2006.

[LEE200501] Lee, H. K. *Understanding IPv6.* New York: Springer-Verlag, 2005.

[LOS200301] Loshin, P. *IPv6: Theory, protocol, and practice* (2nd edition). New York: Elsevier, 2003.

[MIL199701] Miller, M. A. *Implementing IPv6: Migrating to the next generation Internet protocol.* New York: Wiley, 1997.

[MIL200001] Miller, M., and P. E. Miller. *Implementing IPV6: Supporting the next generation Internet protocols* (2nd edition). Hungry Minds, 2000.

[MIN200601] Minoli, D. *VoIP over IPv6.* New York: Elsevier, 2006.

[MSD200401] Microsoft Corporation. *Internet protocol.* MSDN Library, 2004. http://msdn.microsoft.com.

[MUR200501] Murphy, N. R., and D. Malone. *IPv6 network administration.* O'Reilly & Associates, 2005.

[RFC2460] Deering, S., and R. Hinden. Internet Protocol, Version 6 (IPv6) Specification, RFC2460, Dec. 1998. Copyright (C) The Internet Society (1998). All Rights Reserved. This document and translations of it may be copied and furnished to others, and derivative works that comment on or otherwise explain it or assist in its implementation may be prepared, copied, published and distributed, in whole or in part, without restriction of any kind, provided that the above copyright notice and this paragraph are included on all such copies and derivative works.

[RFC2893] Gilligan, R., and E. Nordmark. Transition Mechanisms for IPv6 Hosts and Routers, RFC 2893, Aug. 2000. Copyright (C) The Internet Society (2000). All Rights Reserved. This document and translations of it may be copied and furnished to others, and derivative works that comment on or otherwise explain it or assist in its implementation may be prepared, copied, published and distributed, in whole or in part, without restriction of any kind, provided that the above copyright notice and this paragraph are included on all such copies and derivative works.

[RFC3022] Srisuresh, P., and K. Egevang. Request for Comments: 3022, Traditional IP Network Address Translator (Traditional NAT), RFC 3022, Jan. 2001.

[RFC3315] Droms, R., ed., J. Bound, B. Volz, T. Lemon, C. Perkins, and M. Carney. Dynamic Host Configuration Protocol for IPv6 (DHCPv6), RFC 3315, July 2003. Copyright (C) The Internet Society (2003). All Rights Reserved. This document and translations of it may be copied and furnished to others, and derivative works that comment on or otherwise explain it or assist in its implementation may be prepared, copied, published and distributed, in whole or in part, without restriction of any kind, provided that the above copyright notice and this paragraph are included on all such copies and derivative works.

[RFC3513] Hinden, R., and S. Deering. Internet Protocol Version 6 (IPv6) Addressing Architecture, RFC 3513, Apr. 2003. Copyright (C) The Internet Society (2003). All Rights Reserved. This document and translations of it may be copied and furnished to others, and derivative works that comment on or otherwise explain it or assist in its implementation may be prepared, copied, published and distributed, in whole or in part, without restriction of any kind, provided that the above copyright notice and this paragraph are included on all such copies and derivative works.

[RFC3879] Huitema, C., and B. Carpenter. Request for Comments: 3879, Deprecating Site Local Addresses, RFC 3879, Sept. 2004.

[RFC4038] Shin, M-K., ed., Y-G. Hong, J. Hagino, P. Savola, and E. M. Castro. Request for Comments: 4038, Application Aspects of IPv6 Transition, RFC 4038, Mar. 2005.

[SOL200401] Soliman, H. S. *Mobile IPv6*. Englewood Cliffs, NJ: Pearson Education, 2004.

[TEA200401] Teare, D., and C. Paquet. CCNP self-study: Advanced IP addressing. Cisco Press, June 11, 2004.

[WEG199901] Wegner, J. D. *IP addressing and subnetting, including IPv6*. New York: Elsevier, 1999.

Chapter 3

More Advanced IPv6 Protocol Mechanisms

Introduction

The previous two chapters provided an introduction to IPv6. This chapter provides additional details. This allows us to focus on security-related issues starting with the chapter that follows.

As we have seen, like IPv4, IPv6 is a connectionless datagram protocol used primarily for addressing and routing packets between hosts. Connectionless means that a session is not established before exchanging data. Connectionless protocols are "unreliable" in the sense that delivery is not automatically guaranteed. IPv6 always makes a best-effort attempt to deliver a packet. An IPv6 packet might be lost, delivered out of sequence, duplicated, or delayed. IPv6 per se does not attempt to recover from these types of errors. The acknowledgment of packets delivered and the recovery of lost packets are done by a higher-layer protocol, such as Transmission Control Protocol (TCP). Other supportive protocols include the following: Internet Control Message Protocol for IPv6 (ICMPv6) (RFC 2463), Neighbor Discovery (ND) (RFC 2461), and Multicast Listener Discovery (MLD) (RFC 2710, RFC 3590, RFC 3810). ICMPv6 is a mechanism that enables hosts and routers that use IPv6 communication to report errors and send simple status messages. ND is a mechanism that is used to manage node-to-node communication on a link. ND uses a series of five ICMPv6 messages. ND replaces Address Resolution Protocol (ARP), ICMPv4 Router Discovery, and the ICMPv4 Redirect message; it also provides additional functions. ND is implemented using the Neighbor Discovery Protocol (NDP). MLD is a mechanism

105

that enables one to manage subnet multicast membership for IPv6. It uses a series of three ICMPv6 messages and replaces the Internet Group Management Protocol (IGMP) v3 that is employed for IPv4.

3.1 IPv6 and Related Protocols (Details)

We introduced a number of basic IPv6 concepts in previous chapters. The sections that follow focus on a more formal description of IPv6. The discussion is based on IETF RFC 2460 [RFC2460]. There is an extensive body of technical research literature on this topic.

IPv6 is a new version of the Internet Protocol, designed as the successor to IP version 4 (IPv4) described in RFC 791. RFC 2460 specifies the basic IPv6 header and the initially defined IPv6 extension headers and options. It also discusses packet size issues, the semantics of flow labels and traffic classes, and the effects of IPv6 on upper-layer protocols. The format and semantics of IPv6 addresses are specified separately in RFC 2373 (now obsoleted by RFC 3513). The IPv6 version of ICMP, which all IPv6 implementations are required to include, is specified in ICMPv6 (RFC 2483). Developers should refer directly to all relevant IETF RFCs for normative guidelines.

The following nomenclature is used in the standard:

Node—a device that implements IPv6;

Router—a node that forwards IPv6 packets not explicitly addressed to itself (see Note below);

Host—any node that is not a router (see Note below);

Upper layer—a protocol layer immediately above IPv6. Examples are transport protocols such as TCP and UDP, control protocols such as ICMP, routing protocols such as Open Shortest Path First (OSPF), and Internet or lower-layer protocols being "tunneled" over (i.e., encapsulated in) IPv6 such as IPX, or IPv6 itself;

Link—a communication facility or medium over which nodes can communicate at the link layer, that is, the layer immediately below IPv6. Examples are Ethernets (simple or bridged), PPP links, Frame Relay, or ATM networks, and Internet (or higher) layer "tunnels," such as tunnels over IPv4 or IPv6 itself;

Neighbors—nodes attached to the same link;

Interface—a node's attachment to a link;

Address—an IPv6-layer identifier for an interface or a set of interfaces;

Packet—an IPv6 header plus payload;

Link Maximum Transmission Unit (MTU)—the maximum transmission unit, that is, maximum packet size in octets that can be conveyed over a link;

Path MTU—the minimum link MTU of all the links in a path between a source node and a destination node.

Note:

It is possible, though unusual, for a device with multiple interfaces to be configured to forward non-self-destined packets arriving from some set (fewer than all) of its interfaces, and to discard non-self-destined packets arriving from its other interfaces. Such a device must obey the protocol requirements for routers when receiving packets from, and interacting with neighbors, the former (forwarding) interfaces. It must obey the protocol requirements for hosts when receiving packets from, and interacting with neighbors over, the latter (nonforwarding) interfaces.

3.2 IPv6 Header Format

Figure 3.1 depicts the IPv6 Header format.

The fields in the header have the following meanings:

Version: 4-bit Internet Protocol version number = 6.
Traffic Class: 8-bit traffic class field.
Flow Label: 20-bit flow label.
Payload Length: 16-bit unsigned integer. Length of the IPv6 payload, that is, the rest of the packet following this IPv6 header, in octets. (Note that any extension headers present are considered part of the payload, that is, included in the length count.)

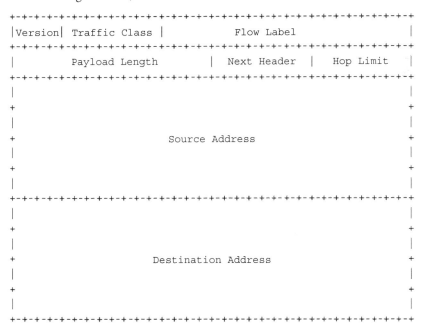

Figure 3.1   IPv6 header format.

Next Header: 8-bit selector. Identifies the type of header immediately following the IPv6 header. Uses the same values as the IPv4 Protocol field.

Hop Limit: 8-bit unsigned integer. Decremented by 1 by each node that forwards the packet. The packet is discarded if Hop Limit is decremented to zero.

Source Address: 128-bit address of the originator of the packet. This is covered later in more detail.

Destination Address: 128-bit address of the intended recipient of the packet (possibly not the ultimate recipient, if a Routing header is present).

3.3 IPv6 Extension Headers

In IPv6, optional Internet-layer information is encoded in separate headers that may be placed between the IPv6 header and the upper-layer header in a packet. There are a small number of such extension headers, each identified by a distinct Next Header value. As illustrated in the examples of Figure 3.2, an IPv6 packet may carry zero, one, or more extension headers, each identified by the Next Header field of the preceding header.

With one exception, extension headers are not examined or processed by any node along a packet's delivery path, until the packet reaches the node (or each of

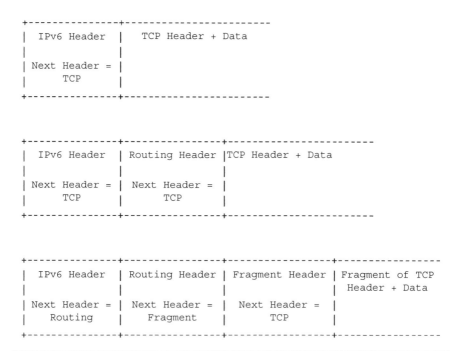

Figure 3.2   Examples of extension headers.

the set of nodes, in the case of multicast) identified in the Destination Address field of the IPv6 header. There, normal demultiplexing on the Next Header field of the IPv6 header invokes the module to process the first extension header, or the upper-layer header if no extension header is present. The contents and semantics of each extension header determine whether or not to proceed to the next header. Therefore, extension headers must be processed strictly in the order they appear in the packet. A receiver must not, for example, scan through a packet looking for a particular kind of extension header and process that header prior to processing all preceding ones.

The exception referred to in the preceding paragraph is the *Hop-by-Hop Options* header, which carries information that must be examined and processed by every node along a packet's delivery path, including the source and destination nodes. The *Hop-by-Hop Options* header, when present, must immediately follow the IPv6 header; its presence is indicated by the value zero in the Next Header field of the IPv6 header.

If, as a result of processing a header, a node is required to proceed to the next header but the Next Header value in the current header is unrecognized by the node, it should discard the packet and send an ICMP Parameter Problem message to the source of the packet, with an ICMP Code value of 1 ("unrecognized Next Header type encountered") and the ICMP Pointer field containing the offset of the unrecognized value within the original packet. The same action should be taken if a node encounters a Next Header value of zero in any header other than an IPv6 header.

Each extension header is an integer multiple of 8 octets long, in order to retain 8-octet alignment for subsequent headers. Multioctet fields within each extension header are aligned on their natural boundaries, that is, fields of width n octets are placed at an integer multiple of n octets from the start of the header, for n = 1, 2, 4, or 8.

A full implementation of IPv6 includes implementation of the following extension headers:

- Hop-by-Hop Options
- Routing (Type 0)
- Fragment
- Destination Options
- Authentication
- Encapsulating Security Payload

The first four are specified in this RFC; the last two are specified in RFC 2402 and RFC 2406, respectively.

3.3.1 Extension Header Order

When more than one extension header is used in the same packet, it is recommended that those headers appear in the following order:

IPv6 header
Hop-by-Hop Options header
Destination Options header (Note 1)
Routing header
Fragment header
Authentication header (Note 2)
Encapsulating Security Payload header (Note 2)
Destination Options header (Note 3)
Upper-layer header

Note 1: for options to be processed by the first destination that appears in the IPv6 Destination Address field plus subsequent destinations listed in the *Routing* header.
Note 2: additional recommendations regarding the relative order of the *Authentication* and *Encapsulating Security Payload* headers are given in RFC 2406.
Note 3: for options to be processed only by the final destination of the packet.

Each extension header should occur at most once, except for the *Destination Options* header, which should occur at most twice (once before a Routing header and once before the upper-layer header).

If the upper-layer header is another IPv6 header (in the case of IPv6 being tunneled over or encapsulated in IPv6), it may be followed by its own extension headers, which are separately subject to the same ordering recommendations.

If and when other extension headers are defined, their ordering constraints relative to the above listed headers must be specified.

IPv6 nodes must accept and attempt to process extension headers in any order and occurring any number of times in the same packet, except for the *Hop-by-Hop Options* header which is restricted to appear immediately after an IPv6 header only. Nonetheless, it is strongly advised that sources of IPv6 packets adhere to the above recommended order until and unless subsequent specifications revise that recommendation.

3.3.2 Options

Two of the currently defined extension headers—the *Hop-by-Hop Options* header and the *Destination Options* header—carry a variable number of type-length-value (TLV) encoded "options," of the format shown in Figure 3.3.

Option Type: 8-bit identifier of the type of option.

Opt Data Len: 8-bit unsigned integer. Length of the Option Data field of this option, in octets.

Option Data: Variable-length field. Option-Type-specific data.

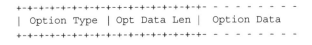

Figure 3.3 **Extension headers options.**

The sequence of options within a header must be processed strictly in the order they appear in the header; a receiver must not, for example, scan through the header looking for a particular kind of option and process that option prior to processing all preceding ones.

The Option Type identifiers are internally encoded such that the highest-order two bits specify the action that must be taken if the processing IPv6 node does not recognize the Option Type:

00 - skip over this option and continue processing the header.

01 - discard the packet.

10 - discard the packet and, regardless of whether or not the packet's Destination Address was a multicast address, send an ICMP Parameter Problem, Code 2, message to the packet's Source Address, pointing to the unrecognized Option Type.

11 - discard the packet and, only if the packet's Destination Address was not a multicast address, send an ICMP Parameter Problem, Code 2, message to the packet's Source Address, pointing to the unrecognized Option Type.

The third-highest-order bit of the Option Type specifies whether or not the Option Data of that option can change en route to the packet's final destination. When an Authentication Header is present in the packet, for any option whose data may change en route, its entire Option Data field must be treated as zero-valued octets when computing or verifying the packet's authenticating value.

0 - Option Data does not change en route

1 - Option Data may change en route

The three high-order bits described above are to be treated as part of the Option Type, not independent of the Option Type. That is, a particular option is identified by a full 8-bit Option Type, not just the low-order 5 bits of an Option Type.

The same Option Type numbering space is used for both the *Hop-by-Hop Options* header and the *Destination Options* header. However, the specification of a particular option may restrict its use to only one of those two headers.

Individual options may have specific alignment requirements, to ensure that multioctet values within Option Data fields fall on natural boundaries. The alignment requirement of an option is specified using the notation xn+y, meaning the Option Type must appear at an integer multiple of x octets from the start of the header, plus y octets. For example:

2n means any 2-octet offset from the start of the header;

8n+2 means any 8-octet offset from the start of the header, plus 2 octets.

There are two padding options which are used when necessary to align subsequent options and to pad out the containing header to a multiple of 8 octets in length. These padding options must be recognized by all IPv6 implementations:

Pad1 option (alignment requirement: none)

```
+-+-+-+-+-+-+-+-+
|       0       |
+-+-+-+-+-+-+-+-+
```

The Pad1 option is used to insert one octet of padding into the Options area of a header.

Note:

The format of the Pad1 option is a special case—it does not have length and value fields.

If more than one octet of padding is required, the PadN option, described next, should be used, rather than multiple Pad1 options.

PadN option (alignment requirement: none)

```
+-+-+-+-+-+-+-+-+-+-+-+-+-+-+-+-+-  - - - - - - -
|    1    |   Opt Data Len   |   Option Data
+-+-+-+-+-+-+-+-+-+-+-+-+-+-+-+-+-  - - - - - - -
```

The PadN option is used to insert two or more octets of padding into the Options area of a header. For N octets of padding, the Opt Data Len field contains the value N-2, and the Option Data consists of N-2 zero-valued octets.

3.3.3 Hop-by-Hop Options Header

The *Hop-by-Hop Options* header is used to carry optional information that must be examined by every node along a packet's delivery path. The *Hop-by-Hop Options* header is identified by a Next Header value of 0 in the IPv6 header, and has the format as shown in Figure 3.4.

The fields are as follows:

Next Header: 8-bit selector. Identifies the type of header immediately following the *Hop-by-Hop Options* header. Uses the same values as the IPv4 Protocol field (RFC 1700.)

Hdr Ext Len: 8-bit unsigned integer. Length of the *Hop-by-Hop Options* header in 8-octet units, not including the first 8 octets.

```
+-+-+-+-+-+-+-+-+-+-+-+-+-+-+-+-+-+-+-+-+-+-+-+-+-+
| Next Header | Hdr Ext Len |                     |
+-+-+-+-+-+-+-+-+-+-+-+-+-+-+                     +
|                                                 |
.                                                 .
.                    Options                      .
.                                                 .
|                                                 |
+-+-+-+-+-+-+-+-+-+-+-+-+-+-+-+-+-+-+-+-+-+-+-+-+-+
```

Figure 3.4   Hop-by-hop options header.

Options: Variable-length field, of length such that the complete *Hop-by-Hop Options* header is an integer multiple of 8 octets long. Contains one or more TLV-encoded options.

3.3.4 Routing Header

The *Routing* header is used by an IPv6 source to list one or more intermediate nodes to be "visited" on the way to a packet's destination. This function is very similar to IPv4's Loose Source and Record Route option. The *Routing* header is identified by a Next Header value of 43 in the immediately preceding header, and has the format of Figure 3.5.

The fields are as follows:

Next Header: 8-bit selector. Identifies the type of header immediately following the Routing header. Uses the same values as the IPv4 Protocol field (RFC 1700).
Hdr Ext Len: 8-bit unsigned integer. Length of the Routing header in 8-octet units, not including the first 8 octets.
Routing Type: 8-bit identifier of a particular Routing header variant.
Segments Left: 8-bit unsigned integer. Number of route segments remaining, that is, number of explicitly listed intermediate nodes still to be visited before reaching the final destination.
Type-specific data: Variable-length field, of format determined by the Routing Type, and of length such that the complete Routing header is an integer multiple of 8 octets long.

If, while processing a received packet, a node encounters a *Routing* header with an unrecognized Routing Type value, the required behavior of the node depends on the value of the Segments Left field, as follows:

If Segments Left is zero, the node must ignore the *Routing* header and proceed to process the next header in the packet, whose type is identified by the Next Header field in the *Routing* header.

If Segments Left is nonzero, the node must discard the packet and send an ICMP Parameter Problem, Code 0, message to the packet's Source Address, pointing to the unrecognized Routing Type.

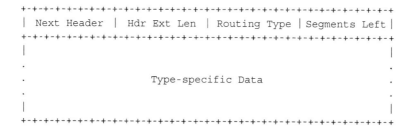

```
+-+-+-+-+-+-+-+-+-+-+-+-+-+-+-+-+-+-+-+-+-+-+-+-+-+-+-+-+-+-+-+-+
|  Next Header  |  Hdr Ext Len  |  Routing Type | Segments Left |
+-+-+-+-+-+-+-+-+-+-+-+-+-+-+-+-+-+-+-+-+-+-+-+-+-+-+-+-+-+-+-+-+
|                                                               |
.                                                               .
.                      Type-specific Data                       .
.                                                               .
|                                                               |
+-+-+-+-+-+-+-+-+-+-+-+-+-+-+-+-+-+-+-+-+-+-+-+-+-+-+-+-+-+-+-+-+
```

Figure 3.5   Routing header.

If, after processing a Routing header of a received packet, an intermediate node determines that the packet is to be forwarded onto a link whose link MTU is less than the size of the packet, the node must discard the packet and send an ICMP Packet Too Big message to the packet's Source Address.

The Type 0 Routing header has the format shown in Figure 3.6.

The fields are as follows:

> **Next Header:** 8-bit selector. Identifies the type of header immediately following the Routing header. Uses the same values as the IPv4 Protocol field (RFC 1700).

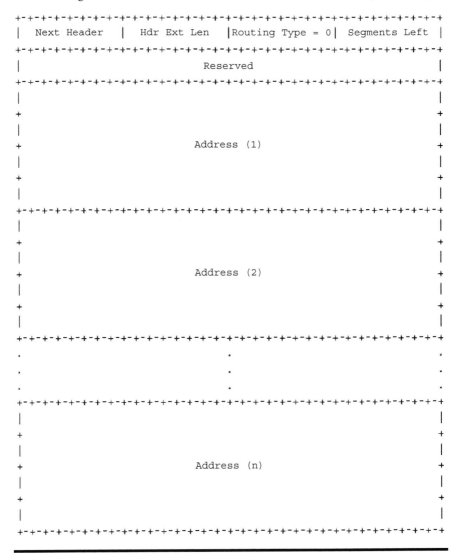

Figure 3.6 Type 0 Routing header.

Hdr Ext Len: 8-bit unsigned integer. Length of the Routing header in 8-octet units, not including the first 8 octets. For the Type 0 Routing header, Hdr Ext Len is equal to two times the number of addresses in the header.

Routing Type: 0.

Segments Left: 8-bit unsigned integer. Number of route segments remaining, that is, number of explicitly listed intermediate nodes still to be visited before reaching the final destination.

Reserved: 32-bit reserved field. This is initialized to zero for transmission and ignored on reception.

Address[1, 2, ..., n]: Vector of 128-bit addresses, numbered 1 to n.

Multicast addresses must not appear in a *Routing* header of Type 0 or in the IPv6 Destination Address field of a packet carrying a Routing header of Type 0.

A Routing header is not examined or processed until it reaches the node identified in the Destination Address field of the IPv6 header. In that node, dispatching on the Next Header field of the immediately preceding header causes the Routing header module to be invoked, which, in the case of Routing Type 0, performs the following algorithm:

```
if Segments Left = 0 {
proceed to process the next header in the packet, whose type is
identified by the Next Header field in the Routing header
}
else if Hdr Ext Len is odd {
send an ICMP Parameter Problem, Code 0, message to the Source
Address, pointing to the Hdr Ext Len field, and discard the
packet
}
else {
compute n, the number of addresses in the Routing header, by
dividing Hdr Ext Len by 2

if Segments Left is greater than n {
send an ICMP Parameter Problem, Code 0, message to the Source
Address, pointing to the Segments Left field, and discard the
packet
}
else {
decrement Segments Left by 1;
compute i, the index of the next address to be visited in
the address vector, by subtracting Segments Left from n

if Address [i] or the IPv6 Destination Address is multicast {
discard the packet
}
else {
swap the IPv6 Destination Address and Address[i]
```

```
if the IPv6 Hop Limit is less than or equal to 1 {
send an ICMP Time Exceeded—Hop Limit Exceeded in
Transit message to the Source Address and discard the
packet
}
else {
decrement the Hop Limit by 1
resubmit the packet to the IPv6 module for transmission
to the new destination
}
}
}
}
```

As an example of the effects of the above algorithm, consider the case of a source node S sending a packet to destination node D, using a Routing header to cause the packet to be routed via intermediate nodes I1, I2, and I3. The values of the relevant IPv6 header and Routing header fields on each segment of the delivery path would be as follows:

As the packet travels from S to I1:

```
    Source Address = S              Hdr Ext Len = 6
    Destination Address = I1        Segments Left = 3
                                    Address[1] = I2
                                    Address[2] = I3
                                    Address[3] = D
```

As the packet travels from I1 to I2:

```
    Source Address = S              Hdr Ext Len = 6
    Destination Address = I2        Segments Left = 2
                                    Address[1] = I1
                                    Address[2] = I3
                                    Address[3] = D
```

As the packet travels from I2 to I3:

```
    Source Address = S              Hdr Ext Len = 6
    Destination Address = I3        Segments Left = 1
                                    Address[1] = I1
                                    Address[2] = I2
                                    Address[3] = D
```

As the packet travels from I3 to D:

```
    Source Address = S              Hdr Ext Len = 6
    Destination Address = D         Segments Left = 0
                                    Address[1] = I1
                                    Address[2] = I2
                                    Address[3] = I3
```

3.3.5 Fragment Header

The *Fragment* header is used by an IPv6 source to send a packet larger than would fit in the path MTU to its destination. (Note: unlike IPv4, fragmentation in IPv6 is performed only by source nodes, not by routers along a packet's delivery path.) The *Fragment* header is identified by a Next Header value of 44 in the immediately preceding header, and has the format shown in Figure 3.7.

The fields are as follows:

Next Header: 8-bit selector. Identifies the initial header type of the Fragmentable Part of the original packet (defined below). Uses the same values as the IPv4 Protocol field (RFC 1700).

Reserved: 8-bit reserved field. This field is initialized to zero for transmission and ignored on reception.

Fragment Offset: 13-bit unsigned integer. The offset, in 8-octet units, of the data following this header, relative to the start of the Fragmentable Part of the original packet.

Res: 2-bit reserved field. This field is initialized to zero for transmission and ignored on reception.

M flag: 1 = more fragments; 0 = last fragment.
Identification: 32 bits. See description below.

In order to send a packet that is too large to fit in the MTU of the path to its destination, a source node may divide the packet into fragments and send each fragment as a separate packet, to be reassembled at the receiver.

For every packet that is to be fragmented, the source node generates an Identification value. The Identification must be different than that of any other fragmented packet sent recently (see Note) with the same Source Address and Destination Address. If a *Routing* header is present, the Destination Address of concern is that of the final destination.

Note:

"Recently" means within the maximum likely lifetime of a packet, including transit time from source to destination and time spent awaiting reassembly with other fragments of the same packet. However, it is not required that a source node know the maximum packet lifetime. Rather, it is assumed that the requirement can be met by maintaining the Identification value as a simple, 32-bit, "wrap-around" counter, incremented each time a packet must be fragmented. It is an implementation choice whether to maintain a single counter for the node or multiple counters, for example, one for each of the node's possible source addresses, or one for each active (source address, destination address) combination.

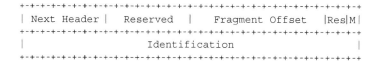

Figure 3.7   Fragment header.

The initial, large, unfragmented packet is referred to as the "original packet," and it is considered to consist of two parts, as seen in Figure 3.8.

The Unfragmentable Part consists of the IPv6 header plus any extension headers that must be processed by nodes en route to the destination, that is, all headers up to and including the Routing header if present, else the *Hop-by-Hop Options* header if present, else no extension headers.

The Fragmentable Part consists of the rest of the packet, that is, any extension headers that need be processed only by the final destination node(s), plus the upper-layer header and data.

The Fragmentable Part of the original packet is divided into fragments, each, except possibly the last ("rightmost") one, being an integer multiple of 8 octets long. The fragments are transmitted in separate "fragment packets" as illustrated in Figure 3.9.

Each fragment packet comprises:

■ The Unfragmentable Part of the original packet, with the Payload Length of the original IPv6 header changed to contain the length of this fragment packet only (excluding the length of the IPv6 header itself), and the Next Header field of the last header of the Unfragmentable Part changed to 44.
■ A Fragment header containing:
  – The Next Header value that identifies the first header of the Fragmentable Part of the original packet.
  – A Fragment Offset containing the offset of the fragment, in 8-octet units, relative to the start of the Fragmentable Part of the original packet. The Fragment Offset of the first ("leftmost") fragment is 0.
  – An M flag value of 0 if the fragment is the last ("rightmost") one, else an M flag value of 1.
  – The Identification value generated for the original packet.
■ The fragment itself.

The lengths of the fragments must be chosen such that the resulting fragment packets fit within the MTU of the path to the packets' destination(s).

At the destination, fragment packets are reassembled into their original, unfragmented form, as illustrated in Figure 3.10.

The following rules govern reassembly:

■ An original packet is reassembled only from fragment packets that have the same Source Address, Destination Address, and Fragment Identification.

```
Original Packet:

+------------------+------------------------//----------------------+
| Unfragmentable |              Fragmentable                      |
|      Part      |                 Part                           |
+------------------+------------------------//----------------------+
```

Figure 3.8 Original packet.

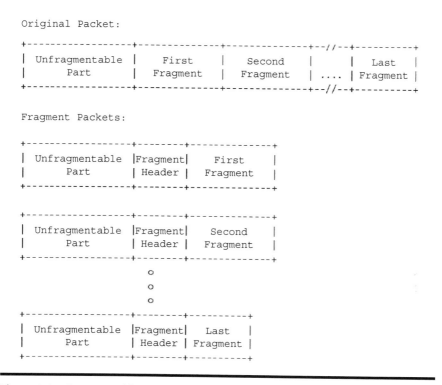

```
Original Packet:

+-----------------+---------------+---------------+--//--+----------+
| Unfragmentable  |    First      |    Second     |      |   Last   |
|     Part        |   Fragment    |   Fragment    | .... | Fragment |
+-----------------+---------------+---------------+--//--+----------+


Fragment Packets:

+-----------------+--------+---------------+
| Unfragmentable  |Fragment|    First      |
|     Part        | Header |   Fragment    |
+-----------------+--------+---------------+


+-----------------+--------+---------------+
| Unfragmentable  |Fragment|    Second     |
|     Part        | Header |   Fragment    |
+-----------------+--------+---------------+
                      o
                      o
                      o
+-----------------+--------+----------+
| Unfragmentable  |Fragment|   Last   |
|     Part        | Header | Fragment |
+-----------------+--------+----------+
```

Figure 3.9 Fragmentable parts.

```
Reassembled Original Packet:

+-----------------+----------------------//----------------------+
|Unfragmentable|                    Fragmentable                 |
|     Part     |                        Part                     |
+-----------------+----------------------//----------------------+
```

Figure 3.10 Reassembled original packet.

■ The Unfragmentable Part of the reassembled packet consists of all headers up to, but not including, the *Fragment* header of the first fragment packet (that is, the packet whose Fragment Offset is zero), with the following two changes:

  – The Next Header field of the last header of the Unfragmentable Part is obtained from the Next Header field of the first fragment's *Fragment* header.

  – The Payload Length of the reassembled packet is computed from the length of the Unfragmentable Part and the length and offset of the last fragment. For example, a formula for computing the Payload Length of the reassembled original packet is:

PL.orig = PL.first − FL.first − 8 + (8 * FO.last) + FL.last
where

PL.orig	= Payload Length field of reassembled packet.
PL.first	= Payload Length field of first fragment packet.
FL.first	= length of fragment following Fragment header of first fragment packet.
FO.last	= Fragment Offset field of Fragment header of last fragment packet.
FL.last	= length of fragment following Fragment header of last fragment packet.

■ The Fragmentable Part of the reassembled packet is constructed from the fragments following the *Fragment* headers in each of the fragment packets. The length of each fragment is computed by subtracting from the packet's Payload Length the length of the headers between the IPv6 header and fragment itself; its relative position in Fragmentable Part is computed from its Fragment Offset value.
■ The Fragment header is not present in the final, reassembled packet.

The following error conditions may arise when reassembling fragmented packets:

■ If insufficient fragments are received to complete reassembly of a packet within 60 seconds of the reception of the first-arriving fragment of that packet, reassembly of that packet must be abandoned and all the fragments that have been received for that packet must be discarded. If the first fragment (i.e., the one with a Fragment Offset of zero) has been received, an ICMP Time Exceeded—Fragment Reassembly Time Exceeded message should be sent to the source of that fragment.
■ If the length of a fragment, as derived from the fragment packet's Payload Length field, is not a multiple of 8 octets and the M flag of that fragment is 1, then that fragment must be discarded and an ICMP Parameter Problem, Code 0, message should be sent to the source of the fragment, pointing to the Payload Length field of the fragment packet.
■ If the length and offset of a fragment are such that the Payload Length of the packet reassembled from that fragment would exceed 65,535 octets, then that fragment must be discarded and an ICMP Parameter Problem, Code 0, message should be sent to the source of the fragment, pointing to the Fragment Offset field of the fragment packet.

The following conditions are not expected to occur, but are not considered errors if they do:

■ The number and content of the headers preceding the *Fragment* header of different fragments of the same original packet may differ. Whatever headers are present, preceding the *Fragment* header in each fragment packet, are processed when the packets arrive, prior to queuing the fragments for reassembly. Only those headers in the Offset zero fragment packet are retained in the reassembled packet.

■ The Next Header values in the *Fragment* headers of different fragments of the same original packet may differ. Only the value from the Offset zero fragment packet is used for reassembly.

3.3.6 *Destination Options Header*

The *Destination Options* header is used to carry optional information that need be examined only by a packet's destination node(s). The *Destination Options* header is identified by a Next Header value of 60 in the immediately preceding header, and has the format shown in Figure 3.11.

Next Header: 8-bit selector. Identifies the type of header immediately following the *Destination Options* header. Uses the same values as the IPv4 Protocol field (RFC 1700).

Hdr Ext Len: 8-bit unsigned integer. Length of the *Destination Options* header in 8-octet units, not including the first 8 octets.

Options: Variable-length field, of length such that the complete *Destination Options* header is an integer multiple of 8 octets long. Contains one or more TLV-encoded options.

Note that there are two possible ways to encode optional destination information in an IPv6 packet: either as an option in the *Destination Options* header, or as a separate extension header. The Fragment header and the Authentication Header are examples of the latter approach. Which approach can be used depends on what action is desired of a destination node that does not understand the optional information:

■ If the desired action is for the destination node to discard the packet and, only if the packet's Destination Address is not a multicast address, send an ICMP Unrecognized Type message to the packet's Source Address, then the information may be encoded either as a separate header or as an option in the

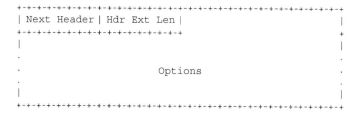

Figure 3.11   Destination options header.

Destination Options header whose Option Type has the value 11 in its highest-order two bits. The choice may depend on such factors as which takes fewer octets, or which yields better alignment or more efficient parsing.

◼ If any other action is desired, the information must be encoded as an option in the *Destination Options* header whose Option Type has the value 00, 01, or 10 in its highest-order two bits, specifying the desired action.

3.3.7 No Next Header

The value 59 in the Next Header field of an IPv6 header or any extension header indicates that there is nothing following that header. If the Payload Length field of the IPv6 header indicates the presence of octets past the end of a header whose Next Header field contains 59, those octets must be ignored, and passed on unchanged if the packet is forwarded.

3.4 Packet Size Issues

IPv6 requires that every link in the Internet have an MTU of 1280 octets or greater. On any link that cannot convey a 1280-octet packet in one piece, link-specific fragmentation and reassembly must be provided at a layer below IPv6.

Links that have a configurable MTU (for example, PPP links defined in RFC 1661) must be configured to have an MTU of at least 1280 octets. It is recommended that they be configured with an MTU of 1500 octets or greater, to accommodate possible encapsulations (i.e., tunneling) without incurring IPv6-layer fragmentation.

From each link to which a node is directly attached, the node must be able to accept packets as large as that link's MTU.

It is strongly recommended that IPv6 nodes implement Path MTU Discovery (RFC 1981) in order to discover and take advantage of path MTUs greater than 1280 octets. However, a minimal IPv6 implementation (e.g., in a boot ROM) may simply restrict itself to sending packets no larger than 1280 octets, and omit implementation of Path MTU Discovery.

In order to send a packet larger than a path's MTU, a node may use the IPv6 *Fragment* header to fragment the packet at the source and have it reassembled at the destination(s). However, the use of such fragmentation is discouraged in any application that is able to adjust its packets to fit the measured path MTU (i.e., down to 1280 octets).

A node must be able to accept a fragmented packet that, after reassembly, is as large as 1500 octets. A node is permitted to accept fragmented packets that reassemble to more than 1500 octets. An upper-layer protocol or application that depends on IPv6 fragmentation to send packets larger than the MTU of a path should not send packets larger than 1500 octets unless it has assurance that the destination is capable of reassembling packets of that larger size.

In response to an IPv6 packet that is sent to an IPv4 destination (i.e., a packet that undergoes translation from IPv6 to IPv4), the originating IPv6 node may receive an ICMP Packet Too Big message reporting a Next-Hop MTU less than 1280. In that case, the IPv6 node is not required to reduce the size of subsequent packets to less than 1280, but must include a *Fragment* header in those packets so that the IPv6-to-IPv4 translating router can obtain a suitable Identification value to use in resulting IPv4 fragments. Note that this means the payload may have to be reduced to 1232 octets (1280 minus 40 for the IPv6 header and 8 for the *Fragment* header), and smaller still if additional extension headers are used.

3.5 Flow Labels

The 20-bit Flow Label field in the IPv6 header may be used by a source to label sequences of packets for which it requests special handling by the IPv6 routers, such as nondefault quality of service or "real-time" service. This aspect of IPv6 is still experimental to a large degree and subject to change as the requirements for flow support in the Internet become clearer (RFC 3697, March 2004, and RFC 3595, September 2003, provide additional information on the topic). Hosts or routers that do not support the functions of the Flow Label field are required to set the field to zero when originating a packet, pass the field on unchanged when forwarding a packet and ignore the field when receiving a packet.

3.6 Traffic Classes

The 8-bit Traffic Class field in the IPv6 header is available for use by originating nodes or forwarding routers to identify and distinguish between different classes or priorities of IPv6 packets. There are a number of experiments under way in the use of the IPv4 Type of Service or Precedence bits to provide various forms of "differentiated service" for IP packets, other than through the use of explicit flow setup. The Traffic Class field in the IPv6 header is intended to allow similar functionality to be supported in IPv6.

The expectation is that experimentation will eventually lead to agreement on what type of traffic classifications will be most useful for IP packets. Detailed definitions of the syntax and semantics of all or some of the IPv6 Traffic Class bits, whether experimental or intended for eventual standardization, are to be provided in separate documents.

The following general requirements apply to the Traffic Class field:

■ The service interface to the IPv6 service within a node must provide a means for an upper-layer protocol to supply the value of the Traffic Class bits in packets originated by that upper-layer protocol. The default value must be zero for all 8 bits.

■ Nodes that support a specific (experimental or eventual standard) use of some or all of the Traffic Class bits are permitted to change the value of those bits in packets that they originate, forward, or receive, as required for that specific use. Nodes should ignore and leave unchanged any bits of the Traffic Class field for which they do not support a specific use.
■ An upper-layer protocol must not assume that the value of the Traffic Class bits in a received packet are the same as the value sent by the packet's source.

3.7 Upper-Layer Protocol Issues

3.7.1 Upper-Layer Checksums

Any transport or other upper-layer protocol that includes the addresses from the IP header in its checksum computation must be modified for use over IPv6, to include the 128-bit IPv6 addresses instead of 32-bit IPv4 addresses. In particular, Figure 3.12 shows the TCP and UDP "pseudoheader" for IPv6.

■ If the IPv6 packet contains a Routing header, the Destination Address used in the pseudoheader is that of the final destination. At the originating node, that address will be in the last element of the Routing header; at the recipient(s), that address will be in the Destination Address field of the IPv6 header.
■ The Next Header value in the pseudoheader identifies the upper-layer protocol (e.g., 6 for TCP or 17 for UDP). It will differ from the Next Header value

Figure 3.12 TCP and UDP "pseudoheader" for IPv6.

in the IPv6 header if there are extension headers between the IPv6 header and the upper-layer header.

■ The Upper-Layer Packet Length in the pseudoheader is the length of the upper-layer header and data (e.g., TCP header plus TCP data). Some upper-layer protocols carry their own length information (e.g., the Length field in the UDP header); for such protocols, that is the length used in the pseudoheader. Other protocols (such as TCP) do not carry their own length information, in which case the length used in the pseudoheader is the Payload Length from the IPv6 header, minus the length of any extension headers present between the IPv6 header and the upper-layer header.

■ Unlike IPv4, when UDP packets are originated by an IPv6 node, the UDP checksum is not optional. That is, whenever originating a UDP packet, an IPv6 node must compute a UDP checksum over the packet and the pseudoheader, and, if that computation yields a result of zero, it must be changed to hex FFFF for placement in the UDP header. IPv6 receivers must discard UDP packets containing a zero checksum, and should log the error.

The IPv6 version of ICMP includes the above pseudoheader in its checksum computation; this is a change from the IPv4 version of ICMP, which does not include a pseudoheader in its checksum. The reason for the change is to protect ICMP from misdelivery or corruption of those fields of the IPv6 header on which it depends, which, unlike IPv4, are not covered by an IP-layer checksum. The Next Header field in the pseudoheader for ICMP contains the value 58, which identifies the IPv6 version of ICMP.

3.7.2 Maximum Packet Lifetime

Unlike IPv4, IPv6 nodes are not required to enforce maximum packet lifetime. That is the reason the IPv4 "Time to Live" (TTL) field was renamed "Hop Limit" in IPv6. In practice, very few, if any, IPv4 implementations conform to the requirement that they limit packet lifetime, so this is not a change in practice; however, it is important to note that TTL has been used in many security attacks and reconnaissance techniques. Any upper-layer protocol that relies on the Internet layer (whether IPv4 or IPv6) to limit packet lifetime ought to be upgraded to provide its own mechanisms for detecting and discarding obsolete packets.

3.7.3 Maximum Upper-Layer Payload Size

When computing the maximum payload size available for upper-layer data, an upper-layer protocol must take into account the larger size of the IPv6 header relative to the IPv4 header. For example, in IPv4, TCP's Maximum Segment Size (MSS) option is computed as the maximum packet size (a default value or a value learned through Path MTU Discovery) minus 40 octets (20 octets for the minimum-length

IPv4 header and 20 octets for the minimum-length TCP header). When using TCP over IPv6, the MSS must be computed as the maximum packet size minus 60 octets, because the minimum-length IPv6 header (i.e., an IPv6 header with no extension headers) is 20 octets longer than a minimum-length IPv4 header.

3.7.4 Responding to Packets Carrying Routing Headers

When an upper-layer protocol sends one or more packets in response to a received packet that included a Routing header, the response packet(s) must not include a Routing header that was automatically derived by "reversing" the received Routing header unless the integrity and authenticity of the received Source Address and Routing header have been verified (e.g., via the use of an Authentication header in the received packet). In other words, only the following kinds of packets are permitted in response to a received packet bearing a Routing header:

- Response packets that do not carry Routing headers;
- Response packets that carry Routing headers that were not derived by reversing the Routing header of the received packet (for example, a Routing header supplied by local configuration); and
- Response packets that carry Routing headers that were derived by reversing the Routing header of the received packet if and only if the integrity and authenticity of the Source Address and Routing header from the received packet have been verified by the responder.

3.8 Semantics and Usage of the Flow Label Field

A flow is a sequence of packets sent from a particular source to a particular (unicast or multicast) destination for which the source desires special handling by the intervening routers. The nature of that special handling might be conveyed to the routers by a control protocol, such as a resource reservation protocol, or by information within the flow's packets themselves, for example, in a *Hop-by-Hop Option*.

There may be multiple active flows from a source to a destination, as well as traffic that is not associated with any flow. A flow is uniquely identified by the combination of a source address and a nonzero flow label. Packets that do not belong to a flow carry a flow label of zero.

A flow label is assigned to a flow by the flow's source node. New flow labels must be chosen (pseudo) randomly and uniformly from the range 1 to FFFFF hex. The purpose of the random allocation is to make any set of bits within the Flow Label field suitable for use as a hash key by routers, for looking up the state associated with the flow.

All packets belonging to the same flow must be sent with the same source address, destination address and flow label. If any of those packets includes a *Hop-by-Hop Options* header, then they all must be originated with the same *Hop-by-Hop Options* header contents (excluding the Next Header field of the *Hop-by-Hop Options* header). If any of those packets includes a Routing header, then they all must be originated with the same contents in all extension headers up to and including the *Routing* header (excluding the Next Header field in the *Routing* header). The routers or destinations are permitted, but not required, to verify that these conditions are satisfied. If a violation is detected, it should be reported to the source by an ICMP Parameter Problem message, Code 0, pointing to the high-order octet of the Flow Label field (i.e., offset 1 within the IPv6 packet).

The maximum lifetime of any flow-handling state established along a flow's path must be specified as part of the description of the state-establishment mechanism, for example, the resource reservation protocol or the flow-setup *Hop-by-Hop Option*. A source must not reuse a flow label for a new flow within the maximum lifetime of any flow-handling state that might have been established for the prior use of that flow label.

When a node stops and restarts (e.g., as a result of a "crash"), it must be careful not to use a flow label that it might have used for an earlier flow whose lifetime may not have expired yet. This may be accomplished by recording flow label usage on stable storage so that it can be remembered across crashes, or by refraining from using any flow labels until the maximum lifetime of any possible previously established flows has expired. If the minimum time for rebooting the node is known, that time can be deducted from the necessary waiting period before starting to allocate flow labels.

There is no requirement that all, or even most, packets belong to flows, and so forth, carry nonzero flow labels. This observation is placed here to remind protocol designers and implementers not to assume otherwise. For example, it would be unwise to design a router whose performance would be adequate only if most packets belonged to flows, or to design a header compression scheme that only worked on packets that belonged to flows.

3.9 Formatting Guidelines for Options

This section addresses how to lay out the fields when designing new options to be used in the *Hop-by-Hop Options* header or the *Destination Options* header. These guidelines are based on the following assumptions:

- One desirable feature is that any multioctet fields within the Option Data area of an option be aligned on their natural boundaries, that is, fields of width n octets should be placed at an integer multiple of n octets from the start of the *Hop-by-Hop* or *Destination Options* header, for n = 1, 2, 4, or 8.
- Another desirable feature is that the *Hop-by-Hop* or *Destination Options* header take up as little space as possible, subject to the requirement that the header be an integer multiple of 8 octets long.
- It may be assumed that, when either of the option-bearing headers are present, they carry a very small number of options, usually only one.

These assumptions suggest the following approach to laying out the fields of an option: order the fields from smallest to largest, with no interior padding, then derive the alignment requirement for the entire option based on the alignment requirement of the largest field (up to a maximum alignment of 8 octets). This approach is illustrated in the following examples:

Example 1

If an option X required two data fields, one of length 8 octets and one of length 4 octets, it would be laid out as follows:

```
                              +-+-+-+-+-+-+-+-+-+-+-+-+-+-+-+-+
                              | Option Type=X |Opt Data Len=12|
+-+-+-+-+-+-+-+-+-+-+-+-+-+-+-+-+-+-+-+-+-+-+-+-+-+-+-+-+-+-+-+-+
|                         4-octet field                         |
+-+-+-+-+-+-+-+-+-+-+-+-+-+-+-+-+-+-+-+-+-+-+-+-+-+-+-+-+-+-+-+-+
|                                                               |
+                        8-octet field                          +
|                                                               |
+-+-+-+-+-+-+-+-+-+-+-+-+-+-+-+-+-+-+-+-+-+-+-+-+-+-+-+-+-+-+-+-+
```

Its alignment requirement is 8n+2, to ensure that the 8-octet field starts at a multiple-of-8 offset from the start of the enclosing header. A complete *Hop-by-Hop* or *Destination Options* header containing this one option would look as follows:

```
+-+-+-+-+-+-+-+-+-+-+-+-+-+-+-+-+-+-+-+-+-+-+-+-+-+-+-+-+-+-+-+-+
| Next Header | Hdr Ext Len=1 | Option Type=X |Opt Data Len=12|
+-+-+-+-+-+-+-+-+-+-+-+-+-+-+-+-+-+-+-+-+-+-+-+-+-+-+-+-+-+-+-+-+
|                         4-octet field                         |
+-+-+-+-+-+-+-+-+-+-+-+-+-+-+-+-+-+-+-+-+-+-+-+-+-+-+-+-+-+-+-+-+
|                                                               |
+                        8-octet field                          +
|                                                               |
+-+-+-+-+-+-+-+-+-+-+-+-+-+-+-+-+-+-+-+-+-+-+-+-+-+-+-+-+-+-+-+-+
```

Example 2

If an option Y required three data fields, one of length 4 octets, one of length 2 octets, and one of length 1 octet, it would be laid out as follows:

```
                              +-+-+-+-+-+-+-+-+
                              | Option Type=Y |
+-+-+-+-+-+-+-+-+-+-+-+-+-+-+-+-+-+-+-+-+-+-+-+-+-+-+-+-+-+-+-+-+
|Opt Data Len=7 | 1-octet field |        2-octet field          |
+-+-+-+-+-+-+-+-+-+-+-+-+-+-+-+-+-+-+-+-+-+-+-+-+-+-+-+-+-+-+-+-+
|                         4-octet field                         |
+-+-+-+-+-+-+-+-+-+-+-+-+-+-+-+-+-+-+-+-+-+-+-+-+-+-+-+-+-+-+-+-+
```

Its alignment requirement is 4n+3, to ensure that the 4-octet field starts at a multiple-of-4 offset from the start of the enclosing header. A complete *Hop-by-Hop* or *Destination Options* header containing this one option would look as follows:

```
+-+-+-+-+-+-+-+-+-+-+-+-+-+-+-+-+-+-+-+-+-+-+-+-+-+-+-+-+-+-+-+-+
| Next Header   | Hdr Ext Len=1 | Pad1 Option=0 | Option Type=Y |
+-+-+-+-+-+-+-+-+-+-+-+-+-+-+-+-+-+-+-+-+-+-+-+-+-+-+-+-+-+-+-+-+
|Opt Data Len=7 | 1-octet field |            2-octet field      |
+-+-+-+-+-+-+-+-+-+-+-+-+-+-+-+-+-+-+-+-+-+-+-+-+-+-+-+-+-+-+-+-+
|                         4-octet field                         |
+-+-+-+-+-+-+-+-+-+-+-+-+-+-+-+-+-+-+-+-+-+-+-+-+-+-+-+-+-+-+-+-+
| PadN Option=1 |Opt Data Len=2 |        0      |       0       |
+-+-+-+-+-+-+-+-+-+-+-+-+-+-+-+-+-+-+-+-+-+-+-+-+-+-+-+-+-+-+-+-+
```

Example 3

A *Hop-by-Hop* or *Destination Options* header containing both options X and Y from Examples 1 and 2 would have one of the two following formats, depending on which option appeared first:

```
+-+-+-+-+-+-+-+-+-+-+-+-+-+-+-+-+-+-+-+-+-+-+-+-+-+-+-+-+-+-+-+-+
| Next Header   | Hdr Ext Len=3 |Option Type=X|Opt Data Len=12 |
+-+-+-+-+-+-+-+-+-+-+-+-+-+-+-+-+-+-+-+-+-+-+-+-+-+-+-+-+-+-+-+-+
|                         4-octet field                         |
+-+-+-+-+-+-+-+-+-+-+-+-+-+-+-+-+-+-+-+-+-+-+-+-+-+-+-+-+-+-+-+-+
|                                                               |
+                         8-octet field                         +
|                                                               |
+-+-+-+-+-+-+-+-+-+-+-+-+-+-+-+-+-+-+-+-+-+-+-+-+-+-+-+-+-+-+-+-+
| PadN Option=1 | Opt Data Len=1 |        0      | Option Type=Y|
+-+-+-+-+-+-+-+-+-+-+-+-+-+-+-+-+-+-+-+-+-+-+-+-+-+-+-+-+-+-+-+-+
|Opt Data Len=7 | 1-octet field |            2-octet field      |
+-+-+-+-+-+-+-+-+-+-+-+-+-+-+-+-+-+-+-+-+-+-+-+-+-+-+-+-+-+-+-+-+
|                         4-octet field                         |
+-+-+-+-+-+-+-+-+-+-+-+-+-+-+-+-+-+-+-+-+-+-+-+-+-+-+-+-+-+-+-+-+
| PadN Option=1 | Opt Data Len=2 |        0      |       0       |
+-+-+-+-+-+-+-+-+-+-+-+-+-+-+-+-+-+-+-+-+-+-+-+-+-+-+-+-+-+-+-+-+

+-+-+-+-+-+-+-+-+-+-+-+-+-+-+-+-+-+-+-+-+-+-+-+-+-+-+-+-+-+-+-+-+
| Next Header   | Hdr Ext Len=3 | Pad1 Option=0 |Option Type=Y |
+-+-+-+-+-+-+-+-+-+-+-+-+-+-+-+-+-+-+-+-+-+-+-+-+-+-+-+-+-+-+-+-+
|Opt Data Len=7 | 1-octet field |            2-octet field      |
+-+-+-+-+-+-+-+-+-+-+-+-+-+-+-+-+-+-+-+-+-+-+-+-+-+-+-+-+-+-+-+-+
|                         4-octet field                         |
+-+-+-+-+-+-+-+-+-+-+-+-+-+-+-+-+-+-+-+-+-+-+-+-+-+-+-+-+-+-+-+-+
```

```
| PadN Option=1 |Opt Data Len=4 |       0       |      0       |
+-+-+-+-+-+-+-+-+-+-+-+-+-+-+-+-+-+-+-+-+-+-+-+-+-+-+-+-+-+-+-+-+
|        0       |       0       | Option Type=X |Opt Data Len=12|
+-+-+-+-+-+-+-+-+-+-+-+-+-+-+-+-+-+-+-+-+-+-+-+-+-+-+-+-+-+-+-+-+
|                         4-octet field                        |
+-+-+-+-+-+-+-+-+-+-+-+-+-+-+-+-+-+-+-+-+-+-+-+-+-+-+-+-+-+-+-+-+
|                                                              |
+                         8-octet field                        +
|                                                              |
+-+-+-+-+-+-+-+-+-+-+-+-+-+-+-+-+-+-+-+-+-+-+-+-+-+-+-+-+-+-+-+-+
```

3.10 IPv6 Infrastructure

The IPv6 Specification (RFC 2460) and the IPv6 Addressing Architecture (RFC 2373) provide the base architecture and design of IPv6; we covered some of these key concepts in earlier sections. Here we look at basic IPv6 network constructs, specifically routing processes. Because there are differences on some of the details of how these IPv6 processes operate compared with IPv4, it is worth looking at some of these issues. Related work in IPv6 that needs to be mastered by implementers and network designers (covered in chapters that follow) includes the IPv6 Stateless Address Autoconfiguration (RFC 2462); the IPv6 Neighbor Discovery (ND) Processing (RFC 2461); the Dynamic Host Configuration Protocol for IPv6 (DHCPv6) (RFC 3315); and, the Dynamic Updates to DNS (RFC 2136). Some portions of this discussion are based on [MSD200401].

3.10.1 Protocol Mechanisms

As we discussed earlier, the IPv6 header consists of two parts: the IPv6 base header, and optional extension headers. The optional extension headers are considered part of the IPv6 payload, as are the TCP/UDP/RTP PDUs. Obviously, IPv4 headers and IPv6 headers are not automatically interoperable; hence, a router operating in a mixed environment must support an implementation of both IPv4 and IPv6 in order to deal with both header formats. Figure 3.13 shows for illustration purposes the flows of IPv6 PDUs in a VoIP environment.

As we noted in passing in the previous chapter, the large size of the IPv6 address allows it to be subdivided into hierarchical routing domains that are supportive of the topology of today's ubiquitous Internet (IPv4-based Internet lacks this flexibility). Conveniently, the use of 128 bits provides multiple levels of hierarchy and flexibility in designing hierarchical addressing and routing.

3.10.2 Protocol-Support Mechanisms

Two support mechanisms are of interest: (i) a mechanism to deal with communication transmission issues; and (ii) a mechanism to support multicast.

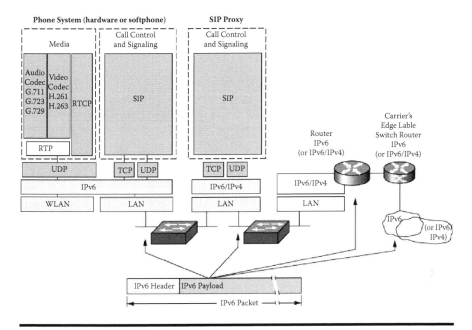

Figure 3.13   Flows of IPv6 packets in a VoIPv6 environment.

Internet Control Message Protocol for IPv6 (ICMPv6) (defined in RFC 2463) is designed to enable hosts and routers that use IPv6 protocols to report errors and forward along other basic status messages. For example, ICMPv6 messages are sent by Network Elements when an IPv6 PDU cannot be forwarded further along to reach its intended destination. ICMPv6 messages are carried as the payload of IPv6 PDUs (see Figure 3.14); hence, there is *no* guarantee on their delivery.

The following list identifies the functionality supported by the basic ICMPv6 mechanisms:

- Destination Unreachable: An error message that informs the sending host that a PDU cannot be delivered.
- Packet Too Big: An error message that informs the sending host that the PDU is too large to forward.
- Time Exceeded: An error message that informs the sending host that the Hop Limit of an IPv6 PDU has expired.
- Parameter Problem: An error message that informs the sending host that an error was encountered in processing the IPv6 header or an IPv6 extension header.
- Echo Request: An informational message that is used to determine whether an IPv6 node is available on the network.
- Echo Reply: An informational message that is used to reply to the ICMPv6 Echo Request message.

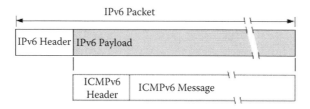

Figure 3.14 ICMPv6 message.

(The ping command is basically an ICMPv6 Echo Request message along with the receipt of an ICMPv6 Echo Reply message. Just as is the case with IPv4, one can use pings to detect network or host communication failures and troubleshoot connectivity problems.)

ICMPv6 also supports MLD. MLD (RFC 2710, RFC 3590, and RFC 3810) enables one to manage subnet multicast membership for IPv6. MLD is a collection of three ICMPv6 messages that replace the Internet Group Management Protocol (IGMP) version 3 that is employed in IPv4. MLD messages are used to determine group membership on a network segment, also known as a link or subnet. As implied, MLD messages are sent as ICMPv6 messages. They are used in the context of multicast communications (see below):

- Multicast Listener Query: Message issued by a multicast router to poll a network segment for group members. Queries can be general, requesting group membership for all groups, or can request group membership for a specific group.
- Multicast Listener Report: Message issued by a host when it joins a multicast group, or in response to an MLD Multicast Listener Query sent by a router.
- Multicast Listener Done: Message issued by a host when it leaves a host group and is the last member of that group on the network segment.

ICMPv6 also supports Neighbor Discovery (ND). ND (RFC 2461) is a collection of five ICMPv6 messages that manage node-to-node communication on a link. Nodes on the same link are also called neighboring nodes. ND replaces Address Resolution Protocol (ARP), ICMPv4 Router Discovery, and the ICMPv4 Redirect message. Table 3.1 identifies key ND processes [MSD200401]. Hosts (e.g., servers, SIP proxies, H.323 gatekeepers, etc.) make use of ND to discover neighboring routers, addresses, address prefixes, and other configuration parameters. Routers make use of ND to advertise their presence, host configuration parameters, and on-link prefixes. Routers also use ND to inform hosts of a better next-hop address to forward PDUs for a specific destination. Nodes make use of ND to resolve the link-layer address of a neighboring node to which an IPv6 PDU is being forwarded. Nodes also use ND to determine when the link-layer address of a neighboring node has changed and whether IPv6 PDUs can be sent to and received from a neighbor. See Appendix A for more information.

Table 3.1　Key ND Processes

Process	Description
Address Autoconfiguration	The process for configuring IP addresses for interfaces in the absence of a stateful address configuration server, e.g., via Dynamic Host Configuration Protocol version 6 (DHCPv6).
Address Resolution	The process by which a node resolves a neighboring node's IPv6 address to its link-layer address. The resolved link-layer address becomes an entry in a neighbor cache in the node. The link layer address is equivalent to ARP in IPv4, and the neighbor cache is equivalent to the ARP cache. The neighbor cache displays the interface identifier for the neighbor cache entry, the neighboring node IPv6 address, the corresponding link-layer address, and the state of the neighbor cache entry.
Duplicate Address Detection	The process by which a node determines that an address considered for use is not already in use by a neighboring node. This is equivalent to the use of ARP frames in IPv4.
Dynamic Updates to DNS (RFC 2136)	A process that supports the dynamic update of DNS records for both IPv4 and IPv6. DHCP can use the dynamic updates to DNS to integrate addresses and name space to not only support autoconfiguration but also autoregistration in IPv6 [RFC3315].
IPv6 Neighbor Discovery (RFC 2461)	The node discovery process/protocol in IPv6 that replaces and enhances functions of ARP. To understand IPv6 and stateless address autoconfiguration, implementers and network designers need to understand IPv6 Neighbor Discovery [RFC3315].
Neighbor Unreachability Detection	The process by which a node determines that neighboring hosts or routers are no longer available on the local network segment. After the link-layer address for a neighbor has been determined, the state of the entry in the neighbor cache is tracked. If the neighbor is no longer receiving and sending back PDUs, the neighbor cache entry is eventually removed.
	(Continued)

Table 3.1 Key ND Processes (Continued)

Process	Description
Next-Hop Determination	The process by which a node determines the IPv6 address of the neighbor to which a PDU is being forwarded. The determination is made based on the destination address. The forwarding or next-hop address is either the destination address of the PDU being sent or the address of a neighboring router. The resolved next-hop address for a destination becomes an entry in a node's destination cache, also known as a route cache. The route cache displays the destination address, the interface identifier and next-hop address, the interface identifier and address used as a source address when sending to the destination, and the path maximum transmission unit (MTU) for the destination.
Parameter Discovery	The process by which a host discovers additional operating parameters, including the link MTU and the default hop limit for outbound PDUs.
Prefix Discovery	The process by which a host discovers the network prefixes for local destinations.
Redirect Function	The process by which a router informs a host of a better first-hop IPv6 address to reach a destination. This is equivalent to the function of the IPv4 ICMP Redirect message.
Router Discovery	The process by which a host discovers the local routers on an attached link and automatically configures a default router. In IPv4, this is equivalent to using ICMPv4 router discovery to configure a default gateway.

3.11 Routing and Route Management

Routing is the process of forwarding PDUs between connected network segments (also known as links or subnets.) Routing is a primary function of a network layer protocol, whether it is IP version 4 or version 6. IPv6 routers provide the primary means for joining together two or more IPv6 network segments. Network segments are identified by using an IPv6 network prefix and prefix length. Routers pass IPv6 PDUs from one network segment to another. IPv6 routers are attached to two or more IPv6 network segments and enable hosts on those segments to forward IPv6 PDUs. IPv6 PDUs are exchanged and processed on each host by using IPv6 at layer 3 (the Internet layer.).

Datagrams with a source and destination IP address identified in the header are handed to the IP protocol engine/layer. Above the IPv6 layer, transport services on the source host pass data in the form of TCP segments or UDP PDUs down to the IPv6 layer. IPv6 layer services on each sending host examine the destination address of each PDU, compare this address to a locally maintained routing table, and then determine what additional forwarding is required. The IPv6 layer creates IPv6 PDUs with source and destination address information that is used to route the data through the network. The IPv6 layer then passes PDUs down to the link layer, where the PDUs are converted into frames for transmission over network-specific media on a physical network. This process occurs in reverse order on the destination host [MSD200401].

IPv6 hosts utilize routing tables to maintain information about other IPv6 networks and IPv6 hosts. The routing tables provide important information about how to communicate with remote networks and hosts. Every device that implements IPv6 determines how to forward PDUs based on the contents of the IPv6 routing table. The following information is contained in the IPv6 routing table:

■ An address prefix
■ The interface over which PDUs that match the address prefix are sent
■ A forwarding or next-hop address
■ A preference value used to select between multiple routes with the same prefix
■ The lifetime of the route
■ The specification of whether the route is published (advertised in a Routing Advertisement)
■ The specification of how the route is aged
■ The route type

The IPv6 routing table is built automatically, based on the current IPv6 configuration of the router. When forwarding IPv6 PDUs, the router searches the routing table for an entry that is the most specific match to the destination IPv6 address. A route for the link-local prefix (FE80::/64) is not displayed.

Typically, a default route is used by an end device because it is not practical for an end device to maintain a routing table for each communication device on an IPv6 network. The default route (a route with a prefix of ::/0) is typically used to forward an IPv6 PDU to a default router on the local link. Because the router that corresponds to the default router contains information about the network prefixes of the other IPv6 subnets within the larger IPv6 internetwork, it forwards the PDU to other routers until the PDU is eventually delivered to the destination.

The following steps occur during the routing process [MSD200401]:

1. Before a communication device sends an IPv6 PDU, it inserts its source IPv6 address and the destination IPv6 address (for the recipient) into the IPv6 header.
2. The device then examines the destination IPv6 address, compares it to a locally maintained IPv6 routing table, and takes appropriate action. The device does one of the following:
   ■ It passes the PDU to a protocol layer above IPv6 on the local host.
   ■ It forwards the PDU through one of its attached network interfaces.
   ■ It discards the PDU.
3. IPv6 searches the routing table for the route that is the closest match to the destination IPv6 address. The most specific to the least specific route is determined in the following order:
   ■ A route that matches the destination IPv6 address (a host route with a 128-bit prefix length).
   ■ A route that matches the destination with the longest prefix length.
   ■ The default route (the network prefix ::/0).
4. If a matching route is not found, the destination is determined to be an on-link destination.

3.12 Configuration Methods

IPv6 Stateless Address Autoconfiguration (RFC 2462) specifies procedures by which a node may autoconfigure addresses based on router advertisements and the use of a valid lifetime to support renumbering of addresses on the Internet. In addition, the protocol interaction by which a node begins stateless or stateful autoconfiguration is specified. DHCP is one vehicle to perform stateful autoconfiguration; compatibility with stateless address autoconfiguration is a design requirement of DHCP [RFC3315].

As we have seen earlier, the IPv6 protocol can use two address configuration methods: (i) Automatic configuration; and, (ii) Manual configuration. Autoconfigured addresses exist in one or more of the states depicted in Figure 3.15: tentative, preferred, deprecated, valid (= preferred + deprecated), and, invalid. IPv6 nodes (hosts and routers) automatically create unique link-local addresses for all LAN interfaces that appear to be Ethernet interfaces. IPv6 hosts use received Router Advertisement messages to automatically configure the following parameters [MSD200401]:

■ A default router.
■ The default setting for the Hop Limit field in the IPv6 header.
■ The timers used in Neighbor Discovery processes.
■ The MTU of the local link.

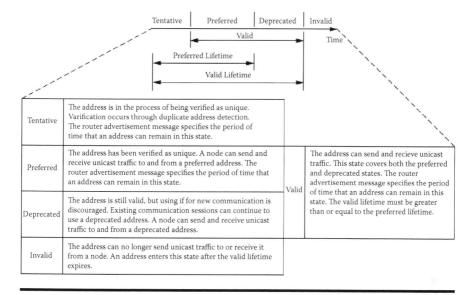

Figure 3.15   Address states.

- The list of network prefixes that are defined for the link. Each network prefix contains both the IPv6 network prefix and its valid and preferred lifetimes. If indicated, a network prefix is combined with the interface identifier to create a stateless IPv6 address configuration for the receiving interface. A network prefix also defines the range of addresses for nodes on the local link.
- 6to4 addresses on a 6to4 tunneling interface for all public IPv4 addresses that are assigned to the computer (some implementations).
- Intrasite Automatic Tunnel Addressing Protocol (ISATAP) addresses on an automatic interface for all IPv4 addresses that are assigned to the computer (some implementations).
- The stack to query for IPv6 ISATAP routers in an IPv4 environment (some implementations).
- Routes to off-link prefixes, if the off-link address prefix is advertised by a router (some implementations).

DHCP is *not* utilized in IPv6 to configure a link-local scope IP address: the link-local scope of an IPv6 addresses is always configured automatically. Addresses with other scopes are configured by router advertisements. Specifically, unique link-local addresses are automatically configured for each interface on each IPv6 node (host or router). To communicate with IPv6 nodes that are not on attached links, the host must have additional global unicast addresses. Additional addresses for hosts are obtained from router advertisements while additional addresses for routers must be assigned manually. To communicate with IPv6 nodes on other network segments, IPv6 uses a default router. A default router is automatically assigned based on the receipt of a router advertisement. Alternately, one can add a default route to the IPv6 routing table. Note that one does not need to configure a default router for a network that consists of a single network segment.

The following sequence identifies the address autoconfiguration process for an IPv6 node, such as an IPv6-based VoIP phone:

1. A tentative link-local address is derived, based on the link-local prefix of FE80::/64 and the 64-bit interface identifier.
2. Duplicate address detection is performed to verify the uniqueness of the tentative link-local address.
3. If duplicate address detection fails, one must manually configure the node.
   or

If duplicate address detection succeeds, the tentative address is assumed to be valid and unique. The link-local address is initialized for the interface. The corresponding solicited-node multicast link-layer address is registered with the network adapter.

For an IPv6 host, address autoconfiguration continues as follows:

1. The host sends a Router Solicitation message.
2. If a Router Advertisement message is received, the configuration information that is included in the message is set on the host.
3. For each stateless autoconfiguration address prefix that is included, the following processes occurs:

   The address prefix and the appropriate 64-bit interface identifier are used to derive a tentative address.

4. Duplicate address detection is used to verify the uniqueness of the tentative address. If the tentative address is in use, the address is not initialized for the interface. If the tentative address is not in use, the address is initialized. This includes setting the valid and preferred lifetimes based on information included in the Router Advertisement message.

Other configuration processes are shown in Table 3.2 [MSD200401].

3.13 Dynamic Host Configuration Protocol for IPv6

The Dynamic Host Configuration Protocol for IPv6 (DHCPv6 or more simply DHCP) enables DHCP servers to pass configuration parameters such as IPv6 network addresses to IPv6 nodes. DHCP provides both robust stateful autoconfiguration and autoregistration of DNS Host Names.

Table 3.2 Configurations of Interest

Configuration	Description
Single Subnet with Link-Local Addresses	This configuration supports the installation of the IPv6 protocol on at least two nodes on the same network segment without intermediate routers.
IPv6 Traffic Between Nodes on Different Subnets of an IPv6 Internetwork	This configuration includes two separate network segments (also known as links or subnets), and an IPv6-capable router that connects the network segments and forwards IPv6 Protocol Data Units (PDUs) between the hosts.
IPv6 Traffic Between Nodes on Different Subnets of an IPv4 Internetwork	This configuration supports IPv6 traffic that is carried as the payload of an IPv4 PDU (treating the IPv4 infrastructure as an IPv6 link-layer) without the deployment of IPv6 routers.
IPv6 Traffic Between Nodes in Different Sites Across the Internet	This configuration supports the 6to4 tunneling technique. The IPv6 traffic is encapsulated with an IPv4 header before it is sent over an IPv4 internetwork such as the Internet.

DHCP offers the capability of automatic allocation of reusable network addresses and additional configuration flexibility. This protocol is a stateful counterpart to "IPv6 Stateless Address Autoconfiguration" (RFC 2462) and can be used separately or concurrently with the latter to obtain configuration parameters. DHCP is a client/server protocol that provides managed configuration of devices. DHCP can provide a device with addresses assigned by a DHCP server and other configuration information. The operational models and relevant configuration information for DHCPv4 and DHCPv6 are significantly different [RFC3315].

IPv6 clients and servers exchange DHCP messages using UDP. The client uses a link-local address or an address determined through other mechanisms for transmitting and receiving DHCP messages. DHCP servers receive messages from clients using a reserved, link-scoped multicast address. A DHCP client transmits most messages to this reserved multicast address so that the client need not be configured with the address or addresses of DHCP servers [RFC3315].

DHCP makes use of the following multicast addresses:

All_DHCP_Relay_Agents_and_Servers (FF02::1:2) A link-scoped multicast address used by a client to communicate with neighboring (i.e., on-link) relay agents and servers. All servers and relay agents are members of this multicast group.

All_DHCP_Servers (FF05::1:3) A site-scoped multicast address used by a relay agent to communicate with servers, either because the relay agent wants to send messages to all servers or because it does not know the unicast addresses of the servers. Note that in order for a relay agent to use this address, it must have an address of sufficient scope to be reachable by the servers. All servers within the site are members of this multicast group.

To allow a DHCP client to send a message to a DHCP server that is not attached to the same link, a DHCP relay agent on the client's link will relay messages between the client and server. The operation of the relay agent is transparent to the client and the discussion of message exchanges in the remainder of this section will omit the description of message relaying by relay agents. Once the client has determined the address of a server, it may under some circumstances send messages directly to the server using unicast [RFC3315].

The following list provides basic DHCP terminology:

Appropriate to the link: An address is "appropriate to the link" when the address is consistent with the DHCP server's knowledge of the network topology, prefix assignment, and address assignment policies.

Identity Association (IA): A collection of addresses assigned to a client. Each IA has an associated IAID. A client may have more than one IA assigned to it; for example, one for each of its interfaces. Each IA holds one type of address; for example, an identity association for temporary addresses (IA_TA) holds temporary addresses (see "identity association for temporary addresses"). Throughout this section, "IA" is used to refer to an identity association without identifying the type of addresses in the IA.

DUID: A DHCP Unique Identifier for a DHCP participant; each DHCP client and server has exactly one DUID.

Binding: A binding (or, client binding) is a group of server data records containing the information the server has about the addresses in an IA or configuration information explicitly assigned to the client. Configuration information that has been returned to a client through a policy—for example, the information returned to all clients on the same link—does not require a binding. A binding containing information about an IA is indexed by the tuple <DUID, IA-type, IAID> (where IA-type is the type of address in the IA; for example, temporary). A binding containing configuration information for a client is indexed by <DUID>.

Configuration parameter: An element of the configuration information set on the server and delivered to the client using DHCP. Such parameters may be used to carry information to be used by a node to configure its network subsystem and enable communication, for example on a link or internetwork.

DHCP client (or client): A node that initiates requests on a link to obtain configuration parameters from one or more DHCP servers.

DHCP domain: A set of links managed by DHCP and operated by a single administrative entity.

DHCP realm: A name used to identify the DHCP administrative domain from which a DHCP authentication key was selected.

DHCP relay agent (or relay agent): A node that acts as an intermediary to deliver DHCP messages between clients and servers, and is on the same link as the client.

DHCP server (or server): A node that responds to requests from clients, and may or may not be on the same link as the client(s).

Identity Association Identifier (IAID): An identifier for an IA, chosen by the client. Each IA has an IAID, which is chosen to be unique among all IAIDs for IAs belonging to that client.

Identity Association for Nontemporary Addresses (IA_NA): An IA that carries assigned addresses that are not temporary addresses (see "identity association for temporary addresses").

Identity Association for Temporary Addresses (IA_TA): An IA that carries temporary addresses.

Message: A unit of data carried as the payload of a UDP datagram; exchanged among DHCP servers, relay agents, and clients.

Reconfigure key: A key supplied to a client by a server used to provide security for Reconfigure messages.

Relaying: A DHCP relay agent relays DHCP messages between DHCP participants.

Transaction ID: An opaque value used to match responses with replies initiated either by a client or server.

Clients listen for DHCP messages on UDP port 546. Servers and relay agents listen for DHCP messages on UDP port 547. DHCP defines and make use of the following message types [RFC3315]:

SOLICIT: A client sends a Solicit message to locate servers.

ADVERTISE: A server sends an Advertise message to indicate that it is available for DHCP service, in response to a Solicit message received from a client.

REQUEST: A client sends a Request message to request configuration parameters, including IP addresses, from a specific server.

CONFIRM: A client sends a Confirm message to any available server to determine whether the addresses it was assigned are still appropriate to the link to which the client is connected.

RENEW: A client sends a Renew message to the server that originally provided the client's addresses and configuration parameters to extend the lifetimes on the addresses assigned to the client and to update other configuration parameters.

REBIND: A client sends a Rebind message to any available server to extend the lifetimes on the addresses assigned to the client and to update other configuration parameters; this message is sent after a client receives no response to a Renew message.

REPLY: A server sends a Reply message containing assigned addresses and configuration parameters in response to a Solicit, Request, Renew, or Rebind message received from a client. A server sends a Reply message containing configuration parameters in response to an Information-request message. A server sends a Reply message in response to a Confirm message confirming or denying that the addresses assigned to the client are appropriate to the link to which the client is connected. A server sends a Reply message to acknowledge receipt of a Release or Decline message.

RELEASE: A client sends a Release message to the server that assigned addresses to the client to indicate that the client will no longer use one or more of the assigned addresses.

DECLINE: A client sends a Decline message to a server to indicate that the client has determined that one or more addresses assigned by the server are already in use on the link to which the client is connected.

RECONFIGURE: A server sends a Reconfigure message to a client to inform the client that the server has new or updated configuration parameters, and that the client is to initiate a Renew/Reply or Information-request/Reply transaction with the server in order to receive the updated information.

INFORMATION-REQUEST: A client sends an Information-request message to a server to request configuration parameters without the assignment of any IP addresses to the client.

RELAY-FORW: A relay agent sends a Relay-forward message to relay messages to servers, either directly or through another relay agent. The received message, either a client message or a Relay-forward message from another relay agent, is encapsulated in an option in the Relay-forward message.

RELAY-REPL: A server sends a Relay-reply message to a relay agent containing a message that the relay agent delivers to a client. The Relay-reply message may be relayed by other relay agents for delivery to the destination relay agent. The server encapsulates the client message as an option in the Relay-reply message, which the relay agent extracts and relays to the client.

3.14 More on Transition Approaches and Mechanisms

Although most technical aspects of IPv6 have been defined for some time, deployment of IPv6 is occurring gradually. Initially, IPv6 is being deployed within isolated islands with interconnectivity among the islands being achieved by the existing IPv4 infrastructure, and a number of transition mechanisms have been defined to interconnect such islands.

There is an additional need for support for IPv6 hosts and routers that need to interoperate with legacy IPv4 hosts, and an overview of such mechanisms for this purpose is provided in RFC 2893. That RFC defines the following types of nodes with respect to the transition to IPv6.

IPv4-only node: A host or router that implements only IPv4. An IPv4-only node does not understand IPv6. The installed base of IPv4 hosts and routers are examples of IPv4-only nodes.

IPv6/IPV4 node: A host or router that implements both the IPv4 and IPv6 protocols.

IPv6-only node: A host or router that implements IPv6 and does not implement IPv4.

IPv6 node: Any host or router that implements IPv6. IPv6/IPv4 and IPv6-only nodes are both IPv6 nodes.

IPv4 node: Any host or router that implements IPv4. IPv6/IPv4 and IPv4-only nodes are both IPv4 nodes.

The RFC also defines the IPv4-compatible IPv6 address, e.g., ::156.55.23.5, discussed previously in the section on IPv6 address space. IPv4-compatible IPv6 addresses are used to implement a simple automatic tunneling mechanism.

In addition to connectivity issues at the IP layer, the transition to IPv6 is also not entirely transparent to the networking layers above IP. As discussed previously, IPv6 addresses are significantly longer in size than IPv4 addresses and thus will require a change in application programming interfaces (APIs) or service primitive parameters that include IP addresses. Applications must also be extended to select the appropriate protocol, IPv4 or IPv6, when a DNS lookup returns both types of addresses. In general, legacy applications written for IPv4 either need to be rewritten or amended to support IPv6. For example, the application layer file transfer protocol (FTP) embeds IP addresses in its protocol fields, and could thus require changes to both the client and server FTP applications.

The IETF has defined a number of specific mechanisms to assist in transitioning to IPv6. These mechanisms are generally classified as belonging to the following categories:

Dual-Stack—The principal building block for transitioning is the *dual-stack* approach. Dual-stack nodes, as the name suggests, maintain two protocol stacks that operate in parallel and thus allow the end system or router to operate via either protocol. In end systems they enable both IPv4 and IPv6 capable applications to operate on the same node. Dual-stack capabilities in routers allow handling of both IPv4 and IPv6 packet types.

Translation—Translation refers to the direct conversion of protocols (e.g., between IPv4 and IPv6) and may include transformation of both the protocol header and the protocol payload. Translation can occur at several layers in the protocol stack, including IP, transport, and application layers. Note that protocol translation can results in feature loss where there is no clear mapping between the features provided by translated protocols. For instance, translation of an IPv6 header into an IPv4 header will lead to the loss of the IPv6 flow label and its accompanying functionality.

Tunneling (or Encapsulation)—Tunneling is used to interconnect compatible networking nodes or domains across incompatible networks. It can be viewed technically as the transfer of a payload protocol data unit by an encapsulating carrier protocol. For IPv6 transition, the IPv6 protocol data unit is generally carried as the payload of an IPv4 packet. Encapsulation of the payload protocol data unit is performed at the tunnel entrance and de-encapsulation is performed at the tunnel exit point.

Note that a transition mechanism may employ techniques from more than one of these categories. For example, when an end system or router creates an IPv6 in IPv4 tunnel, this could be classified as both dual stack (having both an IPv4 and IPv6 address) and tunneling.

References

[CIS200801] Cisco Documentation. *Enabling IPv6 routing and configuring IPv6 addressing.* www.cisco.com.

[MSD200401] Microsoft Corporation. *Internet protocol.* MSDN Library, 2004. http://msdn.microsoft.com.

[RFC2460] Deering, S., and R. Hinden Internet Protocol, Version 6 (IPv6) Specification, RFC 2460, Dec. 1998. Copyright (C) The Internet Society (1998). All Rights Reserved. This document and translations of it may be copied and furnished to others, and derivative works that comment on or otherwise explain it or assist in its implementation may be prepared, copied, published and distributed, in whole or in part, without restriction of any kind, provided that the above copyright notice and this paragraph are included on all such copies and derivative works.

[RFC2461] Narten, T., E. Nordmarket, and W. Simpson. Request for Comment: 2461, Neighbor Discovery for IPv6, RFC 2461, Dec. 1998.

[RFC2893] Gilligan, R., and E. Nordmark. Transition Mechanisms for IPv6 Hosts and Routers, RFC 2893, Aug. 2000. Copyright (C) The Internet Society (2000). All Rights Reserved. This document and translations of it may be copied and furnished to others, and derivative works that comment on or otherwise explain it or assist in its implementation may be prepared, copied, published and distributed, in whole or in part, without restriction of any kind, provided that the above copyright notice and this paragraph are included on all such copies and derivative works.

[RFC3022] Srisuresh, P., and K. Egevang. Request for Comments: 3022, Traditional IP Network Address Translator (Traditional NAT), RFC 3022, Jan. 2001.

[RFC3315] Droms, R., ed., J. Bound, B. Volz, T. Lemon, C. Perkins, and M. Carney. Dynamic Host Configuration Protocol for IPv6 (DHCPv6), RFC 3315, July 2003. Copyright (C) The Internet Society (2003). All Rights Reserved. This document and translations of it may be copied and furnished to others, and derivative works that comment on or otherwise explain it or assist in its implementation may be prepared, copied, published and distributed, in whole or in part, without restriction of any kind, provided that the above copyright notice and this paragraph are included on all such copies and derivative works.

[RFC3513] Hinden, R., and S. Deering. Internet Protocol Version 6 (IPv6) Addressing Architecture, RFC 3513, Apr. 2003. Copyright (C) The Internet Society (2003). All Rights Reserved. This document and translations of it may be copied and furnished to others, and derivative works that comment on or otherwise explain it or assist in its implementation may be prepared, copied, published and distributed, in whole or in part, without restriction of any kind, provided that the above copyright notice and this paragraph are included on all such copies and derivative works.

[RFC3775] Johnson, D., C. Perkins, and J. Arkko. Request for Comments: 3775, Mobility Support in IPv6, RFC 3775, June 2004.

[RFC3879] Huitema, C., and B. Carpenter. Request for Comments: 3879, Deprecating Site Local Addresses, Sept. 2004.

[RFC4038] Shin, M-K., ed., Y-G. Hong, J. Hagino, P. Savola, and E. M. Castro. Request for Comments: 4038, Application Aspects of IPv6 Transition, RFC 4038, Mar. 2005.

Appendix A: Neighbor Discovery for IP Version 6 (IPv6) Protocol

This section provides a brief overview of the Neighbor Discovery for IP Version 6 (IPv6) protocol, also known as Neighbor Discovery Protocol (NDP) based directly on RFC 2461 [RFC2461].

Functionality

As covered briefly earlier in the chapter, the Neighbor Discovery for IP Version 6 (IPv6) protocol solves a set of problems related to the interaction between nodes attached to the same link. It defines mechanisms for solving each of the following problems:

Router Discovery: How hosts locate routers that reside on an attached link.

Prefix Discovery: How hosts discover the set of address prefixes that define which destinations are on-link for an attached link. (Nodes use prefixes to distinguish destinations that reside on-link from those only reachable through a router.)

Parameter Discovery: How a node learns such link parameters as the link MTU or such Internet parameters as the hop limit value to place in outgoing packets.

Address Autoconfiguration: How nodes automatically configure an address for an interface.

Address resolution: How nodes determine the link-layer address of an on-link destination (e.g., a neighbor), given only the destination's IP address.

Next-hop determination: The algorithm for mapping an IP destination address into the IP address of the neighbor to which traffic for the destination should be sent. The next-hop can be a router or the destination itself.

Neighbor Unreachability* Detection: How nodes determine that a neighbor is no longer reachable. For neighbors used as routers, alternate default routers can be tried. For both routers and hosts, address resolution can be performed again.

Duplicate Address Detection: How a node determines that an address it wishes to use is not already in use by another node.

Redirect: How a router informs a host of a better first-hop node to reach a particular destination.

Neighbor Discovery defines five different ICMP packet types: A pair of Router Solicitation and Router Advertisement messages, a pair of Neighbor Solicitation and Neighbor Advertisements messages, and a Redirect message. The messages serve the following purpose:

Router Solicitation (RS): When an interface becomes enabled, hosts may send out Router Solicitations that request routers to generate Router Advertisements immediately rather than at their next scheduled time.

Router Advertisement (RA): Routers advertise their presence together with various link and Internet parameters either periodically, or in response to a Router Solicitation message. Router Advertisements contain prefixes that are used for on-link determination or address configuration, a suggested hop limit value, and so forth.

Neighbor Solicitation (NS): Sent by a node to determine the link-layer address of a neighbor, or to verify that a neighbor is still reachable via a cached link-layer address. Neighbor Solicitations are also used for Duplicate Address Detection.

Neighbor Advertisement (NA): A response to a Neighbor Solicitation message. A node may also send unsolicited Neighbor Advertisements to announce a link-layer address change.

Redirect: Used by routers to inform hosts of a better first hop for a destination.

On multicast-capable links, each router periodically multicasts a Router Advertisement packet announcing its availability. A host receives Router Advertisements from all routers, building a list of default routers. Routers generate Router Advertisements frequently enough that hosts will learn of their presence within a few minutes, but not frequently enough to rely on an absence of adver-

---

* For neighboring routers, reachability means that packets sent by a node's IP layer are delivered to the router's IP layer, and the router is indeed forwarding packets (i.e., it is configured as a router, not a host). For hosts, reachability means that packets sent by a node's IP layer are delivered to the neighbor host's IP layer. Unreachability means being in a state where reachability is not achieved at the time in question.

tisements to detect router failure; a separate Neighbor Unreachability Detection algorithm provides failure detection.

Router Advertisements contain a list of prefixes used for on-link determination or autonomous address configuration; flags associated with the prefixes specify the intended uses of a particular prefix. Hosts use the advertised on-link prefixes to build and maintain a list that is used in deciding when a packet's destination is on-link or beyond a router. Note that a destination can be on-link even though it is not covered by any advertised on-link prefix. In such cases a router can send a Redirect informing the sender that the destination is a neighbor.

Router Advertisements (and per-prefix flags) allow routers to inform hosts how to perform Address Autoconfiguration. For example, routers can specify whether hosts should use stateful (DHCPv6) or autonomous (stateless) address configuration.

Router Advertisement messages also contain Internet parameters such as the hop limit that hosts should use in outgoing packets and, optionally, link parameters such as the link MTU. This facilitates centralized administration of critical parameters that can be set on routers and automatically propagated to all attached hosts.

Nodes accomplish address resolution by multicasting a Neighbor Solicitation that asks the target node to return its link-layer address. Neighbor Solicitation messages are multicast to the solicited-node multicast address of the target address. The target returns its link-layer address in a unicast Neighbor Advertisement message. A single request-response pair of packets is sufficient for both the initiator and the target to resolve each other's link-layer addresses; the initiator includes its link-layer address in the Neighbor Solicitation.

Neighbor Solicitation messages can also be used to determine if more than one node has been assigned the same unicast address.

Neighbor Unreachability Detection detects the failure of a neighbor or the failure of the forward path to the neighbor. Doing so requires positive confirmation that packets sent to a neighbor are actually reaching that neighbor and being processed properly by its IP layer. Neighbor Unreachability Detection uses confirmation from two sources: When possible, upper-layer protocols provide a positive confirmation that a connection is making "forward progress," that is, previously sent data is known to have been delivered correctly (e.g., new acknowledgments were received recently). When positive confirmation is not forthcoming through such "hints," a node sends unicast Neighbor Solicitation messages that solicit Neighbor Advertisements as reachability confirmation from the next hop. To reduce unnecessary network traffic, probe messages are only sent to neighbors to which the node is actively sending packets.

In addition to addressing the above general problems, Neighbor Discovery also handles the following situations:

Link-layer address change—A node that knows its own link-layer address has changed can multicast a few (unsolicited) Neighbor Advertisement packets to all nodes to quickly update cached link-layer addresses that have become invalid. Note that the sending of unsolicited advertisements is a performance enhancement only (e.g., unreliable). The Neighbor Unreachability Detection algorithm ensures that all nodes will reliably discover the new address, though the delay may be somewhat longer.

Inbound load balancing—Nodes with replicated interfaces may want to load balance the reception of incoming packets across multiple network interfaces on the same link. Such nodes have multiple link-layer addresses assigned to the same interface. For example, a single network driver could represent multiple network interface cards as a single logical interface having multiple link-layer addresses.

Load balancing is handled by allowing routers to omit the source link-layer address from Router Advertisement packets, thereby forcing neighbors to use Neighbor Solicitation messages to learn link-layer addresses of routers. Returned Neighbor Advertisement messages can then contain link-layer addresses that differ depending on who issued the solicitation.

Anycast addresses—Anycast addresses identify one of a set of nodes providing an equivalent service, and multiple nodes on the same link may be configured to recognize the same Anycast address. Neighbor Discovery handles anycasts by having nodes expect to receive multiple Neighbor Advertisements for the same target. All advertisements for anycast addresses are tagged as being non-Override advertisements. This invokes specific rules to determine which of potentially multiple advertisements should be used.

Proxy advertisements—A router willing to accept packets on behalf of a target address that is unable to respond to Neighbor Solicitations can issue non-Override Neighbor Advertisements. There is currently no specified use of proxy, but proxy advertising could potentially be used to handle cases like mobile nodes that have moved off-link. However, it is not intended as a general mechanism to handle nodes that, for example, do not implement this protocol.

A short comparison with IPv4 follows.

The IPv6 Neighbor Discovery protocol corresponds to a combination of the IPv4 protocols ARP, ICMP Router Discovery, and ICMP Redirect. In IPv4 there is no generally agreed upon protocol or mechanism for Neighbor Unreachability Detection, although Hosts Requirements does specify some possible algorithms for Dead Gateway Detection (a subset of the problems Neighbor Unreachability Detection tackles).

■ The Neighbor Discovery protocol provides a multitude of improvements over the IPv4 set of protocols:

■ Router Discovery is part of the base protocol set; there is no need for hosts to "snoop" the routing protocols.

■ Router advertisements carry link-layer addresses; no additional packet exchange is needed to resolve the router's link-layer address.

- Router advertisements carry prefixes for a link; there is no need to have a separate mechanism to configure the "netmask."
- Router advertisements enable Address Autoconfiguration.
- Routers can advertise an MTU for hosts to use on the link, ensuring that all nodes use the same MTU value on links lacking a well-defined MTU.
- Address resolution multicasts are "spread" over 4 billion (2^{32}) multicast addresses greatly reducing address resolution related interrupts on nodes other than the target. Moreover, non-IPv6 machines should not be interrupted at all.
- Redirects contain the link-layer address of the new first hop; separate address resolution is not needed upon receiving a redirect.
- Multiple prefixes can be associated with the same link. By default, hosts learn all on-link prefixes from Router Advertisements. However, routers may be configured to omit some or all prefixes from Router Advertisements. In such cases hosts assume that destinations are off-link and send traffic to routers. A router can then issue redirects as appropriate.

Unlike IPv4, the recipient of an IPv6 redirect assumes that the new next-hop is on-link. In IPv4, a host ignores redirects specifying a next-hop that is not on-link according to the link's network mask. The IPv6 redirect mechanism is expected to be useful on nonbroadcast and shared media links in which it is undesirable or not possible for nodes to know all prefixes for on-link destinations.

Neighbor Unreachability Detection is part of the base significantly improving the robustness of packet delivery in the presence of failing routers, partially failing or partitioned links, and nodes that change their link-layer addresses. For instance, mobile nodes can move off-link without losing any connectivity due to stale ARP caches.

Unlike ARP, Neighbor Discovery detects half-link failures (using Neighbor Unreachability Detection) and avoids sending traffic to neighbors with which two-way connectivity is absent.

Unlike IPv4 Router Discovery, the Router Advertisement messages do not contain a preference field. The preference field is not needed to handle routers of different "stability"; the Neighbor Unreachability Detection will detect dead routers and switch to working ones.

The use of link-local addresses to uniquely identify routers (for Router Advertisement and Redirect messages) makes it possible for hosts to maintain the router associations in the event of the site renumbering to use new global prefixes.

Using the Hop Limit equal to 255 trick, Neighbor Discovery is immune to off-link senders that accidentally or intentionally send ND messages. In IPv4, off-link senders can send both ICMP Redirects and Router Advertisement messages.

Placing address resolution at the ICMP layer makes the protocol more media-independent than ARP and makes it possible to use standard IP authentication and security mechanisms as appropriate.

Appendix B: Mobile IP Version 6 (MIPv6)

This appendix provides a short introduction to MIPv6, based directly on RFC 3775 [RFC3775]. RFC 3775 is a lengthy RFC due to the complexity of the topic. Only the most basic capabilities are covered here, and the reader and developer should refer to the RFC for a complete view.

MIPv6 is a protocol that allows nodes to remain reachable while moving around in the IPv6 Internet. Each mobile node is always identified by its home address, regardless of its current point of attachment to the Internet. While situated away from its home, a mobile node is also associated with a care-of address, which provides information about the mobile node's current location. IPv6 packets addressed to a mobile node's home address are transparently routed to its care-of address. The protocol enables IPv6 nodes to cache the binding of a mobile node's home address with its care-of address, and to then send any packets destined for the mobile node directly to it at this care-of address. To support this operation, MIPv6 defines a new IPv6 protocol and a new destination option. All IPv6 nodes, whether mobile or stationary, can communicate with mobile nodes.

RFC 3775 specifies a protocol, known as Mobile IPv6, that allows nodes to remain reachable while moving around in the IPv6 Internet. Without specific support for mobility in IPv6, packets destined to a mobile node would not be able to reach it while the mobile node is away from its home link. In order to continue communication in spite of its movement, a mobile node could change its IP address each time it moves to a new link, but the mobile node would then not be able to maintain transport and higher-layer connections when it changes location. Mobility support in IPv6 is particularly important, as mobile computers are likely to account for a majority or at least a substantial fraction of the population of the Internet during the lifetime of IPv6.

The protocol defined in the RFC allows a mobile node to move from one link to another without changing the mobile node's "home address." Packets may be routed to the mobile node using this address regardless of the mobile node's current point of attachment to the Internet. The mobile node may also continue to communicate with other nodes (stationary or mobile) after moving to a new link. The movement of a mobile node away from its home link is thus transparent to transport and higher-layer protocols and applications.

The Mobile IPv6 protocol is just as suitable for mobility across homogeneous media as for mobility across heterogeneous media. For example, Mobile IPv6 facilitates node movement from one Ethernet segment to another as well as it facilitates node movement from an Ethernet segment to a wireless LAN cell, with the mobile node's IP address remaining unchanged in spite of such movement.

One can think of the Mobile IPv6 protocol as solving the network-layer mobility management problem. Some mobility management applications,—such as handover among wireless transceivers, each of which covers only a very small geographic area—have been solved using link-layer techniques. For example, in many current wireless LAN products, link-layer mobility mechanisms allow a "handover" of a mobile node from one cell to another, re-establishing link-layer connectivity to the node in each new location.

The design of Mobile IP support in IPv6 (that is, Mobile IPv6) benefits both from the experiences gained from the development of Mobile IP support in IPv4 (Mobile IPv4), and from the opportunities provided by IPv6. Mobile IPv6 thus shares many features with Mobile IPv4, but is integrated into IPv6 and offers many other improvements. The major differences between Mobile IPv4 and Mobile IPv6 are as follows:

- There is no need to deploy special routers as "foreign agents," as in Mobile IPv4. Mobile IPv6 operates in any location without any special support required from the local router.
- Support for route optimization is a fundamental part of the protocol, rather than a nonstandard set of extensions.
- Mobile IPv6 route optimization can operate securely even without prearranged security associations. It is expected that route optimization can be deployed on a global scale between all mobile nodes and correspondent nodes.
- Support is also integrated into Mobile IPv6 for allowing route optimization to coexist efficiently with routers that perform "ingress filtering."
- The IPv6 Neighbor Unreachability Detection assures symmetric reachability between the mobile node and its default router in the current location.
- Most packets sent to a mobile node while away from home in Mobile IPv6 are sent using an IPv6 routing header rather than IP encapsulation, reducing the amount of resulting overhead compared to Mobile IPv4.
- Mobile IPv6 is decoupled from any particular link layer, as it uses IPv6 Neighbor Discovery instead of ARP. This also improves the robustness of the protocol.
- The use of IPv6 encapsulation (and the routing header) removes the need in Mobile IPv6 to manage "tunnel soft state."
- The dynamic home agent address discovery mechanism in Mobile IPv6 returns a single reply to the mobile node. The directed broadcast approach used in IPv4 returns separate replies from each home agent.

Table B1 provides some basic terminology that is used in MIPv6.

Basic Operation of Mobile IPv6

A mobile node is always expected to be addressable at its home address, whether it is currently attached to its home link or is away from home. The "home address" is an IP address assigned to the mobile node within its home subnet prefix on its home link.

Table B1   Basic Terminology Used in MIPv6

Term	Definition
Destination option	Destination options are carried by the IPv6 *Destination Options* extension header. Destination options include optional information that need be examined only by the IPv6 node given as the destination address in the IPv6 header, not by routers in between. Mobile IPv6 defines one new destination option, the Home Address destination option.
Routing header	A routing header may be present as an IPv6 header extension, and indicates that the payload has to be delivered to a destination IPv6 address in some way that is different from what would be carried out by standard Internet routing. In MIPv6, use of the term "routing header" typically refers to use of a type 2 routing header.
Home address	A unicast routable address assigned to a mobile node, used as the permanent address of the mobile node. This address is within the mobile node's home link. Standard IP routing mechanisms will deliver packets destined for a mobile node's home address to its home link. Mobile nodes can have multiple home addresses; for instance, when there are multiple home prefixes on the home link.
Home subnet prefix	The IP subnet prefix corresponding to a mobile node's home address.
Home link	The link on which a mobile node's home subnet prefix is defined.
Mobile node	A node that can change its point of attachment from one link to another, while still being reachable via its home address.
Movement	A change in a mobile node's point of attachment to the Internet such that it is no longer connected to the same link as it was previously. If a mobile node is not currently attached to its home link, the mobile node is said to be "away from home."
L2 handover	A process by which the mobile node changes from one link-layer connection to another. For example, a change of wireless access point is an L2 handover.
L3 handover	Subsequent to an L2 handover, a mobile node detects a change in an on-link subnet prefix that would require a change in the primary care-of address. For example, a change of access router subsequent to a change of wireless access point typically results in an L3 handover.
	(Continued)

Table B1   Basic Terminology Used in MIPv6 (Continued)

Term	*Definition*
Correspondent node	A peer node with which a mobile node is communicating. The correspondent node may be either mobile or stationary.
Foreign subnet prefix	Any IP subnet prefix other than the mobile node's home subnet prefix.
Foreign link	Any link other than the mobile node's home link.
Care-of address	A unicast routable address associated with a mobile node while visiting a foreign link; the subnet prefix of this IP address is a foreign subnet prefix. Among the multiple care-of addresses that a mobile node may have at any given time (e.g., with different subnet prefixes), the one registered with the mobile node's home agent for a given home address is called its "primary" care-of address.
Home agent	A router on a mobile node's home link with which the mobile node has registered its current care-of address. While the mobile node is away from home, the home agent intercepts packets on the home link destined to the mobile node's home address, encapsulates them, and tunnels them to the mobile node's registered care-of address.
Binding	The association of the home address of a mobile node with a care-of address for that mobile node, along with the remaining lifetime of that association.
Registration	The process during which a mobile node sends a Binding Update to its home agent or a correspondent node, causing a binding for the mobile node to be registered.
Mobility message	A message containing a Mobility Header.
Binding authorization	Correspondent registration needs to be authorized to allow the recipient to believe that the sender has the right to specify a new binding.
Return routability procedure	The return routability procedure authorizes registrations by the use of a cryptographic token exchange.
Correspondent registration	A return routability procedure followed by a registration, run between the mobile node and a correspondent node.
Home registration	A registration between the mobile node and its home agent, authorized by the use of IPsec.

(Continued)

Table B1   Basic Terminology Used in MIPv6 (Continued)

Term	Definition
Nonce	Nonces are random numbers used internally by the correspondent node in the creation of keygen tokens related to the return routability procedure. The nonces are not specific to a mobile node, and are kept secret within the correspondent node.
Cookie	A cookie is a random number used by a mobile node to prevent spoofing by a bogus correspondent node in the return routability procedure.
Care-of init cookie	A cookie sent to the correspondent node in the Care-of Test Init message, to be returned in the Care-of Test message.
Home init cookie	A cookie sent to the correspondent node in the Home Test Init message, to be returned in the Home Test message.
Keygen token	A keygen token is a number supplied by a correspondent node in the return routability procedure to enable the mobile node to compute the necessary binding management key for authorizing a Binding Update.
Care-of keygen token	A keygen token sent by the correspondent node in the Care-of Test message.
Home keygen token	A keygen token sent by the correspondent node in the Home Test message.
Binding management key (Kbm)	A binding management key (Kbm) is a key used for authorizing a binding cache management message (e.g., Binding Update or Binding Acknowledgement). Return routability provides a way to create a binding management key.

While a mobile node is at home, packets addressed to its home address are routed to the mobile node's home link, using conventional Internet routing mechanisms.

While a mobile node is attached to some foreign link away from home, it is also addressable at one or more care-of addresses. A care-of address is an IP address associated with a mobile node that has the subnet prefix of a particular foreign link. The mobile node can acquire its care-of address through conventional IPv6 mechanisms, such as stateless or stateful autoconfiguration. As long as the mobile node stays in this location, packets addressed to this care-of address will be routed to the mobile node. The mobile node may also accept packets from several care-of addresses, such as when it is moving but still reachable at the previous link.

The association between a mobile node's home address and care-of address is known as a "binding" for the mobile node. While away from home, a mobile node registers its primary care-of address with a router on its home link, requesting this router to function as the "home agent" for the mobile node. The mobile node performs this binding registration by sending a "Binding Update" message to the home agent. The home agent replies to the mobile node by returning a "Binding Acknowledgement" message.

Any node communicating with a mobile node is referred to in this document as a "correspondent node" of the mobile node, and may itself be either a stationary node or a mobile node. Mobile nodes can provide information about their current location to correspondent nodes. This happens through the correspondent registration. As a part of this procedure, a return routability test is performed in order to authorize the establishment of the binding.

There are two possible modes for communications between the mobile node and a correspondent node. The first mode, bidirectional tunneling, does not require Mobile IPv6 support from the correspondent node and is available even if the mobile node has not registered its current binding with the correspondent node. Packets from the correspondent node are routed to the home agent and then tunneled to the mobile node. Packets to the correspondent node are tunneled from the mobile node to the home agent ("reverse tunneled") and then routed normally from the home network to the correspondent node. In this mode, the home agent uses proxy Neighbor Discovery (ND) to intercept any IPv6 packets addressed to the mobile node's home address (or home addresses) on the home link. Each intercepted packet is tunneled to the mobile node's primary care-of address. This tunneling is performed using IPv6 encapsulation.

The second mode, "route optimization," requires the mobile node to register its current binding at the correspondent node. Packets from the correspondent node can be routed directly to the care-of address of the mobile node. When sending a packet to any IPv6 destination, the correspondent node checks its cached bindings for an entry for the packet's destination address. If a cached binding for this destination address is found, the node uses a new type of IPv6 routing header to route the packet to the mobile node by way of the care-of address indicated in this binding.

Routing packets directly to the mobile node's care-of address allows the shortest communications path to be used. It also eliminates congestion at the mobile node's home agent and home link. In addition, the impact of any possible failure of the home agent or networks on the path to or from it is reduced.

When routing packets directly to the mobile node, the correspondent node sets the Destination Address in the IPv6 header to the care-of address of the mobile node. A new type of IPv6 routing header is also added to the packet to carry the desired home address. Similarly, the mobile node sets the Source Address in the packet's IPv6 header to its current care-of addresses. The mobile node adds a new

IPv6 "Home Address" destination option to carry its home address. The inclusion of home addresses in these packets makes the use of the care-of address transparent above the network layer (e.g., at the transport layer).

Mobile IPv6 also provides support for multiple home agents, and a limited support for the reconfiguration of the home network. In these cases, the mobile node may not know the IP address of its own home agent, and even the home subnet prefixes may change over time. A mechanism, known as "dynamic home agent address discovery" allows a mobile node to dynamically discover the IP address of a home agent on its home link, even when the mobile node is away from home. Mobile nodes can also learn new information about home subnet prefixes through the "mobile prefix discovery" mechanism.

The reader and developer(s) should refer to RFC 3775 for a detailed view of these concepts and for all protocol details.

Appendix C: Enabling IPv6 in Cisco Routers

Given the wide penetration of Cisco Systems router technology, we briefly summarize below some basic configuration information on these platforms, based directly on vendor documentation [CIS200801].

Enabling IPv6 Routing and Configuring IPv6 Addressing

In principle, IPv6 routing is disabled in the Cisco IOS software (however, this is not always the case). To enable IPv6 routing, one must first enable the forwarding of IPv6 traffic globally on the router and then one must assign IPv6 addresses to individual interfaces in the router. The tasks described in the following sections explain how to enable IPv6 routing on a Cisco router. Each task in the list is identified as either required or optional:

Enabling IPv6 Processing Globally on the Router (required)
Configuring IPv6 Addresses (required)
Verifying IPv6 Operation and Address Configuration (optional)

Enabling IPv6 Processing Globally on the Router

To enable the forwarding of IPv6 traffic globally on the router, use the following command in global configuration mode:

Command	Purpose
`Router(config)# ipv6 unicast-routing`	Enables the forwarding of IPv6 unicast datagrams.

Configuring IPv6 Addresses

An IPv6 address must be configured on an interface for the interface to forward IPv6 traffic. Configuring a site-local or global IPv6 address on an interface automatically configures a link-local address and activates IPv6 for that interface. Additionally, the configured interface automatically joins the following required multicast groups for that link:

■ Solicited-node multicast group FF02:0:0:0:0:1:FF00::/104 for each unicast and anycast address assigned to the interface
■ All-nodes multicast group FF02:0:0:0:0:0:0:1 (scope is link-local)
■ All-routers multicast group FF02:0:0:0:0:0:0:2 (scope is link-local)
(The solicited-node multicast address is used in the neighbor discovery process.)

To configure an IPv6 address on an interface, use the following commands, as shown on pages 158 and 159, beginning in global configuration mode.

Verifying IPv6 Operation and Address Configuration

To verify that IPv6 processing of packets is enabled globally on the router and on applicable interfaces, and that an IPv6 address is configured on applicable interfaces, enter the show **running-config** EXEC command:

```
Router# show running-config
Building configuration...
Current configuration : 22324 bytes
!
! Last configuration change at 14:59:38 PST Tue Jan 16 2001
! NVRAM config last updated at 04:25:39 PST Tue Jan 16 2001
!
hostname cat
!
ipv6 unicast-routing
!
interface Ethernet0
no ip route-cache
no ip mroute-cache
no keepalive
media-type 10BaseT
ipv6 address 3FFE:C00:0:1::/64 eui-64
!
```

	Command	Purpose
Step 1	Router(config)# **interface** *interface-type* *interface-number*	Specifies an interface type and number, and enters interface configuration mode.
Step 2	Router(config-if)# **ipv6 address** *ipv6-prefix/prefix-length* [**eui-64**]	Specifies an IPv6 network assigned to the interface and enables IPv6 processing on the interface. Specifying the **ipv6 address** *ipv6-prefix*/prefix-length interface configuration command without the **eui-64** keyword configures site-local and global IPv6 addresses. Specifying the **ipv6 address** *ipv6-prefix*/prefix-length command with the **eui-64** keyword configures site-local and global IPv6 addresses with an interface identifier (ID) in the low-order 64 bits of the IPv6 address. Only the 64-bit network prefix for the address needs to be specified; the last 64 bits are automatically computed from the interface ID. The link-local address for an interface is automatically configured when IPv6 is enabled on the interface.
	Router(config-if)# **ipv6 address** *ipv6-address* {*/prefix-length* **link-local**}	Specifies an IPv6 address assigned to the interface and enables IPv6 processing on the interface. Specifying the **ipv6 address** *ipv6-address* interface configuration command without the **link-local** keyword configures site-local and global IPv6 addresses. (The link-local address for an interface is automatically configured when IPv6 is enabled on that interface.) Specifying the **ipv6 address** command with the link-local keyword configures a link-local address on the interface that is used instead of the **link-local** address that is automatically configured when IPv6 is enabled on the interface.

Command	Purpose
`Router(config-if)# ipv6 unnumbered interface-type interface-number`	Specifies an unnumbered interface and enables IPv6 processing on an interface. The global IPv6 address of the interface specified with the *interface-type interface-number* argument is used as the source address in packets generated from the unnumbered interface. (A link-local address is automatically configured on an unnumbered interface when IPv6 is enabled on the interface.)
`Router(config-if)# ipv6 enable`	Automatically configures an IPv6 link-local address on the interface while also enabling the interface for IPv6 processing. The link-local address can be used only to communicate with nodes on the same link.

Notes:

The ipv6-address argument in the ipv6 address command must be in the form documented in RFC 2373 where the address is specified in hexadecimal using 16-bit values between colons.

The ipv6-prefix argument in the ipv6 address command must be in the form documented in RFC 2373 where the address is specified in hexadecimal using 16-bit values between colons.

The /prefix-length argument in the ipv6 address command is a decimal value that indicates how many of the high-order contiguous bits of the address comprise the prefix (the network portion of the address). A slash mark must precede the decimal value.

In Cisco IOS Release 12.2(4)T or later releases, Cisco IOS Release 12.0(21)ST, and Cisco IOS Release 12.0(22)S or later releases, the ipv6 address or ipv6 address eui-64 command can be used to configure multiple IPv6 global and site-local addresses within the same prefix on an interface. Multiple IPv6 link-local addresses on an interface are not supported.

Prior to Cisco IOS Releases 12.2(4)T, 12.0(21)ST, and 12.0(22)S, the Cisco IOS command-line interface (CLI) displays the following error message when multiple IPv6 addresses within the same prefix on an interface are configured:

`Prefix <prefix-number> already assigned to <interface-type>`

To verify that IPv6 addresses are configured correctly, enter the show **ipv6 interface** EXEC command. The following example shows the IPv6 addresses configured for Ethernet interface 0:

```
Router# show ipv6 interface ethernet 0
Ethernet0 is up, line protocol is up
IPv6 is enabled, link-local address is FE80::260:3EFF:FE11:6770
Global unicast address(es):
3FFE:C00:0:1:260:3EFF:FE11:6770, subnet is 3FFE:C00:0:1::/64
Joined group address(es):
FF02::1
FF02::2
FF02::1:FF11:6770
MTU is 1500 bytes
ICMP error messages limited to one every 500 milliseconds
ND reachable time is 30,000 milliseconds
ND advertised reachable time is 0 milliseconds
ND advertised retransmit interval is 0 milliseconds
ND router advertisements are sent every 200 seconds
ND router advertisements live for 1800 seconds
Hosts use stateless autoconfig for addresses.
```

IPv6 Routing and IPv6 Address Configuration Example

In the following example, IPv6 is enabled on the router with both a link-local address and a global address based on the IPv6 prefix 3ffe:c00:c18:1::/64. The EUI-64 interface ID is used in the low-order 64 bits of both addresses. Output from the **show ipv6 interface** EXEC command is included to show how the interface ID (260:3EFF:FE47:1530) is appended to the link-local prefix FE80::/64 of Ethernet interface 0.

```
ipv6 unicast-routing
interface ethernet 0
ipv6 address 3ffe:c00:c18:1::/64 eui-64
Router# show ipv6 interface ethernet 0
Ethernet0 is up, line protocol is up
IPv6 is enabled, link-local address is FE80::260:3EFF:FE47:1530
Global unicast address(es):
3FFE:C00:C18:1:260:3EFF:FE47:1530, subnet is 3FFE:C00:C18:1::/64
Joined group address(es):
FF02::1
FF02::2
FF02::1:FF47:1530
FF02::9
MTU is 1500 bytes
ICMP error messages limited to one every 500 milliseconds
ND reachable time is 30,000 milliseconds
```

```
ND advertised reachable time is 0 milliseconds
ND advertised retransmit interval is 0 milliseconds
ND router advertisements are sent every 200 seconds
ND router advertisements live for 1800 seconds
Hosts use stateless autoconfig for addresses.
```

In the following example, multiple IPv6 global addresses within the prefix 3000::/64 are configured on Ethernet interface 0:

```
interface ethernet 0
ipv6 address 3000::1/64
ipv6 address 3000::/64 eui-64
```

Chapter 4

Security Mechanisms and Approaches

Introduction

This chapter starts the discussion on IPv6 security, which continues over the chapters that follow. The IPv6 features and capabilities described up to now all play a role in the various areas of security concern, potential vulnerabilities, and mitigation approaches. We begin with a short review of traditional firewall-based perimeter security and then begin looking at IPv6.

4.1 Security 101

Information security is defined as the set of mechanisms, techniques, measures, and administrative processes employed to protect information assets from unintentional disclosure or from unauthorized access, appropriation, use manipulation, modification, or destruction of these assets. The term "information asset" refers here to actual data elements, records, files, and so forth, while the term "information technology asset" refers to the broader set of assets including the hardware, the media, the communications elements, and the actual environment. Information security spans the areas of confidentiality, integrity, and availability. Confidentiality is protection against unauthorized access, appropriation, or use of assets. Integrity is protection against unauthorized manipulation, modification, or loss of assets. Availability is protection against blockage, limitation, or diminution of benefit from an asset that is owed. The Computer Crime and Intellectual Property Section

(CCIPS) Computer Intrusion Cases, of the U.S. Department of Justice defines these terms (and considers respective infractions as crimes), as follows:

Confidentiality—A breach of confidentiality occurs when a person knowingly accesses a computer without authorization or exceeding authorized access. Confidentiality is compromised when an attacker views or copies proprietary or private information, such as a credit card number or trade secret.

Integrity—A breach of integrity occurs when a system or data has been accidentally or maliciously modified, altered or destroyed without authorization. For example, viruses and worms alter source code in order to allow an attacker to gain unauthorized access to a computer.

Availability—A breach of availability occurs when an authorized user is prevented from timely, reliable access to data or a system. An example of this is a denial of service attack.

Table 4.1 enumerates some key security infraction mechanisms. Analysis shows, however, that only a subset of all firms have a comprehensive, high-assurance institution-wide mechanism in place. Table 4.2 provides a basic glossary of related terms (reference [MIN200601] contains over 5,500 terms for any interested reader). While many types of infractions exist, *some* that are of concern in IPv6 include the following:

Intrusion into the private network of an institution with the goal of misappropriating information, altering data, or placing a Trojan horse or other malware to achieve future breaches

Session hijacking (active, while the session is underway, or statically, say via an inappropriate DNS resolution)

Redirection: compromise of the IP routing mechanism where packets for any destination can be redirected arbitrarily to any (undesired/unintended) location

Denial of service

Also see Table 4.3 [RFC2401]. Appendix A provides other examples of possible infractions, but a large book could be written just on this topic alone.

A pragmatic concern is that while the IPv6 protocol itself appears to have increased security and there are no known weaknesses in the protocol itself, this does not matter if a vendor (Cisco, Apple, Juniper, Check Point) implements it poorly.

An alarming fraction of companies spend relatively little on security, even in the face of the avalanche of increased threats (caused by geopolitical events, higher penetration of Internet access to "rogue" countries, greater deployment of "weak" Web-based software, etc.). Furthermore, today when people talk security most people simply talk about writing a few lines of filtering code on a router or perimeter firewall based on Transmission Control Protocol (TCP) ports to prevent a few kinds of transport-layer flows to be admitted into an intranet. This clearly only gives a false sense of security and provides nothing for business continuity and disaster/infraction recovery. For

Table 4.1 Basic Infraction Mechanisms

Mechanism	Description
Hoax	Usually an e-mail that gets sent in chain-letter mode describing some devastating, but highly unlikely virus. Hoaxes are detectable as having no file attachment, no reference to a third party who can validate the claim, and by the general tone of the message.
Joke	A harmless program that causes various benign activities to display on your computer (for example, an unexpected screen saver).
Trojan Horse	A program that neither replicates nor copies itself but causes damage or compromises the security of the computer. Typically, an individual e-mails a Trojan Horse to a recipient (it does not e-mail itself) and it may arrive in the form of a joke program or software of some sort.
Virus	A program or code that replicates itself. A virus infects another program, boot sector, partition sector, or document that supports macros, by inserting itself or attaching itself to that medium. Most viruses only replicate, though many do a large amount of damage as well.
Worm	A program that makes copies of itself; for example, from one disk drive to another or by copying itself using e-mail or another transport mechanism. The worm may do damage and compromise the security of the computer. It may arrive in the form of a joke program or software of some sort.
Physical Access	Direct access to systems or networks, allowing passive or active intrusion.
Intrusion	Penetration into an organization's network (be it the intranet, the extranet, the wireless LAN, etc.) or computer systems (hosts).

Courtesy: Symantec

example, while excluding some flows, the filter might allow an e-mail (SMTP) flow; however, a virus or other security-damaging code might sneak in under that flow. Or, other damaging code is admitted under a normally accepted mundane TCP flow. Malicious code giving rise to what are called "blended threats" is now very common. Blended threats combine the characteristics of viruses, worms, Trojan horses, and malicious code with server and Internet vulnerabilities to initiate, transmit, and spread an attack. Since these threats utilize multiple methods and techniques, the damaging code often spreads rapidly and can cause widespread infractions.

Table 4.2 Basic Glossary of Terms

Term	Definition
Attack	An attempt to gain unauthorized access to an information system's services, resources, or information, or the attempt to compromise an information system's confidentially, integrity, or availability [NIC200001].
Audit	The process of examining the history of a transaction to find out what happened. An operational audit can be an examination of ongoing activities to determine what is happening. It can also be an independent review and examination [NIC200001].
Business Continuity Planning	Written plan describing the procedures the company takes in case of potentially disruptive events short of a disaster (for which the Disaster Recovery Plan is applicable) to assure that the operations of the company can continue unimpeded.
Compromise	Disclosure of information to unauthorized persons or a violation of the security policy of a system in which unauthorized intentional or unintentional disclosure, modification, destruction, or loss of an object may have occurred [NIC200001].
Denial of Service	The result of any action or series of actions that prevents any part of an information system from functioning [NIC200001].
Disaster Recovery Planning	Written plan describing the steps company would take to restore computer operations in the event of a disaster containing four components: the emergency plan, the backup plan, the recovery plan, and the test plan [INF200801].
Disaster Recovery Testing	Written plan describing the steps to test the Disaster Recovery Plan.
Fraud Discovery and Interdiction	Fraud: Computer-related crimes involving deliberate misrepresentation or alteration of data in order to obtain something of value [INF200801]. Fraud discovery: mechanisms and processes to identify fraud. Fraud interdiction: actions to recover from or prevent future fraud.
	(Continued)

Table 4.2   Basic Glossary of Terms (Continued)

Information Asset	Information an organization must have to conduct its mission or business.
Information Security	The protection of information systems against unauthorized access to, or modification of, information, whether in storage, processing, or transit, and against the denial of service to authorized users or the provision of service to unauthorized users, including those measures necessary to detect, document, and counter such threats [GOV200801] (Reference NSTISSI 4009.
Information Systems (IS)	The discipline of informatics; the collection of assets used to support computer-based data acquisition, storage, processing, distribution, etc. Synonym: IT system. The term "IT system" refers to a general support system (e.g., mainframe computer, mid-range computer, local area network, agency-wide backbone) or a major application that can run on a general support system and whose use of information resources satisfies a specific set of user requirements [STO200201].
Man-in-the-Middle	A form of active wiretapping attack in which the attacker intercepts and selectively modifies communicated data in order to masquerade as one or more of the entities involved in a communication association. For example, suppose Alice and Bob try to establish a session key by using the Diffie-Hellman algorithm without data origin authentication service. A "man in the middle" could block direct communication between Alice and Bob and then masquerade as Alice sending data to Bob, masquerade as Bob sending data to Alice, establish separate session keys with each of them, and function as a clandestine proxy server between them in order to capture or modify sensitive information that Alice and Bob think they are sending only to each other [RFC2828].
Masquerade	An action of an unauthorized entity that entails posing as an authorized user. Such action is by the unauthorized entity to gain access to a system ("spoof") or to perform a malicious act ("malicious logic"). In context of masquerade malicious logic is any hardware, firmware, or software (e.g., Trojan horse) that appears to perform a useful or desirable function, but actually gains unauthorized access to system resources or tricks a user into executing other malicious logic.
	(Continued)

Table 4.2   Basic Glossary of Terms (Continued)

Masquerade Attack	(aka spoofing) A type of attack in which one system entity illegitimately poses as (assumes the identity of) another entity.
Private-Key Encryption (symmetric)	A cryptographic method of encryption where the same key is used to encrypt and decrypt. The issue here is that the process for delivering and updating these keys can become cumbersome with large networks. One private-key authentication approach used today is Kerberos; this is a branch of cryptography involving algorithms that use the same key for two different steps of the algorithm (such as encryption and decryption, or signature creation and signature verification). A modern example of a symmetric encryption algorithm is the U.S. Government's Data Encryption Algorithm. Symmetric cryptography is sometimes called "secret-key cryptography" (versus public-key cryptography) because the entities that share the key, such as the originator and the recipient of a message, need to keep the key secret. For example, when Alice wants to ensure confidentiality for data she sends to Bob, she encrypts the data with a secret key, and Bob uses the same key to decrypt. Keeping the shared key secret entails both cost and risk when the key is distributed to both Alice and Bob. Thus, symmetric cryptography has a key management disadvantage compared to asymmetric cryptography [RFC2828].
Public Key Infrastructure (PKI)	A system of Certification Authorities (CAs) (and, optionally, registration authorities (RAs) and other supporting servers and agents) that perform some set of certificate management, archive management, key management, and token management functions for a community of users in an application of asymmetric cryptography [RFC2828]. The core PKI functions are (a) to register users and issue their public-key certificates, (b) to revoke certificates when required, and (c) to archive data needed to validate certificates at a much later time. Key pairs for data confidentiality may be generated (and perhaps escrowed) by CAs or RAs, but requiring a PKI client to generate its own digital signature key pair helps maintain system integrity of the cryptographic system, because then only the client ever possesses the private key it uses. Also, an authority may be established to approve or coordinate Certificate Policy Statement (CPSs), which are security policies under which components of a PKI operate [RFC2828].
	(Continued)

Table 4.2 Basic Glossary of Terms (Continued)

	A number of other servers and agents may support the core PKI, and PKI clients may obtain services from them. The full range of such services is not yet fully understood and is evolving, but supporting roles may include archive agent, certified delivery agent, confirmation agent, digital notary, directory, key escrow agent, key generation agent, naming agent (who ensures that issuers and subjects have unique identifiers within the PKI), repository, ticket-granting agent, and time stamp agent [RFC2828].
Public-Key Encryption (asymmetric)	A cryptographic method of encryption where the data is encrypted using a symmetric public key provided by the user for whom the data is destined. Authentication occurs when the recipient of data is able to decrypt that data using the sender's public key. A public key cryptosystem consists of three algorithms: K, E, and D. The key generation algorithm K is an efficient algorithm that takes a security parameter as input and outputs a public key, p_k, and private key, s_k. The public key specifies, among other things, a finite set of possible messages and a finite set of possible ciphertexts, denoted by p_kM and p_kC. The encryption algorithm E is an efficient algorithm that takes a public key and a message as input and outputs a ciphertext. The decryption algorithm D is a deterministic polynomial-time algorithm that takes a private key and a ciphertext as input and outputs either a message or the special symbol. One requirement is that for any public-private key pair (p_k, s_k) and any message m the set of messages specified by p_k, the following holds true $D(s_k, E(p_k,m)) = m$ [GJO200401].
Residual Risk	The portion of risk remaining after security measures have been applied [NIC200001].
Risk	A risk is the probability that a threat will materialize. The probability that a vulnerability may be exploited or that a threat may become harmful [NIC200001]. Risk is the net negative impact of the exercise of a vulnerability, considering both the probability and the impact of occurrence [STO200201].
Risk Analysis	Process of analyzing a target environment and the relationships of its risk-related attributes. The analysis should identify threat vulnerabilities, associate these vulnerabilities of affected assets, identify the potential nature of an undesirable result, and identify and evaluate risk-reducing countermeasures [TIP200001].

(Continued)

Table 4.2 Basic Glossary of Terms (Continued)

Risk Assessment	A study of vulnerabilities, threats, probabilistic likelihood, impact, or loss, and theoretical effectiveness of security measures. The process of evaluating threats and vulnerabilities, known and postulated, to determine expected loss and establish the degree of acceptability to system operations [INF200801]. Term represents the assignment of value to assets, threat frequency (annualized), consequence (i.e., exposure factors) and other elements of chance. The reported results of risk analysis can be said to provide an assessment or measurement of risk, regardless of the degree to which quantitative techniques are applied. For consistency in this chapter, the term risk assessment hereafter is used to characterize both the process and the results of analyzing and assessing risk [TIP200001]. The process of analyzing threats to and vulnerabilities of an information system and the potential impact the loss of information or capabilities of a system would have on national security. The resulting analysis is used as a basis for identifying appropriate and cost-effective countermeasures [NIC200001].
Risk Management	The process established to identify, control, and minimize the impact of uncertain events [INF200801]. Risk management is the process of identifying risk, analyzing and assessing risk, and taking steps to reduce risk to an acceptable level. Risk management, when properly practiced, positions an organization to accomplish its mission(s) by (1) better securing the IT systems that store, process, or transmit organizational information; (2) enabling management to make well-informed risk management decisions to justify the expenditures that are part of an IT budget; and (3) assisting management in authorizing (or accrediting) the IT systems on the basis of the supporting documentation resulting from the performance of risk management [STO200201]. Term characterizes the overall process. The first phase, risk assessment, includes identification of the assets at risk and their value, risks that threaten a loss of that value, risk-reducing measures, and the budgetary impact of implementing decisions related to the acceptance, mitigation, or transfer of risk. The second phase of risk management includes the process of assigning priority to, budgeting, implementing, and maintaining appropriate risk-reducing measures. Risk management is a continuous process [TIP200001].
	(Continued)

Table 4.2 Basic Glossary of Terms (Continued)

	The process concerned with the identification, measurement, control, and minimization of security risks in information systems to a level commensurate with the value of the assets protected [NIC200001].
Risk Mitigation	Techniques and principles to address risk and either eliminate it or minimize it. Techniques to ascertain that future reoccurrences of the same event will result is no or less damage. Methods to increase security assurance. Involves risk identification, risk analysis, risk assessment, and risk management.
Safeguard	Term represents a risk-reducing measure that acts to detect, prevent, or minimize loss associated with the occurrence of specified threat or category of threats. Safeguards are also often described as controls or countermeasures [TIP200001].
Security Architecture Development	A company-wide blueprint that describes the target multitiered security plan for the organization.
Threats and Threat Identification	A threat is an event or activity that has the potential to cause harm to the information systems. Term defines an event (tornado, theft, or computer virus infection) the occurrence of which could have an undesirable impact [NIC200001].
Vulnerability and Vulnerability Identification	A vulnerability, or weakness, is a lack of a safeguard which may be exploited by a threat, causing harm to the information systems. A software flaw that permits an exogenous agent to use a computer system without authorization or to use it with authorization in excess of that which the system owner specifically granted said agent. Term characterizes a weakness in an information system (procedures, hardware design, internal controls, software) that can be exploited [NIC200001].

Figure 4.1 depicts the basic approach of layered security. Some of the classic tools that may be used to secure company assets include the following:

- Firewalls
- VPNs (virtual private networks)
- Secure private networks (SPNs)
- Intrusion detection systems (IDS) / Intrusion Protection Systems (IPS)

Table 4.3   Security Issues of Specific Concern in IPv6 (Partial List)

Security Capability	Definition (from RFC2401 [RFC2401])
Access Control	Access control is a security service that prevents unauthorized use of a resource, including the prevention of use of a resource in an unauthorized manner.
Confidentiality	Confidentiality is the security service that protects data from unauthorized disclosure. The primary confidentiality concern in most instances is unauthorized disclosure of application level data, but disclosure of the external characteristics of communication also can be a concern in some circumstances. Traffic flow confidentiality is the service that addresses this latter concern by concealing source and destination addresses, message length, or frequency of communication.
Data Origin Authentication	A security service that verifies the identity of the claimed source of data. This service is usually bundled with connectionless integrity service.
Encryption	A security mechanism used to transform data from an intelligible form (plaintext) into an unintelligible form (ciphertext), to provide confidentiality. The inverse transformation process is designated decryption.
Integrity	Integrity is a security service that ensures that modifications to data are detectable. Integrity comes in various flavors to match application requirements.
Traffic Analysis	The analysis of network traffic flow for the purpose of deducing information that is useful to an adversary. Examples of such information are frequency of transmission, the identities of the conversing parties, sizes of packets, flow identifiers, etc.
Traffic Flow Confidentiality	A security service that addresses traffic concerns by concealing source and destination addresses, message length, or frequency of communication.

- DHCP servers/port-forwarding Network Address Translation (NAT) (typically in IPv4 today one uses some form of address translation to hide the identity of the specific host within a site; only the site can be identified based on the IP address [RFC4218])
- Anti-virus screening/disinfectant software
- E-mail security

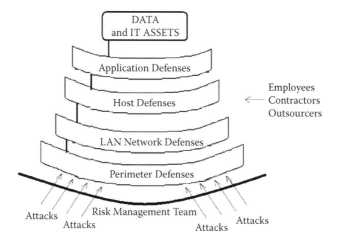

Figure 4.1   Tiered security measures.

- Instant messaging security
- Secure file deletion
- File encryption
- Folder encryption
- Content encryption
- Text encryption
- Digital signing of documents/files
- Digitally signing parts of documents
- Voice security (e.g., voice encryption mechanisms)
- Wireless security (e.g., data encryption mechanisms)
- Videoconferencing security (e.g., video encryption mechanisms)

Two types of attacks typically seen by network administrators include the following, for which protection is sought in IPv4, IPv6, and mixed environments [ICA200701]:

Exploitation attacks use maliciously crafted packets and traffic streams to identify and exploit a flaw in the programming logic of a targeted application and cause the application to fail (cease operation) or respond in an unintended manner; in particular, attackers use exploitation attacks with the expectation that the application will somehow provide them with a means to take administrative control of the target system. Such attacks are called *escalated privilege attacks*. Once an attacker gains administrative control of a system, the attacker may install malicious executables that can communicate back to an attacker's *command and control system* (C&C). The C&C can order remotely controlled systems to perform virtually any service (host a Web server, send spam, etc.).

Exploitation and attacks resulting from "gaining root or admin" on exploited or compromised systems are examples of host and network intrusions.

Flooding attacks are designed to exhaust the resources (processing, memory, or bandwidth capacity) of a targeted application, system or network, and thus deny service to users. Flooding attacks are the most commonly recognized forms of denial of service attacks and vendors call specific attention to a product's ability to block the popular variants of denial and distributed denial of service (DDoS) attacks.

(See Appendix A for additional discussion.)

In the discussion below and in the chapters that follow, the following terminology is used [RFC4218]:

Link—a communication facility or medium over which nodes can communicate at the link layer, that is, the layer immediately below IPv6. Examples are Ethernets (simple or bridged); PPP links; X.25, Frame Relay, or Asynchronous Transfer Mode (ATM) networks; and Internet (or higher) layer "tunnels," such as tunnels over IPv4 or IPv6 itself.

Interface—a node's attachment to a link.

Address—an IP layer name that has both topological significance (i.e., a locator) and identifies an interface. There may be multiple addresses per interface. Normally an address uniquely identifies an interface, but there are exceptions: the same unicast address can be assigned to multiple interfaces on the same node, and an anycast address can be assigned to different interfaces on different nodes.

Locator—an IP layer topological name for an interface or a set of interfaces. There may be multiple locators per interface.

Identifier—an IP layer identifier for an IP layer endpoint, that is, something that might be commonly referred to as a "host." The transport endpoint name is a function of the transport protocol and would typically include the IP identifier plus a port number. There might be use for having multiple identifiers per stack/per host. An identifier continues to function regardless of the state of any one interface.

Address field—the source and destination address fields in the IPv6 header. As IPv6 is currently specified, these fields carry "addresses." If identifiers and locators are separated, these fields will contain locators.

Fully Qualified Domain Name (FQDN)—A fully qualified domain name consists of a host and domain name, including the top-level domain.

4.2 Review of Firewall-Based Perimeter Security

It is now generally accepted by most organizations that "the network" cannot be trusted. Security has been a requirement for years; however, instead of controls being built into critical applications, they are typically bolted on after the fact, usually at the network layer. Firewalls are in most cases the mechanism utilized to support network security, and their notoriety and popularity have grown with their increased usage over the past several years. However, prior to firewalls being installed in almost every home and organization, the security landscape of the network was much different. It was common even for mid- to large-size organizations to be directly connected to the Internet. This allowed easy access to private networks for attackers with little effort. Attackers would probe organizations looking for open ports and then take their pick of the numerous ways they could gain access to critical assets.

Firewalls were eventually installed; this provided protection to organizations by allowing traffic to be passed or denied based on a security policy. Even with this control put in place, attackers still found it easy to gain access, as knowledge about network security and firewalls was quite limited within user organization. Firewalls were purchased and installed but typically improperly configured; this created more of a false sense of security than the protection organizations believed they had in place. Organizations realized that large network segments and hosts could be protected by perimeter firewalls and would allow security controls to be implemented quickly. The investment in this space increased and attackers found access to an organization's assets a bit more challenging. When firewalls finally became common and were configured properly, attackers discovered that open ports and unfiltered access to private networks were becoming harder to find. Attackers realized that organizations were only allowing access to services that they wanted to publish to the world, such as e-mail and Web site access. This is the point when attackers realized that they would need to start attacking applications directly. Most firewalls at that point intime were only making basic filtering decisions (some a bit more intelligent than others, as will be discussed later in this section), but access to common services had to be allowed through the firewall by the network administrator. This type of new attack challenged the approach many organizations implemented by only focusing security controls on the network. [CRU200001] [KLA199701].

Firewalls are still the basic foundation of an information security program and provide the most fundamental protection for organizations. It is widely accepted that firewalls alone are not the only mechanism needed to ensure that organizations are safe from attacks. However, it can be argued that any good information security program begins with network security, and a strong firewall infrastructure is at its core. Installing a firewall and then walking away is not going to ensure that the organization is secure; the firewall itself, whether it is hardware- or software-based, will need to be maintained. Many firewalls run as a hardened appliance but there are quite a few that run on well-known operating systems such as Solaris, Linux, or Windows. This requires that a security administrator maintain patches and configurations on the operating system, given that it is the core that runs the application. It is most important that firewall policies that are installed on the firewall are appropriate to the challenge at hand. Many organizations install a firewall and believe they are safe from attackers but pay little attention to the traffic that they are allowing to pass through the firewall, whether it be initiated from internal going outbound or from the external coming back inside the company [STA200801], [WEN200101], [TEA199901].

Figure 4.2 depicts the basic concept of a firewall.

4.2.1 Firewall Capabilities

Firewall technology and uses have gone through substantial changes and improvements over the years. However, simply defined, a firewall is a network security device that enforces an organization's security policy by approving or denying network traffic. In order for a firewall to function properly, it requires that a security administrator uses the organization's security policy to create a detailed firewall ruleset. The ruleset is what the firewall will use to examine data packets that pass through the device, and is the basis for making packet-forwarding decisions. In addition to enforcing the security policy, firewalls also have the capability to log traffic that passes through the firewall, making it a powerful security tool [WEN200101], [TEA199901].

In addition, firewalls have the following capabilities:

Network address translation
Virtual private networks
Demilitarized zones
Antispoofing

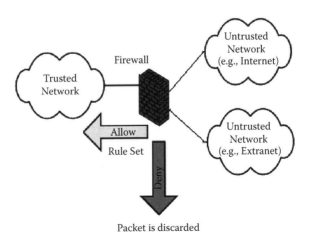

Figure 4.2 Basic arrangement.

4.2.1.1 Network Address Translation (NAT)

In a traditional IPv4 environment, NAT helps to facilitate communication between endpoints and also provides increased security functionality. NAT provides a solution to the lack of available IP addresses under the current IPv4 protocol by rewriting the contents of the IP packet header so that it appears to have come from a single (different) IP address. This capability also allows organizations to hide the details of their internal network topology by making all internal endpoints appear to come from a single IP address, typically the firewall.

Static NAT—maps a specific single address to another specific single address.
Pooled NAT—dynamically maps all specific single addresses to a pool or range of external addresses.
Port Level NAT/Hide NAT—dynamically maps all specific single internal addresses to a specific single external address. The internal address is mapped or identified by the specific external address in combination with a unique port number.

4.2.1.2 Virtual Private Network (VPN)

A Virtual Private Network (VPN) is a private network that uses a public network (usually the Internet) to connect remote sites or users together. Instead of using a dedicated, real-world connection such as a leased line, a VPN uses "virtual" connections routed through the Internet from the company's private network to the remote site or employee. See Figure 4.3.

4.2.1.3 Demilitarized Zones (DMZ)

In a world where instant communication is critical, organizations need to be able to connect with anyone and everyone. In order to make this happen, one must allow applications and services to communicate as necessary; this typically requires the implementation of a DMZ to provide public service while protecting an organization's assets. A DMZ is based on the military usage of the term that defines a demarcation zone or buffer between two networks that are untrusted (see Figure 4.4). A key capability of a firewall is to be able to create a DMZ and then control access in and out of the network protecting the public services that are offered.

4.2.1.4 Antispoofing

As discussed previously, firewalls implement security policies based on rulesets that are defined by security administrators. The core of the ruleset is the description of the network topology on the firewall so that decision can be made based on where

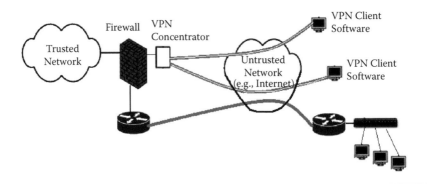

Figure 4.3   Virtual private networks.

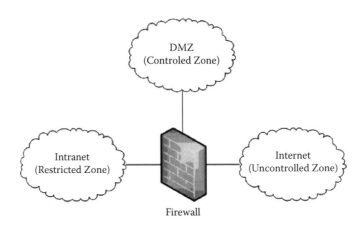

Figure 4.4.   Demilitarized zones (DMZ).

the endpoints exist; specifically, the ruleset examines IP addresses in order to establish the origination point of packets. Antispoofing is a capability some firewalls possess to ensure that an attacker cannot spoof or impersonate the source address of a connection to trick a firewall to allow a connection that should be denied. Firewalls typically implement antispoofing by checking the source address of every packet against a predefined view of the network topology that is specifically defined in the firewall. The most basic example of a spoofing attack on a firewall is to send traffic that appears to come from an internal address or an external network, thus tricking the firewall to think it is a valid corporate internal IP and allowing the traffic to pass the firewall.

4.2.2 Firewall Types

When an organization is looking to deploy strong network security, the type of firewall that is selected should be based on specific requirements. The type of assets being protected will determine the type of firewall that should be implemented. There have been multiple advancements in the firewall technology in recent years, and while there may be some niche technologies, most firewalls can now be grouped in the following categories [POR200501], [STA200801]:

Packet filter
Proxy or application level filtering
Stateful inspection

As seen in Figure 4.5, each firewall type operates at different levels of the Open Systems Interconnection Reference Model (OSIRM).

4.2.2.1 Packet Filter

Packet filter firewalls function by examining packets and focus on gathering header information to make filtering decisions. This type of firewall typically operates by only evaluating source and destination addresses and service ports. While packet-filtering firewalls do not provide sophisticated features or a high level of security, they are inexpensive and are able to handle a significant amount of traffic.

4.2.2.2 Proxy

Proxy firewalls are considered by many to be the most complex but secure firewall technology. The fundamental difference with this technology compared to packet filtering is that there is no direct communication between a client and server.

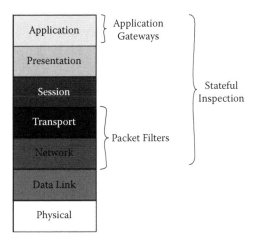

Figure 4.5　Layer coverage by different types of firewalls.

The proxy effectively acts as an intermediary between two endpoints that need to communicate and only allows connections by going through the proxy firewall.

It is generally accepted that there are two categories of proxy firewalls:

Application level proxy—operates at the application layer of the OSI model and is capable of making decisions based on specific packet payload. This offers substantial security benefits as users cannot run nonstandard services on permitted standard ports.

Circuit-level proxies—Unlike a packet-filtering firewall, a circuit-level gateway does not examine individual packets. Instead, circuit-level gateways monitor TCP or UDP sessions. Once a session has been established, it leaves the port open to allow all other packets belonging to that session to pass. The port is closed when the session is terminated. In many respects this method of packet screening resembles application gateways/proxies and adaptive proxies, but circuit-level gateways operate at the transport layer (layer 4) of the OSI model.

4.2.2.3 Stateful Inspection

Stateful inspection (also known as Dynamic Packet Filter) firewalls function by keeping track of the state of all network connections that traverse it. The firewall operates by keeping track of connections and being able to distinguish and enforce legitimate traffic based on the TCP Three-Way Handshake. This is a critical security improvement and makes it in most cases a better choice over packet-filter firewalls. Stateful inspection firewalls also evaluate much more than header information and examine traffic all the way up through the application layer of the OSI model. Performance considerations, however, are important: based on the additional packet information that is being evaluated, and considering that the state of each connection is tracked, the performance of this type of firewall technology can be an issue, and proper sizing is critical.

Deep packet inspection (or sometimes called multilayered stateful inspection) is a form of stateful inspection that builds on stateful inspection technology and further examines the data and header part of a packet. Packets are inspected from layer 2 all the way up to layer 7. Firewalls using deep packet inspection have the ability to provide additional intrusion detection and prevention capabilities. Deep packet inspection has led to the development of firewalls that consolidate multiple security functions into a single platform that is being called a Unified Threat Management firewall [POR200501]. Security functions that may be provided include the following:

Traditional stateful firewalling technology
Intrusion detection and prevention
Antivirus
Antispyware
IPsec and SSL VPN

Content filtering
Web application firewalling technology

4.2.3 *Firewall Architecture*

Just as important as selecting the proper type of firewall to be implemented is the placement of firewalls within the organization's network. Prior to having a solid strategy as to where to install firewalls by defining security architecture zones, most organizations looked to deploy firewalls at key perimeter points, specifically between untrusted Internet and vendor network borders. As the security industry has matured and the need increased for security of critical assets, additional segmentation has been extended to internal corporate networks. Even though for the most part the internal network is considered trusted, in many cases there is a need for additional security policies to be enforced, and a layered network defense must be implemented. As described previously, firewalls were typically installed to protect an organization's network perimeter. While there are many variations, the two basic firewall architectures that are most commonly used today are as follows [RAN199301]:

Dual homed firewall. This configuration, also known as a bastion host, is typically the most common as it is simple yet secure. The firewall acts as the dividing line and enforcement point between two networks, such as an organization's trusted internal network and the untrusted Internet. The firewall is positioned to intercept all traffic coming in and out and is typically configured to allow very little or no traffic at all into the trusted network.

Screened subnet. This configuration creates an isolated network segment also, called a DMZ, that the access into and out of can be explicitly controlled and monitored. A screened subnet can be created using multiple interfaces (at least three) on a single firewall, or also can be implemented by using multiple firewalls to create the environment. For protection of critical assets, using multiple firewalls is recommended, and in some cases it may provide benefit to use multiple firewall vendors.

Security practitioners still contend that implementing defense in depth and using the principle of least privilege for access control is critical when determining an organization's security architecture. Firewalls should be deployed between each of the security zones defined for your organization or as described in Chapter 1 and Figure 1.11. This provides security administrators the granularity and more flexibility to implement the required controls based on the criticality of the assets.

Just as critical as the type of firewall and the placement is ensuring that the appropriate ruleset and security policies are applied to the firewall. Unless a security administrator understands the type of traffic and flows that should be allowed on a particular network, the firewall may just provide a false sense of security. This is true in any environment, whether it be IPv4 or IPv6. Given that security has been installed and typically only managed at perimeters up until this point will force organizations to look at ways to enhance their architectures with IPv6. In Chapter 7, we review hybrid firewall deployments in an IPv6 environment and also include a look at the importance of host-based firewalls. Most firewalls with IPv6 support have separate rulesets for IPv6 and IPv4. It follows that, regardless of the environment (pure IPv4, pure IPv6, mixed IPv4/IPv6), these rulesets must be coordinated and consistent to be properly managed and to avoid an unintended security exposure.

4.3 IPv6 Areas of Security Concerns: Addresses

This section starts the discussion on IPv6 security, which continues over several chapters. While IPsec and other security protocols developed by the IETF operate with both IPv4 and IPv6, not all existing IPv4 systems incorporate these mechanisms, and modifications to these systems could be costly, particularly in very large deployment environments (for example, in global or government applications). Given the choice of either retrofitting these capabilities onto the IPv4 infrastructure or deploying a new IPv6 infrastructure (where IPsec is considered mandatory from the get-go), the latter choice may be more strategic and more effective in the long term. According to proponents, transitioning to IPv6 provides stakeholders a chance to significantly modify and enhance their current enterprise architecture around the capabilities of IPv6. In fact, it provides the opportunity to implement new security architectures and could significantly improve an organization's overall security posture [JUN200801]. However, as we noted in Chapter 1, since many network administrators have yet to take advantage of IPv6, they may be unaware of IPv6 traffic that has tunneled into their networks. Practitioners observe that "black hats" often have deeper expertise and better tools than many "white hats" and security professionals trying to protect their networks [WAR200401].

4.3.1 IPv6 Addressing Security

As we have seen, IPv6 enjoys a very large address space with a /64 usually being the smallest block for a Local Area Network (LAN). This large address space can be beneficial from a security perspective because detailed address and port scanning a subnet *can* be a lot more difficult and time consuming.

As noted, the IPv6 address has two parts: a subnet prefix representing the network to which the interface is connected, and a local identifier. IPv6 stateless address auto-configuration facilitates IP address management, but raises some concerns since the Ethernet address is encoded in the low-order 64 bits of the IPv6 address. This could potentially be used to track a host as it moves around the network, using different

Internet Service Providers (ISPs), and so forth. IPv6 supports temporary addresses that allow applications to control whether they need long-lived IPv6 addresses or desire the improved privacy of using temporary addresses [RFC4218].

Autoconfiguration operates as follows at a high level: For an Ethernet device, the local identifier is usually derived from the EUI-48 Media Access Control (MAC) (as described in Chapter 3, the EUI-64 standard allows one to stretch IEEE 802 addresses from 48 to 64 bits by inserting the 16 bits 0xFFFE at the 24th bit of the IEEE 802*.) To automatically create a link-local address, the system prepends the well-known prefix FE80::/64 to the identifier just described—the subnet prefix is a fixed 64-bit length for all current definitions. During the initialization phase of IPv6 NICs, this process allows the system to build automatically a link-local address. This address is associated with the interface and tagged "tentative." After uniqueness verification,[†] this system can communicate with other IPv6 hosts on that link without any other manual operation [DON200401]. Obviously, in order to exchange information over the Internet, it is necessary to obtain a global prefix. Usually the identifier built during the first step of the automatic link-local autoconfiguration process is appended to this global prefix.[‡] Generally, global prefixes are made available by ISPs.

---

* Example: transforming MAC address 00-0C-29-C2-52-FF using the EUI-64 standards leads to 00-0C-29-FF-FE-C2-52-FF. Then, it is necessary (RFC 3513) to invert the universal bit ("u" bit is set to 0) in the 6th position of the first octet. The result is 020C:29FF:FEC2:52FF.

† Before final association, the system needs to verify the uniqueness of the autogenerated address on the link (in case that some vendors have shipped batches of cards with the same MAC addresses.) This is the goal of the Duplicate Address Detection (DAD) phase. A node that intends to assign a new address to one of its interfaces first runs the DAD procedure to verify that no other node is using the same address. As the rules forbid the use of an address until it has been found unique, no higher-layer traffic is possible until this procedure has been completed. Thus, preventing attacks against DAD can help ensure the availability of communications for the node in question [RFC3971]. The system sends ICMPv6 packets on the link where this detection has to occur. Those packets contain Neighbor Solicitation messages. Their source address is the undefined address "::" and the target address is the tentative address. A node already using this tentative address replies with a Neighbor Advertisement message. In that case, the address cannot be assigned to the interface. If there is no response, it is assumed that the address is unique and can be assigned to the interface. This phase removes the "tentative" tag and formally assigns the address to the network interface. The system can now communicate with its neighbors on the link.

‡ IPv6 routers consistently advertise (every ten seconds or so) information on the links to which they are connected using ICMPv6 Router Advertisement (RA) messages (these sent to multicast group FF02::1). All the systems on a segment must belong to a specific group; hence, nodes configured via autoconfiguration analyze these messages to determine if they contain any routing prefix(es) for this segment. Upon reception of an RA message, a node that used autoconfiguring but not already configured with the corresponding global address will prepend the advertised prefix to the unique identifier built previously.

The EUI-48-to-EUI-64 transform is simple to implement; however, as stated above, it gives rise to a security concern. Because a MAC address follows the interface it is attached to, the identifier of an IPv6 address does not change with the physical location of the Internet connection. Hence, it is possible to trace the movements of a laptop or other mobile IPv6 device. This can be mitigated given that RFC 3041 allows the generation of a random identifier with a limited lifetime. Considering the fact that the IPv6 architecture permits multiple suffixes per interface, a single network interface is *assigned two global addresses*, one derived from the MAC address and one from a random identifier. A typical policy for use of these two addresses would be to keep the MAC-derived global address for inbound connections and the random address for outbound connections (a reason for not using it for inbound connections is the need to update the DNS just as frequently as it changes). Such a system, with two different global addresses—one of which changes regularly—becomes difficult to trace. (For example, Microsoft enables this feature on Windows XP and Windows Server 2003. The random-identifier-based global addresses of Microsoft systems have the address type "temporary." EUI-64 global addresses have type "public." [DON200401].) Note that IPv6 routers are usually manually configured.

In summary, autoconfiguration (self-generated addresses) may present some security risks since breaking into the LAN typically implies having "insider privileges." Autoconfiguration makes the creation of rogue gateways on IPv6 relatively simple [WAR200401]. RFC 2462-based autoconfig addresses can be "stolen" by others, thereby resulting in Denial of Service (DoS). RFC 3041 allows randomized host identifiers addresses, but these cannot have pre-established IPsec keys and may make ingress filtering harder.

The use of a Crypto-Generated Address (CGA) as defined in SEcure Neighbor Discovery (SEND, [RFC3971]) may also possibly be deployed to mitigate this risk. CGAs are used to make sure that the sender of a Neighbor Discovery (ND) message is the "owner" of the claimed address. A public-private key pair is generated by all nodes before they can claim an address. CGA is a technique whereby an IPv6 address of a node is cryptographically generated by using a one-way hash function from the node's public key and some other parameters. Crypto-generated addresses can be bound to a public key. To accomplish this, each node creates a Public Key (PK) and a Private (secret) Key (SK). To derive its IPv6 address using a cryptographically generated interface identifier (CG IID) the node proceeds as follows:

```
CGA = 64-bit prefix + 64-bit_hash_function(PK)
```

(See Table 4.4 for definitions related to hashing [MIN200601].) In effect, the interface identifier is equivalent to its PK. A node "proves" its right to use its CGA by signing with SK.

In a dual-stack mode, the device needs to track multiple prefixes simultaneously. It should be a policy that to map from old (IPv4) to new (IPv6) addresses permissions must be granted administratively.

Table 4.4 Hashing Functions

Hash	A fixed-length cryptographic output of variables. Often used as term describing the output of a hash function.
Hash Function	An algorithm (e.g., Message Digest 2 (MD2), MD4, MD5, Secure Hash Algorithm One (SHA-1)) that computes a value based on a data object (such as a message or file, which is usually variable length and possibly very large), thereby mapping the data object to a smaller data object (the "hash result") which is usually a fixed-size value [RFC2828]. This (mathematical) function maps values from a large (possibly very large) domain into a smaller range. A "good" hash function is such that the results of applying the function to a (large) set of values in the domain will be evenly distributed (and apparently at random) over the range [ITU199001]. The kind of hash function needed for security applications is called a cryptographic hash function, an algorithm for which it is computationally infeasible to find either a data object that maps to a prespecified hash result (the "one-way" property) or two data objects that map to the same hash result (the "collision-free" property) [RFC2828]. Typical uses of hash functions are to use a one-way hash function to protect passwords in storage or to produce cryptographic message digests of documents (in order to ensure data integrity).
Hash function Reliability	Message Digest 4 (MD4), Message Digest 5 (MD5), and Secure Hash Algorithm One (SHA-1) have been broken. MD4 and MD5 should be considered insecure. SHA-1 is still widely used, although its stronger counterparts, SHA-256, SHA-384, and SHA-512 are likely to replace it in the future [SSH200601].
Hash Result	The output (result) of a hash function.
Hashing	The act of putting data through a hash function.
Hashing for Message Authentication (HMAC)	A keyed hash that can be based on any iterated cryptographic hash (e.g., Message Digest 5 (MD5) or Secure Hash Algorithm One (SHA-1)) [RFC2104], [RFC2828]. The cryptographic strength of HMAC depends on the properties of the selected cryptographic hash [RFC2202], [RFC2403], [RFC2404].

(Continued)

Table 4.4   Hashing Functions (Continued)

Hashing for Message Authentication (HMAC)-Based One Time Password (HOTP) algorithm	A proposed algorithm to generate one-time password values, based on keyed-hash message authentication code (HMAC). The proposed algorithm can be used across a wide range of network applications ranging from remote Virtual Private Network (VPN) access, wireless logon, to transaction-oriented Web applications. Intended as a common and shared algorithm that will facilitate adoption of two-factor authentication on the Internet by enabling interoperability across commercial and open-source implementations [MRA200401].

4.3.2 IPv6 Anycast Address Security

There are also security issues related to anycast addresses. For example, reserved anycast addresses may provide an attacker with a well-known target (however, globally reachable anycast is only defined for routers and not end systems). Since no authorization mechanism exists for anycast destination addresses, it is possible to be subjected to spoofing and masquerade. It is difficult to use IPsec since security associations have to be set up in advance and IPsec associations need specific destination addresses.

The sections that follow discuss other key IPv6 areas of focus from a security perspective.

4.4 Documented Issues for IPv6 Security

As we have seen thus far, IPv6 has clear advantages over IPv4, but organizations must recognize that migration is recommended but it is not a silver bullet to address all security issues. It is imperative that a strong information security program has been implemented and proper risk assessments are conducted to manage the transition and evaluate controls required for an organization's assets. More and more vulnerabilities that are being disclosed are in specific applications, whether they be off the shelf or homegrown, and are not related to weaknesses in specific network protocols. In addition, IPv6 by itself does not protect against misconfigurations of networks and servers, nor will it provide adequate protection for information technology assets that have not been hardened, that are missing patches, are poorly designed, or generally lack the required security controls.

According to the Open Source Vulnerability Database (OSVDB), a project that maintains a master copy of security vulnerabilities, there have been 51 documented IPv6 security vulnerabilities as of April 06, 2008 [OSV200802].* Initially, this

---

* The list of issues presented here is not purported to be exhaustive.

may appear to be a significant amount, but given that IPv6 has been available and used for the past 15 years, this number actually appears to be quite low. OSVDB has the first documented IPv6 vulnerability being disclosed on December 07, 2000 [OSV200001]. Given that the inclusion of IPv6 support in many vendors' products has been slow to progress, this could potentially be the justification. Even with the protocol providing increased security by introducing IPv6 functionality, vendors must implement new code into their existing products. It is important for organizations to recognize that the root vulnerabilities are not necessarily in the IPv6 protocol but in the vendor product deployments. Organizations should conduct a full risk assessment on any vendors, including products and versions, prior to implementing their IPv6 functionalities.

IPv6 security weaknesses due to poor vendor implementation have been documented and they have been exploited; these weaknesses have the potential for serious impact. A high profile IPv6 exploit was demonstrated at the Black Hat security conference in 2005 [EVE200506]. The vulnerability allowed an attacker to gain full access to a Cisco device from a remote endpoint [OSV200501]. At the time this issue was disclosed, the initial workaround suggested for most network administrators was to disable support for IPv6 (IPv6 support is often—but not always—enabled on most versions of IOS by default). If the IPv6 protocol were more widely deployed, this solution would not have been sufficient. In addition, this event was significant as it was the first time that it was demonstrated that a remote attacker could completely compromise a Cisco device. Additional high profile IPv6 vulnerabilities have been disclosed in late 2007 and early 2008. Cisco, Apple, and Juniper have all had issues that have a potential impact that range from a DoS to much more serious vulnerabilities that allow remote code execution [OSV200801], [OSV2007101], [OSV2007102].

IPv6 implementations and migrations, specifically when they affect an organization's most valuable assets or are applied in the core backbone of Internet's infrastructure, have the potential to create havoc and cause serious impact. At press time, there have not been documented security vulnerabilities in the IPv6 protocol itself. In April 2004 a vulnerability was discovered in many vendor implementations of TCP/IPv4 (specifically RFC 793) that allowed a denial of service due to a blind reset spoofing attack [OSV200401]. This vulnerability allowed attackers to reset connections including core networks within seconds and had the potential to bring down or massively interrupt the entire Internet.

RFC 793 utilizes sequence checking to ensure proper ordering of received packets. RFC 793 requires that sequence numbers are checked against the window size before accepting data or control flags as valid. RFC 793 also specifies that RST (reset the connection) control flags should be processed immediately, without waiting for out-of-sequence packets to arrive. Furthermore, RFC 793 allows a TCP implementation to verify both sequence and acknowledgement numbers prior to accepting an RST control flag as valid. No TCP stack implementation tested at the time implemented checking of both sequence and acknowledgement. All tested

TCP stacks verified only the sequence number. This allowed connections to be reset with dramatically less effort than previously believed. This risk is compounded by the easy prediction of source port selection used in TCP connections.

References

[AMI200801] Amir, E. *The case for deep packet inspection. IT business edge*. http://www.itbusinessedge.com/item/?ci=35275.

[CHE200301] Cheswick, W. R., S. M. Bellovin, and A. D. Rubin. *Firewalls and Internet security: Repelling the wily attacker*. 2nd edition. Boston: Addison-Wesley, 2003.

[CRU200001] Crume, Jeff. *Inside Internet security*. Boston: Addison-Wesley, 2000.

[DON200401] Donzé, F. IPv6 autoconfiguration, *The Internet Protocol Journal* 7, no. 2 (June 2004).

[EVE200506] Evers, Joris. *Attackers rally behind Cisco flaw finder*. http://www.news.com/Attackers-rally-behind-Cisco-flaw-finder/2100-1002_3-5812044.html?tag=item.

[GJO200401] Gjøsteen, K. Subgroup membership problems and public key cryptosystems, Dr. ing. Thesis, Department of Mathematical Sciences, Norwegian University of Science and Technology, 2004.

[GOV200801] *U.S. National Information Systems Security Glossary, 2008.*

[ICA200701] ICANN Security and Stability Advisory Committee (SSAC), *Survey of IPv6 support in commercial firewalls*, Oct. 2007.

[INF200801] *Infosec@UGA*, The University of Georgia, Office of Information Security, Athens, GA, 30602-1911, 2008.

[ITU199001] International Telecommunications Union–Telecommunication Standardization Sector (formerly CCITT). Recommendation X.509, *Information technology—open systems interconnection—The directory: Authentication framework*. (Equivalent to ISO 9594-8.)

[JUN200801] *An IPv6 Security Guide for U.S. Government Agencies—Executive Summary*, The IPv6 World Report Series, Volume 4, February 2008, Juniper Networks, Sunnyvale, CA, www.juniper.net

[KLA199701] Klander, Lars. *Attacker proof*. Gulf Publishing Company, 1997.

[MIC200801] Microsoft. *Using IPv6 and Teredo*. Microsoft TechNet. http://www.microsoft.com/technet/network/ipv6/ipv6_teredo.mspx.

[MIN200601] Minoli, D., and J. Codovana. *Minoli-Cordovana authoritative computer and network security dictionary*. New York: Wiley, 2006.

[MRA200401] M'Raihi, D., M. Bellare, F. Hoornaert, D. Naccache, and O. Ranen. *HOTP: An HMAC-based one time password algorithm*. IETF Internet Draft draft-mraihi-oath-hmac-otp-03.txt, Oct. 2004.

[NIC200001] Nichols, R. K. *Defending your digital assets*. New York: McGraw-Hill, 2000.

[OSV200001] Open Source Vulnerability Database (OSVDB). *KAME sin6_scope_id Mismatch IPv6 address spoofing disclosed: Dec. 7, 2000*. http://osvdb.org/7411.

[OSV200401] Open Source Vulnerability Database (OSVDB). *TCP/IP sequence prediction blind reset spoofing DoS, disclosed: Apr. 20, 2004*. http://osvdb.org/4030.

[OSV200501] Open Source Vulnerability Database (OSVDB). *Cisco IOS crafted IPv6 packet remote code execution disclosed: July 27, 2005*. http://osvdb.org/18332.

[OSV2007101] Open Source Vulnerability Database (OSVDB). Apple Mac OS X networking component crafted IPv6 packets remote code execution disclosed: Nov. 15, 2007. http://osvdb.org/40670.

[OSV2007102] Open Source Vulnerability Database (OSVDB). Juniper JUNOS IPv6 traffic handling unspecified remote overflow dos disclosed: Dec. 14, 2007. http://osvdb.org/39158.

[OSV200801] Open Source Vulnerability Database (OSVDB). Cisco IOS crafted IPv6 UDP delivery remote DoS, disclosed: Mar. 26, 2008. http://osvdb.org/43797.

[OSV200802] Open Source Vulnerability Database (OSVDB). http://www.osvdb.org/.

[POR200501] Porter, T. The perils of deep packet inspection. Jan. 11, 2005. http://www.securityfocus.com/infocus/1817.

[RAN199301] Ranum, M. J. *Thinking about firewalls.* 1993. http://www.vtcif.telstra.com.au/pub/docs/security/ThinkingFirewalls/ThinkingFirewalls.html.

[REN200701] Renard, K. *Security issues in IPv6.* San Diego, CA: WareOnEarth Communications Inc., 2007.

[RFC2104] Krawczyk, H., M. Bellare, and R. Canetti. Request for Comments: 2104, HMAC: Keyed-Hashing for Message Authentication, RFC 2104, Feb. 1997.

[RFC2202] Cheng P., and R. Glenn. Request for Comments: 2202, Test Cases for HMAC-MD5 and HMAC- SHA-1, RFC 2202, Sep. 1997.

[RFC2401] Kent, S., and R. Atkinson. Request for Comments: 2401, Security Architecture for the Internet Protocol, RFC 2401, Nov. 1998.

[RFC2403] Madson, C., and R. Glenn. Request for Comments: 2403, The Use of HMAC-MD5-96 within ESP and AH, RFC 2403, Nov. 1998.

[RFC2404] Madson, C., and R. Glenn. Request for Comments: 2404, The Use of HMAC-SHA-1-96 within ESP and AH, RFC 2404, Nov. 1998.

[RFC2828] Shirey, R. Internet Security Glossary, RFC 2828, May 2000. Copyright (C) The Internet Society (2000). All Rights Reserved. This document and translations of it may be copied and furnished to others, and derivative works that comment on or otherwise explain it or assist in its implementation may be prepared, copied, published and distributed, in whole or in part, without restriction of any kind, provided that the above copyright notice and this paragraph are included on all such copies and derivative works.

[RFC3971] Arkko, J., ed. Request for Comments: 3971, SEcure Neighbor Discovery (SEND), RFC 3971, Mar. 2005.

[RFC4218] Nordmark, E., and T. Li. Request for Comments: 4218, Threats Relating to IPv6 Multihoming Solutions, RFC 4218, Oct. 2005.

[SSH200601] *Cryptography white papers*, Valimotie 17, FI-00380 Helsinki, Finland.

[STA200801] Staff. *An introduction to network firewalls and the firewall selection process.* The Missouri Research and Education Network (MOREnet), White paper. http://www.more.net/technical/netserv/tcpip/firewalls/.

[STO200201] Stoneburner, G., Alice Goguen, and Alexis Feringa. *Risk management guide for information technology systems: Recommendations of the national institute of standards and technology*, Special Publication 800-30, July 2002, Computer Security Division, Information Technology Laboratory, National Institute of Standards and Technology, Gaithersburg, MD 20899-8930. [This document may be used by non-governmental organizations on a voluntary basis. It is not subject to copyright.]

[TEA199901] Teare, Diane. *Designing Cisco Networks.* Cisco Press, 1999.

[TIP200001] Tipton, H. F., and M. Krause. *Information Security Management Handbook* (4th edition). Auerbach, 2000.

[WAR200401] Warfield, M. H. *Security implications of IPv6.* X-Force, Internet Security Systems, Inc. (ISS), 16th Annual FIRST Conference on Computer Security Incident Handling, June 13–18, 2004, Budapest, Hungary. www.iss.net, http://www.first.org/conference/2004/papers/c06.pdf.

[WEN200101] Wenstrom, Michael. *Managing Cisco network security.* Cisco Press, 2001.

Appendix A: Risks and Vulnerabilities

This section, based directly on RFC 4218 [RFC4218], identifies some areas of possible security concerns—this is only a partial list. Typically, commercial environments tend to be more concerned with intrusion into the intranet and preventing (potential) corruption of data confidentiality or integrity. Government and military applications also worry about data redirection and availability (however, sophisticated businesses should worry about these too).

Static Session Hijacking

An entity that wishes to communicate (over the Internet or in a private IP network) either starts with an FQDN, which it looks up in the DNS, or already has an IP address from somewhere. For the FQDN to perform IP address lookup, the sender effectively places trust in the DNS. Once it has the IP address, the application places trust in the routing system delivering packets to that address. Applications that use security mechanisms, such as IPsec, have the ability to bind an address or FQDN to cryptographic keying material. Compromising the DNS or routing system can result in packets being dropped or delivered to an attacker, but since the attacker does not possess the encryption keys, the application will not trust the attacker, and the attacker cannot decrypt the data received.

At the responding (non-initiating) end of communication, one finds that the security configurations used by different applications fall into five classes, where a single application might use different classes of configurations for different types of communication.

1. Using the set of public content servers. These systems provide data to any and all systems and are not particularly concerned with confidentiality, as they make their content available to all. However, they are interested in data integrity and denial of service attacks. Having someone manipulate the results of a search engine, for example, or prevent certain systems from reaching a search engine would be a serious security issue. There are also public content servers that provide services available to any and all systems but must protect confidential information. They implement the appropriate level of authentication and authorization access controls to ensure data is only available to appropriate users.

2. Using existing IP source addresses from outside of their immediate local site as a means of authentication without any form of verification. Today, with source IP address spoofing and TCP sequence number guessing as rampant attacks, such applications are effectively opening themselves for public connectivity and are reliant on other systems, such as firewalls, for overall security.

3. Receiving existing IP source addresses, but attempting some verification using the DNS, effectively using the FQDN for access control. (This is typically done by performing a reverse lookup from the IP address, followed by a forward lookup and verifying that the IP address matches one of the addresses returned from the forward lookup.) These applications are already subject to a number of attacks using techniques like source address spoofing and TCP sequence number guessing since an attacker, knowing this is the case, can simply create a DoS attack using a forged source address that has authentic DNS records.

4. Using cryptographic security techniques to provide nonrepudiation by implementing both a strong identity for the peer and data integrity with or without confidentiality. Such systems are still potentially vulnerable to denial of service attacks.

5. Using cryptographic security techniques, but without strong identity (such as opportunistic IPsec). Thus, data integrity with or without confidentiality is provided when communicating with an unknown/unauthenticated principal. Just like the first category above, such applications cannot perform access control based on network layer information since they do not know the identity of the peer. However, they might perform access control using higher-level notions of identity. The availability of IPsec (and similar solutions) together with channel bindings allows protocols (which, in themselves, are vulnerable to man-in-the-middle (MITM) attacks) to operate with a high level of confidentiality in the security of the identification of the peer. A typical example is the Remote Direct Data Placement Protocol (RDDP), which, when used with opportunistic IPsec, works well if channel bindings are available. Channel bindings provide a link between the IP-layer identification and the application protocol identification.

Redirection Attacks

Next, we enumerate some of the redirection attacks that are possible. If routing can be compromised, packets for any destination can be redirected to any location. This can be done by injecting a long prefix into global routing, thereby causing the longest match algorithm to deliver packets to the attacker. Similarly, DNS can be compromised, and a change can be made to an advertised resource record to advertise a different IP address for a hostname, effectively taking over that hostname. Any system that is along the path from the source to the destination host can be compromised and used to redirect traffic. Systems may be added to the best path to accomplish this attack. In general, these attacks work only when the attacker is on the path at the time it is performing the attack. However, in some cases it is possible for an attacker to create a DoS attack that remains at least some time after the attacker has moved off the path. An example of this is an attacker that uses Address Resolution

Protocol (ARP) or ND spoofing while on path to either insert itself or send packets to a black hole (a non-existent L2 address). After the attacker moves away, the ARP/ND entries will remain in the caches in the neighboring nodes for some amount of time (a minute or so in the case of ARP but it may depend on the configuration). This will result in packets continuing to be black-holed until the ARP entry is flushed. Finally, the hosts themselves that terminate the connection can also be compromised and can perform functions that were not intended by the end user. All of these kinds of protocol attacks are the subject of ongoing work to secure them (DNSsec, security for BGP, Secure ND, and routing protocol authentication).

Existing transport layer protocols, such as TCP, use the IP addresses as the identifiers for the communication. In the absence of ingress filtering, the IP layer allows the sender to use an arbitrary source address. This requires that the transport protocols or applications have protection against malicious senders injecting bogus packets into the packet stream between two communicating peers. If this protection can be circumvented, then it is possible for an attacker to cause harm without necessarily needing to redirect the return packets. There are various levels of protection in different transport protocols. For instance, in general TCP packets have to contain a sequence that falls in the receiver's window to be accepted. If the TCP initial sequence numbers are random, then it is very hard for an off-path attacker to guess the sequence number close enough for it to belong to the window, and as a result be able to inject a packet into an existing connection. How hard this is depends on the size of the available window, whether the port numbers are also predictable, and the lifetime of the connection. Note that there is ongoing work to strengthen TCP's protection against this broad class of attacks, but this has been the source of denial service attacks in recent years. IPsec provides cryptographically strong mechanisms that prevent attackers, on or off path, from injecting packets once the security associations have been established. When ingress filtering is deployed between the potential attacker and the path between the communicating peers, it can prevent the attacker from using the peer's IP address as source. In that case, the packet injection will fail.

Denial of Service (Flooding Attacks)

There are several ways for an attacker to use a redirection mechanism to launch DoS attacks that cannot easily be traced to the attacker. Reflection without amplification can be accomplished by an attacker sending a TCP SYN packet to a well-known server with a spoofed source address; the resulting TCP SYN ACK packet will be sent to the spoofed source address. Devices on the path between two communicating entities can also launch DoS attacks. For example, if A is communicating with B, then A can try to overload the path from B to A. If TCP is used, A could do this by sending ACK packets for data that it has not yet received (but it suspects B has already sent) so that B would send at a rate that would cause persistent congestion on the path towards A. Such an attack would seem self-destructive since A would only make its own corner of the network suffer by overloading the path from the Internet towards A. At first glance one would question whether an attacker could generate enough traffic in order cause a denial of service. However, with increased bandwidth available by broadband connectivity (cable modem, DSL, etc) and the usage of botnets, this attack is a potential threat.

Address Privacy

Today there is limited ability to track a host as it uses the Internet because in some cases, such as dialup connectivity, the host will acquire different IPv4 addresses each time it connects. However, with increasing use of broadband connectivity, such as DSL or cable, even though these technologies also use dynamic addresses, it is becoming more likely that the host will maintain the same IPv4 over time. Should a host move around in today's Internet, for instance, by visiting WiFi hotspots, it will be configured with a different IPv4 address at each location.

A common practice in IPv4 today is to use some form of address translation. This effectively hides the identity of the specific host within a site; only the site can be identified based on the IP address. In the cases where it is desirable to maintain connectivity as a host moves around, whether using layer 2 technology or Mobile IPv4, the IPv4 address will remain constant during the movement (otherwise the connections would break). Thus, there is somewhat of a fundamental choice today between seamless connectivity during movement and increased address privacy. IPv6 stateless address autoconfiguration raises some concerns since the Ethernet address is encoded in the low-order 64 bits of the IPv6 address. This could potentially be used to track a host as it moves around the network, using different ISPs, and so forth.

Cause Packets to Be Sent to the Attacker

An attacker might want to receive the flow of packets, for instance to be able to inspect or modify the payload or to be able to apply cryptographic analysis to cryptographically protected payload, using redirection attacks. Note that such attacks are always possible today if an attacker is on the path between two communicating parties; hence, the bulk of these concerns relate to off-path attackers.

"Classic" Redirection Attack

While A and B are communicating, X might send packets to B and claim: "Hi, I'm A, send my packets to my new location," where the location is really X's location. "Standard" solutions to this include requiring that the host requesting redirection somehow be verified to be the same host as the initial host that established communication. However, the burdens of such verification must not be onerous, or the redirection requests themselves can be used as a DoS attack. To prevent this type of attack, a solution would need some mechanism that B can use to verify whether a locator belongs to A before B starts using that locator, and be able to do this when multiple locators are assigned to A.

Time-Shifting Attack

The term "time-shifting attack" is used to describe an attacker's ability to perform an attack after no longer being on the path. Thus, the attacker would have been on the path at some point in time, snooping or modifying packets; and later, when the attacker is no longer on the path, it launches the attack. In the current Internet, it is not possible to perform such attacks to redirect packets. But for some time after moving away, the attacker can cause a DoS attack, for example, by leaving a bogus ARP entry in the nodes on the path, or by forging TCP Reset packets based on having seen the TCP Initial Sequence Numbers when it was on the path.

Cause Packets to Be Sent to a Black Hole

This is also a variant of the classic redirection attack. The difference is that the new location is a locator that is nonexistent or unreachable. Thus, the effect is that sending packets to the new locator causes the packets to be dropped by the network somewhere and has the potential to cause a denial of service.

Third Party Denial-of-Service Attacks

An attacker can use the ability to perform redirection to cause overload on an unrelated third party. For instance, if A and B are communicating, then the attacker X might be able to convince A to send the packets intended for B to some third node C. A third party DoS attack might be against the resources of a particular host, or it might be against the network infrastructure towards a particular IP address prefix, by overloading the routers or links even though there is no host at the address being targeted.

This discussion from RFC 4218 identifies some of the issues that need to be addressed by IPv6 network planners.

Chapter 5

Basic IPv6 Security Considerations

Introduction

This chapter continues the discussion on IPv6 security that we started in Chapter 4. The topics of Flows, Neighbor Discovery, and routing headers are covered.

5.1 IPv6 Flow Labels Issues

RFC 3697 defines in IPv6 Flow Labels. The 20-bit Flow Label field in the IPv6 header is used by a source to label packets of a flow. A flow is a sequence of packets sent from a particular source to a particular unicast, anycast, or multicast destination that the source desires to label as a flow. Flows are associated with a source and destination address pair. A flow could consist of all packets in a specific transport connection or a media stream; however, a flow is not necessarily mapped one-to-one to a transport connection. The usage of the 3-tuple of the Flow Label and the Source and Destination Address fields enables efficient IPv6 flow classification, where only IPv6 main header fields in fixed positions are used.* The minimum level of IPv6 flow support consists of labeling the flows. IPv6 source nodes supporting

---

* Traditionally, flow classifiers have been based on the 5-tuple of the source and destination addresses, ports, and the transport protocol type. However, some of these fields may be unavailable due to either fragmentation or encryption, or locating them past a chain of IPv6 option headers may be inefficient.

the flow labeling must be able to label known flows (e.g., Transmission Control Protocol [TCP] connections, application streams), even if the node itself would not require any flow-specific treatment. Doing this enables load spreading and receiver oriented resource reservations, for example. Packet classifiers use the triplet of Flow Label, Source Address, and Destination Address fields to identify which flow a particular packet belongs to. Packets are processed in a flow-specific manner by the nodes that have been set up with flow-specific state [RFC3697].

The security issues raised by the use of a flow include the potential for denial-of-service attacks and the possibility of theft of service by unauthorized traffic. Also, there is no authorization mechanism and there are issues with tunneling via IPsec. Inspection of unencrypted Flow Labels by an intruder may allow some forms of traffic analysis* by revealing some structure of the underlying communications. Even if the Flow Label were encrypted, its presence as a constant value in a fixed position might assist traffic analysis and crypto analysis. In addition, if Flow Labels were to be encrypted, many devices would not be able to read the information to assist with traffic shaping. It is important for security administrators to understand that firewalls cannot trust Flow Labels for decisions.

Denial-of-Service Attacks. Because the mapping of network traffic to flow-specific treatment is triggered by the IP addresses and Flow Label value of the IPv6 header, an intruder may be able to obtain better service by modifying the IPv6 header or by injecting packets with false addresses or labels. This can also give rise to a denial-of-service attack as the possibility exists for a large amount of malicious traffic to be sent with a high priority. A device would then prioritize the malicious traffic and this could potentially impact valid traffic on the network. The treatment of IP headers by nodes is typically unverified in the IPv6 environment and there is no guarantee that Flow Labels sent by a node follow the syntactically correct form specified by the RFCs. Therefore, any assumptions made by the network about header fields such as Flow Labels should be limited to the extent that the upstream nodes are explicitly trusted. Because flows are identified by the 3-tuple of the Flow Label and the Source and Destination Addresses, the risk of theft or denial of service introduced by the Flow Label is related to the risk of theft or denial of service by address spoofing. An intruder who can forge an address is also likely to be able to forge a label, and vice versa. Refer to RFC 3697 [RFC3697] for more details.

IPsec Issues. Note that the IPsec protocol does not include the IPv6 header's Flow Label in any of its cryptographic calculations (in the case of tunnel mode, it is the outer IPv6 header's Flow Label that is not included). Hence, modification of the Flow Label by a network node has no effect on IPsec end-to-end security,

---

* Traffic Analysis is the analysis of network traffic flow in an attempt to extract information that is useful to an intruder. Examples include frequency of transmission, the identities of the conversing parties, sizes of packets, flow identifiers, etc.

because it cannot cause any IPsec integrity check to fail.* As a consequence, IPsec does not provide any defense against an intruder's modification of the Flow Label (i.e., a man-in-the-middle attack). Refer to RFC 3697 [RFC3697] for more details.

5.2 ICMPv6 Issues

Internet Control Message Protocol (ICMP) Version 6 (ICMPv6) plays a key role in IPv6. Capabilities implemented with ICMPv6 include:

Address autoconfiguration
Duplicate address detection
Echo request and echo reply
Error notifications
Neighbor reachability and address resolution
PMTU (Path Maximum Transmission Unit) discovery
Redirect
Router and prefix discovery
Router renumbering

Broadcast amplification is a concern in IPv4 networks. The IPv6 specification removes the concept of dedicated broadcast from the protocol and specifies specific language in RFC 2463 to mitigate these types of attacks by specifying the following [KAE200601]:

"ICMPv6 messages should not be generated as a response to a packet with an IPv6 multicast destination address, a link-layer multicast address, or a link-layer broadcast address."

Security considerations include the following [REN200701]:

Are Router Advertisements coming from an authorized router?
Are there security requirements for Neighbor Advertisements?
Are redirects coming from the router to which the packet was actually sent?

---

* IPsec tunnel mode provides security for the encapsulated IP header's Flow Label because a tunnel mode IPsec packet contains two IP headers: an outer header supplied by the tunnel ingress node and an encapsulated inner header supplied by the original source of the packet. When an IPsec tunnel is passing through nodes performing flow classification, the intermediate network nodes operate on the Flow Label in the outer header. At the tunnel egress node, IPsec processing includes removing the outer header and forwarding the packet (if required) using the inner header. The IPsec protocol requires that the inner header's Flow Label not be changed by this decapsulation processing to ensure that modifications to label cannot be used to launch theft- or denial-of-service attacks across an IPsec tunnel endpoint.

"Unusual" router advertisements, such as, but not limited to, the ones below, need to be filtered at the firewall [WAR200401]:

- Routers advertising the same established prefixes;
- Routers advertising any new prefixes;
- Prefix changes outside of renumbering and transition periods.

Some of these issues are addressed in the sections (and chapters) that follow.

5.3 Neighbor Discovery Issues

As we saw in Chapter 3 (and its appendix), IPv6 nodes use the Neighbor Discovery Protocol (NDP) to discover other nodes on the link, to determine their link-layer addresses to find routers, and to maintain reachability information about the paths to active neighbors. NDP is defined in RFC 2461 and RFC 2462. It turns out that the basic NDP lacks a mechanism for determining authorized neighbors. If not secured, NDP is vulnerable to various attacks: redirection, stealing addresses, denial of service advertisement, and parameter spoofing could occur. A suggestion (RFC 3682) of using a "hop count of 255" has only rather limited value. The use of IPsec Authentication Header (AH) or Encapsulating Security Payload (ESP) only works with manual keying and pre-established security associations [REN200701].

Nodes on the same link use NDP to discover each other's presence and link-layer addresses, to find routers, and to maintain reachability information about the paths to active neighbors. NDP is used by both hosts and routers. Its functions include Neighbor Discovery (ND), Router Discovery (RD), Address Autoconfiguration, Address Resolution, Neighbor Unreachability Detection (NUD) (a mechanism used for tracking the reachability of neighbors), Duplicate Address Detection (DAD), and Redirection. The original NDP specifications called for the use of IPsec to protect NDP messages. However, the RFCs do not give detailed instructions for using IPsec to do this. In this particular application, IPsec can only be used with a manual configuration of security associations because of bootstrapping problems in using the Internet Key Exchange (IKE) Protocol (IKE is a protocol in the IPsec architecture). Furthermore, the number of manually configured security associations needed for protecting NDP can be very large, making that approach impractical for most purposes [RFC3971].

IPv6 Neighbor Discovery Attacks include the following [REN200701]:

- Neighbor Solicitation
  - Redirect traffic to bogus link-layer address
  - Unreachability Detection error
  - Duplicate Address Detection: "Address in Use" DoS
- Malicious Last-Hop Router—bogus router or false parameters for real routers

- Eliminate Legitimate Routers—crash, DoS, bogus Router Advertisement (RAdv) message
  - Nodes send to off-link hosts as if they were on-link—impersonate off-link nodes
- Spoofed redirect—route packets to different link-layer address
- Bogus on-link prefix
  - Impersonate nodes on bogus link
  - Nodes use source with bogus prefix and get no response
- Bogus Parameters—set low hop limit from router, use stateful address configuration (DHCP)
- Replay Attacks—replay any previous neighbor or router discovery packet
- Neighbor Discovery DoS—send packet to unused address and cause router to perform neighbor discovery

To address the issue, RFC 3971 specifies security mechanisms for NDP; unlike those in the original NDP specifications, these mechanisms do not use IPsec. RFC 3971 specifies the SEcure Neighbor Discovery (SEND) protocol, which is designed to counter the threats to NDP. SEND is applicable in environments where physical security on the link is not assured (such as over wireless) and attacks on NDP are a concern. The Neighbor Discovery Protocol has several functions, most of which are implemented using ICMP messages, such as the ICMPv6 Neighbor Advertisement message. The main functions of NDP as discussed in RFC 3971 are: Neighbor Discovery, Router Discovery, Address Autoconfiguration, Address Resolution, Neighbor Unreachability Detection, Duplicate Address Detection, and Redirection. Specifically, [RFC3971]:

- The Router Discovery function allows IPv6 hosts to discover the local routers on an attached link. The main purpose of Router Discovery is to find neighboring routers willing to forward packets on behalf of hosts. Subnet prefix discovery involves determining which destinations are directly on a link; this information is necessary in order to know whether a packet should be sent to a router or directly to the destination node.
- The Redirect function is used for automatically redirecting a host to a better first-hop router, or to inform hosts that a destination is in fact a neighbor (i.e., on-link).
- Address Autoconfiguration is used for automatically assigning addresses to a host. This allows hosts to operate without explicit configuration related to IP connectivity. The default autoconfiguration mechanism is stateless. To create IP addresses, hosts use any prefix information delivered to them during Router Discovery and then test the newly formed addresses for uniqueness. A stateful mechanism, DHCPv6, provides additional autoconfiguration features.
- DAD is used for preventing address collisions during Address Autoconfiguration. A node that intends to assign a new address to one of its interfaces first runs the DAD procedure to verify that no other node is using the same

address. As the rules forbid the use of an address until it has been found unique, no higher-layer traffic is possible until this procedure has been completed. Thus, preventing attacks against DAD can help ensure the availability of communications for the node in question.

■ The Address Resolution function allows a node on the link to resolve another node's IPv6 address to the corresponding link-layer address. Address Resolution is defined in RFC 2461, and it is used for hosts and routers alike. Again, no higher-level traffic can proceed until the sender knows the link-layer address of the destination node or the next hop router. Note that the source link-layer address on link-layer frames is not checked against the information learned through Address Resolution. This allows for an easier addition of network elements such as bridges and proxies and eases the stack implementation requirements, as less information has to be passed from layer to layer.

■ NUD is used for tracking the reachability of neighboring nodes, both hosts and routers. NUD is security sensitive, because an attacker could claim that reachability exists when in fact it does not.

The NDP messages follow the ICMPv6 message format, as shown in Figure 5.1. All NDP functions are realized by using the Router Solicitation (RS), Router Advertisement (RA), Neighbor Solicitation (NS), Neighbor Advertisement (NA), and Redirect messages. An actual NDP message includes an NDP message header, consisting of an ICMPv6 header and ND message-specific data, and zero or more NDP options. The NDP message options are formatted in the Type-Length-Value format.

SEND secures the various functions in NDP, where a set of new Neighbor Discovery options is introduced. These options are used to protect NDP messages. This specification introduces these options, an authorization delegation discovery process, an address ownership proof mechanism, and requirements for the use of these components in NDP. The components of the solution are as follows [RFC3971]:

■ Certification paths, anchored on trusted parties, are expected to certify the authority of routers. A host must be configured with a trust anchor to which

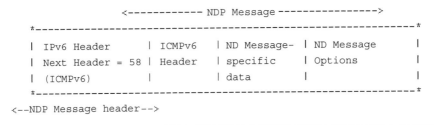

```
              <------------ NDP Message ----------------->
    *------------------------------------------------------------*
    | IPv6 Header      | ICMPv6 | ND Message- | ND Message       |
    | Next Header = 58 | Header | specific    | Options          |
    | (ICMPv6)         |        | data        |                  |
    *------------------------------------------------------------*
  <--NDP Message header-->
```

Figure 5.1 NDP message.

the router has a certification path before the host can adopt the router as its default gateway (router). Certification Path Solicitation and Advertisement messages are used to discover a certification path to the trust anchor without requiring the actual Router Discovery messages to carry lengthy certification paths. The receipt of a protected Router Advertisement message for which no certification path is available triggers the authorization delegation discovery process.

■ Cryptographically Generated Addresses (CGA) are used to make sure that the sender of a Neighbor Discovery message is the "owner" of the claimed address. A public-private key pair is generated by all nodes before they can claim an address. A new NDP option, the CGA option, is used to carry the public key and associated parameters. This specification also allows a node to use non-CGAs with certificates that authorize their use. However, the details of such use are beyond the scope of this specification and are left for future work.

■ A new NDP option, the RSA Signature option, is used to protect all messages relating to Neighbor and Router discovery. Public key signatures protect the integrity of the messages and authenticate the identity of their sender. The authority of a public key is established either with the authorization delegation process, by using certificates, or through the address ownership proof mechanism, by using CGAs, or with both, depending on configuration and the type of the message protected. Note: RSA is mandated because having multiple signature algorithms would break compatibility between implementations or increase implementation complexity by forcing the implementation of multiple algorithms and the mechanism to select among them. A second signature algorithm is only necessary as a recovery mechanism, in case a flaw is found in RSA. If this happens, a stronger signature algorithm can be selected, and SEND can be revised. The relationship between the new algorithm and the RSA-based SEND described in this document would be similar to that between the RSA-based SEND and ND without SEND. Information signed with the stronger algorithm has precedence over that signed with RSA, in the same way that RSA-signed information now takes precedence over unsigned information. Implementations of the current and revised specs would still be compatible.

■ In order to prevent replay attacks, two new Neighbor Discovery options, Timestamp and Nonce, are introduced. Given that Neighbor and Router Discovery messages are in some cases sent to multicast addresses, the Timestamp option offers replay protection without any previously established state or sequence numbers. When the messages are used in solicitation-advertisement pairs, they are protected with the Nonce option. Nonce is a term that means "for the present time" or "for a single occasion or purpose." In the context of security a Nonce is a "number used once," for example, a random or pseudorandom number issued in an authentication protocol to ensure that previous communications cannot be reused to unleash "replay attacks." Hence, it is a random or nonrepeating value that is included in data exchanged by a protocol, usually for the purpose of guaranteeing liveness and thus detecting and protecting against replay attacks [RFC2828].

5.4 Routing Headers

All IPv6 nodes must be able to process Routing Extension Headers. These Routing Extension Headers can be used to evade access controls based on destination address. All nodes can act as routers; a node processes routing header and forwards packets to other destinations. Observers recommend limiting traffic with routing headers to only those nodes that participate in IP mobility or impose strict policies for forwarding on all nodes [REN200701].

The functionality provided by IPv6's Type 0 Routing Header can be exploited in order to achieve traffic amplification over a remote path for the purpose of generating denial-of-service traffic. RFC 5095 deprecates the use of IPv6 Type 0 Routing Headers, in light of this security concern. RFC 2460 defined an IPv6 extension header called "Routing Header," identified by a Next Header value of 43 in the immediately preceding header. A particular Routing Header subtype denoted as "Type 0" (RH0) is also defined. A single RH0 may contain multiple intermediate node addresses, and the same address may be included more than once in the same RH0. This allows a packet to be constructed such that it will oscillate between two RH0-processing hosts or routers many times. In addition, this allows a stream of packets from an attacker to be amplified along the path between two remote routers, which could be used to cause congestion along arbitrary remote paths and hence act as a denial-of-service mechanism. This attack is particularly serious in that it affects the entire path between the two exploited nodes, not only the nodes themselves or their local networks [RFC5095].

RFC 5095 notes that it is to be expected that it will take some time before all IPv6 nodes are updated to remove support for RH0. Some of the uses of RH0 can be mitigated using ingress filtering. A site security policy intended to protect against attacks using RH0 should include the implementation of ingress filtering at the site border.

Note:

Blocking all IPv6 packets that carry Routing Headers (rather than specifically blocking Type 0 and permitting other types) has very serious implications for the future development of IPv6. If even a small percentage of deployed firewalls block other types of Routing Headers by default, it will become impossible in practice to extend IPv6 Routing Headers. For example, Mobile IPv6 [RFC3775] relies upon a Type 2 Routing Header; wide-scale, indiscriminate blocking of Routing Headers will make Mobile IPv6 undeployable but may be required until the controls are more mature. A firewall policy intended to protect against packets containing

RH0 must not simply filter all traffic with a Routing Header; it must be possible to disable forwarding of Type 0 traffic without blocking other types of Routing Headers. In addition, the default configuration must permit forwarding of traffic using a Routing Header other than 0.

5.5 DNS Issues

While security considerations in reference to with DNS* (e.g., DNS Security (DNSSEC)) are not specific to IPv6, improper configuration and use with IPv6 can impact performance.

Practitioners identify the following as points to remember [REN200701]:

- Local addresses should never be published.
- Security models based on source address validation are weak and not recommended.
- Setting up an authorization mechanism (e.g., a shared secret, or public-private keys) between a node and the DNS server has to be done manually and may require quite a bit of time and expertise.
- Setting up the reverse tree is somewhat more complicated, but reverse DNS checks provide weak security at best.
  - The only (questionable) security-related use for them may be in conjunction with other mechanisms when authenticating a user.
  - Reverse chains for 6to4 addresses and Teredo addresses are impractical with Dynamic DNS Updates.

---

* Some of the simplest threats against DNS are various forms of packet interception: man-in-the-middle (MITM) attacks, eavesdropping on requests combined with spoofed responses that beat the real response back to the resolver. In any of these scenarios, the attacker can simply tell either party (usually the resolver) whatever it wants that party to believe. While packet interception attacks are far from unique to DNS, DNS's usual behavior of sending an entire query or response in a single, unsigned, unencrypted UDP packet makes these attacks particularly easy for any "bad guy" with the ability to intercept packets on a shared or transit network. To further complicate things, the DNS query the attacker intercepts may just be a means to an end for the attacker: the attacker might even choose to return the correct result in the answer section of a reply message while using other parts of the message to set the stage for something more complicated; for example, a name chaining attack. While it is possible to sign DNS messages using a channel security mechanism such as Transaction Authentication for DNS (TSIG) or IPsec, or even to encrypt them using IPsec, this would not be a very good solution for interception attacks. First, this approach would impose a fairly high processing cost per DNS message, as well as a very high cost associated with establishing and maintaining bilateral trust relationships between all the parties that might be involved in resolving any particular query. For heavily used name servers (such as the servers for the root zone), this cost would almost certainly be prohibitively high. Even more important, however, is that the underlying trust model in such a design would be wrong, since at best it would only provide a Hop-by-Hop integrity check on DNS messages and would not provide any sort of end-to-end integrity check between the producer of DNS data (the zone administrator) and the consumer of DNS data (the application that triggered the query) [RFC3833].

Note:

Teredo is an IPv6 transition technology that provides address assignment and host-to-host automatic tunneling for unicast IPv6 traffic when IPv6/IPv4 hosts are located behind one or multiple IPv4 network address translation (NAT) devices. The basic NAT operation was defined in RFC 1631 with the intent of conserving IPv4 addresses and involves a mapping between private, internal IPv4 addresses and port numbers within a subnetwork to public, external IP addresses and port numbers assigned by the NAT device. To traverse IPv4 NATs, Teredo specifies IPv6 packets sent as IPv4-based User Datagram Protocol (UDP) messages. Teredo also builds on the techniques defined in RFC 3489 for tunneling UDP traffic through various types of NATs. Like the 6to4 mechanism, Teredo is an automatic tunneling technology but differs from 6to4 in a number of aspects. For example, unlike the 6to4 mechanism, where the automatic tunnel originates in the 6to4 edge router and IPv6 is the subnet technology, the Teredo tunnel originates at the host and uses IPv4 as the subnet technology to route to the NAT device. NAT devices also cause problems for the 6to4 mechanism. 6to4 relies on the 6to4 routing functionality being implemented in the network connectivity device, a functionality that is not common for Small Office/Home Office (SOHO) NAT devices. In cases where the device did implement the 6to4 functionality, the 6to4 function requires the assignment of a public IP address, not possible in cases involving multiple levels of NATs. In addition, NAT devices can usually only deal with TCP, UDP, and limited ICMP messages. 6to4 tunnels make use of IPv4 protocol type 41, which means that it may not be possible for NATed networks to use 6to4 or indeed any other mechanisms using protocol types differing from those of TCP, UDP, or ICMP. The Teredo specification is concerned with identifying the specific type of NAT deployed in a network and specifying procedures for handling these various types.

5.6 Minimum Security Plan

As a minimum, the following steps should be undertaken with regard to IPv6 security by an organization [JUN200801]:

- Develop an IPv6 Security Plan
- Create appropriate policy
- Manage Routers/Switches appropriately
  - Disable IPv6/Tunnels
  - Develop Access Control Lists (ACL) to Block IPv6/Tunnels on core/edge/outside enclave
- Network protection devices/tools
  - Contact vendors for IPv6 advice
- Block IPv6 (Type 41) tunnels
- Enable IPv6 IDS/IPS features

■ Manage End Nodes appropriately:
- Enable IPv6 host firewalls on all end devices
- Disable IPv6 if not used
■ Monitor Core and Enclave Boundaries

In conclusion, one needs to keep in mind that "security in IPv6" is a much broader topic than just a discussion on IPsec. While IPsec is mandatory in IPv6 (as we see in the chapter that follows), the same practical issues with IPsec deployment remain from IPv4, namely configuration complexity and key management. Even when using IPsec, there are numerous threats that still remain issues in IP networking: end-to-end encryption impedes granular visibility in the network (firewalls, SSL offload, IDS), and this may have the effect of countering, removing, or weakening controls that are already put into place. For example, IPv4 ARP attacks are replaced with IPv6 ND attacks; IPv4 DHCP attacks are possibly aggravated by stateless autoconfiguration attacks—this is in addition to traditional DHCP issues for IPv6 [MIL200401]. It follows that detailed planning is needed by the network/security administrator to set up a trustworthy IPv6 environment.

References

[JUN200801] Juniper Networks. An IPv6 security guide for U.S. government agencies: Executive Summary, *The IPv6 World Report Series* 4 (Feb. 2008). Sunnyvale, CA. www.juniper.net.

[KAE200601] Kaeo, M., D. Green, J. Bound, and Y. Pouffary. IPv6 security technology paper, *North American IPv6 Task Force (NAv6TF) Technology Report*, July 22, 2006.

[MIL200401] Miller, D., and S. Convery. *IPv6 Dual Stack Security Implications*. Cisco Systems Presentation, San Jose, CA, 2004.

[REN200701] Renard, K. *Security Issues in IPv6*. San Diego, CA: WareOnEarth Communications Inc., 2007.

[RFC2828] Shirey, R. Internet Security Glossary, RFC 2828, May 2000. Copyright (C) The Internet Society (2000). All Rights Reserved. This document and translations of it may be copied and furnished to others, and derivative works that comment on or otherwise explain it or assist in its implementation may be prepared, copied, published and distributed, in whole or in part, without restriction of any kind, provided that the above copyright notice and this paragraph are included on all such copies and derivative works.

[RFC3697] Rajahalme, J., A. Conta, B. Carpenter, and S. Deering. Request for Comments: 3697, IPv6 Flow Label Specification, RFC 3697, Mar. 2004.

[RFC3775] Johnson, D., Perkins, C., and Arkko, J., Request for comments: 3775, Mobility Support in IPv6, June 2004.

[RFC3833] Atkins, D. Request for Comments: 3833, Threat Analysis of the Domain Name System (DNS), IETF RFC 3833, Aug. 2004.

[RFC3971] Arkko, J., ed. Request for Comments: 3971, SEcure Neighbor Discovery (SEND), RFC 3971, Mar. 2005.

[RFC4218] Nordmark, E., and T. Li. Request for Comments: 4218, Threats Relating to IPv6 Multihoming Solutions, RFC 4218, Oct. 2005.

[RFC5095] Abley, J., P. Savola, and G. Neville-Neil. Request for Comments: 5095 (Updates RFC 2460 and RFC 4294), Deprecation of Type 0 Routing Headers in IPv6, RFC 5095, Dec. 2007.

[WAR200401] Warfield, M. H. *Security Implications of IPv6*. X-Force, Internet Security Systems, Inc. (ISS), 16th Annual FIRST Conference on Computer Security Incident Handling, June 13–18, 2004, Budapest, Hungary.

Chapter 6

IPsec and Its Use in IPv6 Environments

Introduction

IPv6 incorporates security mechanisms at the network layer by making the use of the IPsec* protocols mandatory. IPsec is also available for IPv4, but it has *not* been broadly deployed in that space by organizations except for creating Virtual Private Networks (VPNs).† IPsec is an interoperable (open), reasonably high quality, cryptographically based security mechanism. It provides data origin authentication, connectionless integrity, confidentiality (encryption), replay detection (a form of partial sequence integrity), partial traffic flow confidentiality, and access control (via packet filtering). These capabilities are provided at the IP layer, offering protection for IP or upper-layer protocols.

This chapter provides a high-level overview of IPsec; of particular interest is IPsec in transport mode.

To protect data as it travels across a public or a closed IP network, IPsec supports a combination of the following network security functions: (i) Data confidentiality: it encrypts packets before transmission; (ii) Data integrity: it authenticates packets to help ensure that the data has not been altered during transmission; (iii) Data origin authentication: it authenticates the source of received packets, in conjunction with data integrity service; and, (iv) Anti-replay: it detects aged or duplicate

---

* The term can be expanded to be Internet Protocol Security, but most people do not consider IPsec as an acronym.
† While organizations routinely use IPsec at this time for VPNs over the Internet, they have generally not done so for Wide Area Networks (WAN), links over Frame Relay, Cell Relay, Asynchronous Transfer Mode (ATM), or MPLS.

packets, rejecting them to avoid replay attacks. To make IPsec truly effective on a large scale, one needs a firm-wide (or even Internet-wide) authentication infrastructure, namely a Public Key Infrastructure (PKI); PKI provides the data integrity, user identification and authentication, user nonrepudiation, data confidentiality, encryption, and digital signature services for programs and applications that use a given network. PKI is a service derived from products that provide and manage X.509 certificates for public-key cryptography; certificates identify the entity or individual named in the certificate, and bind that entity or individual to a particular public/private key pair. Note that end-to-end data confidentiality, for example, IPsec, does not protect against denial-of-service (DoS) attacks.

6.1 Overview

The security features of IPv6 are described in the Security Architecture for the Internet Protocol (RFC 2401* [RFC2401], RFC 2402 [RFC2402], and RFC 2406 [RFC2406]), and in other related RFCs as listed in Table 6.1. Implementation of IPsec protocols is optional for IPv4, but it is mandatory for IPv6. As already noted, IPsec includes encryption and authentication techniques. IPsec is actually comprised of two security protocols, the Authentication Header (AH) and the Encapsulating Security Payload (ESP). It also makes use of cryptographic key management procedures and protocols; Internet Key Exchange (IKE) and Internet Security Association and Key Management Protocol (ISAKMP) are application-layer protocols that are used in conjunction with IPsec. AH provides connectionless integrity, data origin authentication, and an optional anti-replay service. ESP provides a combination of security services and may be used by itself, in combination with AH, or in a nested fashion. The choice of the specific IPsec protocol (AH or ESP) is driven by the security and system requirements of the organization and of the application(s) in question.

IPsec supports security of IP-based networks by encrypting portions of the Protocols Data Unit (PDU) at the network layer; by doing so, it protects all upper layers, including both Transmission Control Protocol (TCP) and User Datagram Protocol (UDP). The level (granularity) of protection is host-to-host, host-to-gateway, and gateway-to-gateway. Before an IP datagram is transmitted over the Internet (or any other untrusted network), it is encrypted or signed using an IPsec protocol. When it reaches the destination side, the datagram is decrypted or verified. When a TCP session is transported by an IPsec ESP protocol, the TCP header is encrypted inside the ESP header. Given the sometimes-intense processing requirements, implementing IPsec may require either new hardware or a new protocol stack. IPsec is transparent to user applications; applications running over IPsec

---

* Note that RFC 4301 obsoletes RFC 2401.

Table 6.1   Partial List of RFCs Relevant to IPv6 Security

■ RFC 2401: Security Architecture for the Internet Protocol (*obsoleted by RFC 4301*)
■ RFC 2402: IP Authentication Header (AH) (*obsoleted by RFC 4302*)
■ RFC 2403: The Use of Keyed-Hashing for Message Authentication (HMAC)-Message Digest 5 (MD5)-96 within Encapsulating Security Payload (ESP) and Authentication Header (AH)
■ RFC 2404: The Use of HMAC- Secure Hash Algorithm One (SHA-1)-96 within ESP and AH (*obsoleted by RFC 4305*)
■ RFC 2405: The ESP Data Encryption Standard-Cipher Block Chaining (CBC) (DES-CBC) Cipher Algorithm with Explicit Initialization Vector (IV)
■ RFC 2406: IP Encapsulating Security Payload (ESP) IP Encapsulating Security Payload (ESP) (*obsoleted by RFC 4303 and RFC 4305*).
■ RFC 2407: The Internet IP Security Domain of Interpretation for Internet Security Association and Key Management Protocol (ISAKMP) (*obsoleted by RFC 4306*)
■ RFC 2408: Internet Security Association and Key Management Protocol (ISAKMP)
■ RFC 2409: The Internet Key Exchange (IKE)
■ RFC 2410: The NULL Encryption Algorithm and Its Use with IPsec
■ RFC 2411: IP Security Document Roadmap
■ RFC 2412: The OAKLEY Key Determination Protocol
■ RFC 3602: The AES-CBC Cipher Algorithm and Its Use with IPsec
■ RFC 3686: Using Advanced Encryption Standard (AES) Counter Mode With IPsec Encapsulating Security Payload (ESP)
■ RFC 3715: IPsec-Network Address Translation (NAT) Compatibility Requirements.
■ RFC 3775: Mobility Support in IPv6
■ RFC 3776: Using IPsec to Protect Mobile IPv6 Signaling Between Mobile Nodes and Home Agents
■ RFC 4301: Security Architecture for the Internet Protocol
■ RFC 4302: IP Authentication Header (*obsoletes RFC 2402*)
■ RFC 4303: IP Encapsulating Security Payload (ESP) (*obsoletes RFC 2406*)
(Continued)

Table 6.1   Partial List of RFCs Relevant to IPv6 Security (Continued)

■ RFC 4305: Cryptographic Algorithm Implementation Requirements for Encapsulating Security Payload (ESP) and Authentication Header (AH) *(obsoletes RFC 2404 and RFC 2406)*
■ RFC 4877: Mobile IPv6 Operation with IKEv2 and the Revised IPsec Architecture
■ RFC 4891: Using IPsec to Secure IPv6-in-IPv4 Tunnels.

Note: The IPsec security architecture was previously defined in RFC 2401 and is now superseded by RFC 4301. IKE was originally defined in RFC 2409 (which is called IKEv1) and is now superseded by RFC 4306 (called IKEv2).

do not typically require any changes. Most modern operating systems and many routers have IPsec available [RFC3631], [RFC2401], [RFC4301].

IPsec supports two forms of integrity: (i) connectionless integrity, and (ii) a form of partial sequence integrity. Connectionless integrity is a service that detects modification of an individual IP datagram without regard to the ordering of the datagram in a stream of traffic. The form of partial sequence integrity offered in IPsec is referred to as anti-replay integrity and is capable of detecting the arrival of duplicate IP datagrams (within a constrained window). This is in contrast to connection-oriented integrity, which imposes more stringent sequencing requirements on traffic, for example, to be able to detect lost or reordered messages. Although authentication and integrity services often are cited separately, in practice they are related and almost always offered in conjunction [RFC2401]. See Table 6.2.

The algorithm variation proposed of late for ESP is to use a 168-bit key, consisting of three independent 56-bit quantities used by the Data Encryption Standards (DES) and a 64-bit initialization value. Each datagram contains an initialization value to ensure that each received datagram can be decrypted even when other datagrams are dropped or a sequence of datagrams is reordered in transit [RFC1851], [RFC2828].

6.2 IPsec Modes

IPsec can be used in transport mode or in tunnel mode [RFC2828] (also see Table 6.3 [RFC3884]):

Transport mode: The protection applies to (i.e., the IPsec protocol encapsulates) the *packets of upper-layer protocols*, the ones that are carried above IP. A transport mode Security Association (SA) is always between two hosts.

Tunnel mode: The protection applies to (i.e., the IPsec protocol encapsulates) *IP packets*. In a tunnel mode security association, each end may be either a host or a gateway. Whenever either end of an IPsec security association is a security gateway, the SA is required to be in tunnel mode. An additional set of origination/destination IP addresses are required in this mode.

Table 6.2   IPsec Security Services

Access Control	In the IPsec context, the resource to which access is being controlled is often for a host, computing cycles or data for a security gateway, a network behind the gateway or bandwidth on that network.
Confidentiality	In the IPsec context, using ESP in tunnel mode, especially at a security gateway, can provide some level of traffic flow confidentiality.
Connectionless Integrity	In the IPsec context, connectionless integrity is a service that detects modification of an individual IP datagram, without regard to the ordering of the datagram in a stream of traffic.
Partial Sequence Integrity	In the IPsec context, the form of partial sequence integrity offered is referred to as anti-replay integrity, and it detects arrival of duplicate IP datagrams (within a constrained window).

Table 6.3   IPsec Modes

IPsec Transport Mode	IP security (IPsec) mode as defined in RFC 2401, "Security Architecture for the Internet Protocol." Transport mode is allowed between two end hosts only. Note: tunnel mode is required when at least one of the endpoints is a security gateway (intermediate system that implements IPsec functionality, e.g., a router.)
	Transport mode secures portions of the existing IP header and the *payload data of the packet*. It inserts an IPsec header between the original IP header and the packet payload. The contents of the IPsec header are based on the result of a Security Association (SA) lookup that uses the contents of the original packet header as well as its payload (especially transport layer headers) to locate an SA in the Security Association Database (SAD). When receiving packets secured with IPsec transport mode, a similar SA lookup occurs based on the IP and IPsec headers, followed by a verification step after IPsec processing that checks the contents of the packet and its payload against the respective SA. The verification step is similar to firewall processing.
	(Continued)

Table 6.3 IPsec Modes (Continued)

IPsec Tunnel Mode	IPsec mode as defined in RFC 2401, "Security Architecture (SA) for the Internet Protocol". Tunnel mode is required when at least one of the endpoints is a "security gateway" (intermediate system that implements IPsec functionality, e.g., a router.) Note, by contrast that transport mode is allowed between two end hosts only.
	While transport mode secures portions of the existing IP header and the payload data of the packet by inserting an IPsec header between the IP header and the payload, tunnel mode adds an additional IP header before performing similar operations.
	When using tunnel mode, IPsec prepends an IPsec header and an additional IP header to the outgoing IP packet. In essence, the original packet becomes the payload of another IP packet, which IPsec then secures. This has been described as "a tunnel mode SA is essentially a [transport mode] SA applied to an IP tunnel." In IPsec tunnel mode, the IP header of the original outbound packet together with its payload (especially transport headers) determines the IPsec SA, as for transport mode. However, a tunnel mode SA also contains encapsulation information, including the source and destination IP addresses for the outer tunnel IP header, which is also based on the original outbound packet header and its payload.

IPsec treats everything in an IP datagram after the IP header as one unit. Usually, an IP datagram has three parts: the IP header (for routing purpose only), the upper layer protocol headers (e.g., the TCP header), and the user data (e.g., TCP data). In transport mode, an IPsec header (AH or ESP) is inserted *after the IP header and before the upper-layer protocol header to protect the upper-layer protocols and user data*. In tunnel mode, the entire IP datagram is encapsulated in a new IPsec packet (a new IP header followed by an AH or ESP header). See Figure 6.1. In either mode, the upper-layer protocol headers and data in an IP datagram are protected as one indivisible unit. The keys used in IPsec encryption and authentication are shared only by the sender-side and receiver-side security gateways. All other nodes in the public Internet, whether they are legitimate routers or malicious eavesdroppers, see only the IP header and will not be able to decrypt the content, nor can they tamper it without being detected. Traditionally, the intermediate routers do only one thing: forwarding packets based on the IP header (mainly the destination address field); IPsec's "end-to-end" protection model suits well in this layering paradigm [ZHA200401]. AH and ESP offer complementary capabilities.

Transport Mode

| MAC header | Original IPv4 header | ESP header | TCP header | TCP Data |
| MAC header | Original IPv6 header | ESP header | | |

| MAC header | Original IPv4 header | AH header | TCP header | TCP Data |
| MAC header | Original IPv6 header | AH header | | |

Tunnel Mode

| MAC header | Original IPv4 header | ESP header | Original IPv4 header | TCP header | TCP Data |
| MAC header | Original IPv6 header | ESP header | Original IPv6 header | | |

| MAC header | New IPv4 header | AH header | Original IPv4 header | TCP header | TCP Data |
| MAC header | New IPv6 header | AH header | Original IPv6 header | | |

Figure 6.1   IPsec modes.

6.3 IP Authentication Header (AH)

AH is an IPsec protocol designed to provide connectionless data integrity service and data origin authentication service for IP datagrams, and (optionally) to provide protection against replay attacks. The anti-replay service can be used to prevent denial of service attacks. AH provides for integrity but without confidentiality [RFC2828], [RFC2402]. AH is an appropriate mechanism to employ when confidentiality is not required. AH provides authentication for as much of the IP header as feasible (that is, for selected portions of the IP header) and also for encapsulated protocol data (header and payload.) However, some IP header fields may change in transit and the value of these fields, when the packet arrives at the receiver, may not be predictable by the sender; therefore, these fields cannot be protected by AH. Protection against replays (partial sequence integrity) may be selected by (at the discretion of) the receiver, when an SA is established. (The protocol default requires the sender to increment the sequence number used for anti-replay, but the service is effective only if the receiver checks the sequence number.) Figure 6.2 depicts the AH header. However, to make use of the Extended Sequence Number feature in an interoperable fashion, AH does impose a requirement on SA management protocols to be able to negotiate this feature [RFC2401]. The fields in the header are as follows:

Next header (8 bits): Specifies the next encapsulated protocol
Length (8 bits): Equal to the size of the Authentication Data payload in 32-bit words – 2
SPI, Security Parameters Index (32 bits): Contains a pseudorandom value used to identify the security association for this datagram (if set to zero, a security association does not exist)

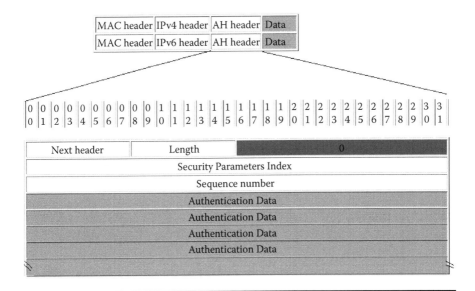

Figure 6.2 AH header.

Sequence number (32 bits)
Authentication Data (Variable length, multiple of 32-bit words)

AH may be used alone, or in combination with the IPsec ESP protocol, or in a nested fashion with tunneling. Security services can be provided between a pair of communicating hosts, between a pair of communicating security gateways, or between a host and a gateway. ESP can provide the same security services as AH, but ESP can also provide data confidentiality service, namely, encryption. The main difference between authentication services provided by ESP and AH is the extent of the coverage; ESP does not protect IP header fields unless they are encapsulated by ESP, as, for example, in tunnel mode [RFC2828].

6.4 IP Encapsulating Security Protocol (ESP)

ESP is an IPsec protocol designed to provide a mix of security services, especially the data confidentiality service, in the Internet Protocol [RFC2406]. ESP can be used to provide confidentiality, data origin authentication, connectionless integrity, an anti-replay service (a form of partial sequence integrity), and (limited) traffic flow confidentiality. ESP supports two modes of operation: tunnel mode and transport mode. ESP may be used alone, or in combination with the IPsec AH protocol or in a nested fashion with tunneling. Security services can be provided between a pair of communicating hosts, between a pair of communicating security gateways, or between a host and a gateway. The ESP header is encapsulated by the IP header, and the ESP header encapsulates either the upper-layer protocol

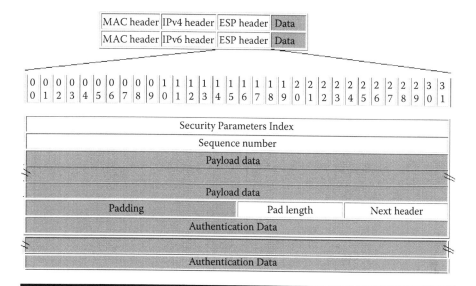

Figure 6.3   ESP header.

header (transport mode) or the original IP header (tunnel mode), as was shown in Figure 6.1. ESP can provide data confidentiality service, data origin authentication service, connectionless data integrity service, an anti-replay service, and limited traffic flow confidentiality [RFC2828]. Figure 6.3 depicts the ESP header. The fields in the header are as follows:

SPI, Security Parameters Index (32 bits): this mandatory field is an arbitrary value that, in combination with the destination IP address and security protocol, uniquely identifies the SA for this datagram. The value is typically selected by the destination system upon establishment of an SA.

Sequence number (32 bits): This mandatory field contains a monotonically increasing counter value. The field is always present even if the receiver does not elect to enable the anti-replay service for a specific SA. Processing of this field is at the discretion of the receiver but the sender must always transmit this field. The sender's counter and the receiver's counter are initialized to 0 when an SA is established. The first packet sent using a given SA will have a Sequence number of 1. If anti-replay is enabled (the default), the transmitted Sequence number must never be allowed to cycle. Thus, the sender's counter and the receiver's counter must be reset (by establishing a new SA and thus a new key) prior to the transmission of the 2^{32}nd packet on an SA.

Payload data (Variable length but an integral number of bytes in length): This field (is mandatory and) contains the data described by the Next header field. If the algorithm used to encrypt the payload requires cryptographic synchronization data, for example, an Initialization Vector (IV), then this data may be carried explicitly in the Payload data field. Any encryption algorithm that requires such explicit, per-packet synchronization data must indicate the length, any structure for such data, and the location of this data as part of a description of how the algorithm is used with ESP.

Padding (Variable length, 0–255 bytes.) Padding as needed to ensure that the resulting ciphertext ends on a 4-byte boundary.

Pad length (8 bits): Specifies the size of the *Padding* field in bytes.

Next header (8 bits): An IPv4/IPv6 protocol number describing the format of the *Payload data* field.

Authentication data (Variable length): Contains an Initial Chaining Vector (ICV), computed over the ESP packet minus the Authentication data. The length of the field is specified by the authentication function selected. This field is optional and is included only if the authentication service has been selected for the SA in question. The authentication algorithm specification must specify the length of the ICV and the comparison rules and processing steps for validation.

In the IPv6 context, the ESP header is an IPv6 extension header and trailer that provide data source authentication, data integrity and confidentiality, and a not-reply service for the loading of the datagram encapsulated by the header and trailer. The ESP header is inserted after the IP header and before the next layer protocol header (transport mode) or before an encapsulated IP header (tunnel mode), this being the original IP header. The set of services provided depends on options selected at the time of SA establishment and on the location of the implementation in a network topology.

ESP supports any type of symmetric encryption, including standard 56-bit DES-CBC (Cipher Block Chaining), the more secure Triple DES (3DES), and the newer Advanced Encryption Standard (AES). The traditional authentication technique used in IPsec is keyed MD5, but other methods have evolved. IPv6 allows for key management to occur either out-of-band or with specifically defined protocols. IPsec parameters are communicated and negotiated between network devices using the IKE protocol. The IPsec protocol provides protection for IP packets by allowing network designers to specify the traffic that needs protection, define how that traffic is to be protected, and control who can receive the traffic. IPsec VPNs replace or augment existing private networks based on traditional WAN infrastructures such as leased-line, Frame Relay, or ATM. They fulfill the same requirements as these WAN alternatives, including the support for multiple protocols. The advantage of IPsec is that it meets network requirements more cost-effectively and with greater flexibility by using today's most pervasive transport technologies: the public Internet and service providers' IP-based networks. When an enterprise out-tasks IPsec VPN service management, the service provider typically configures IPsec in a hub-and-spoke topology, where all branches (spokes) maintain a point-to-point connection to the hub, or headend. IPsec inherently supports IP unicast. Enterprises that need other Layer 3 protocols besides IP, can use protected Generic Routing Encapsulation (GRE) tunnels over IPsec [CIS200601].

6.5 Supportive Infrastructure: IPsec Architecture

As indicated earlier, to make effective use of IPsec, some related infrastructure is required. Table 6.4 enumerates some of this infrastructure. The IPsec architecture specifies the following [RFC2828]:

Table 6.4   Related Infrastructure

Security Association (SA)	A simplex (unidirectional) logical connection created for security purposes and implemented with either AH or ESP (but not both). The security services offered by a security association depend on the protocol selected, the IPsec mode (transport or tunnel), the endpoints, and the election of optional services within the protocol. A security association is identified by a triple consisting of (a) a destination IP address, (b) a protocol (AH or ESP) identifier, and (c) a Security Parameter Index [RFC2828].
Security Parameters Index (SPI)	An arbitrary 32-bit value that assists in the identification of an Authentication, Authorization and Accounting (AAA) or Mobility Security Association. The type of security association identifier used in IPsec protocols. A 32-bit value used to distinguish among different security associations terminating at the same destination (IP address) and using the same IPsec security protocol (AH or ESP). Carried in AH and ESP to enable the receiving system to determine under which Security Association (SA) to process a received packet [RFC3957]. The combination of a destination address, a security protocol, and an SPI uniquely identifies a security association. The SPI enables the receiving system to select the SA under which a received packet will be processed. An SPI has only local significance, as defined by the creator of the SA (usually the receiver of the packet carrying the SPI); thus an SPI is generally viewed as an opaque bit string. However, the creator of an SA may choose to interpret the bits in an SPI to facilitate local processing [RFC2401]. The combination of a destination address, a security protocol, and an SPI uniquely identifies a security association. The SPI is carried in AH and ESP protocols to enable the receiving system to select the SA under which a received packet will be processed. An SPI has only local significance, as defined by the creator of the SA (usually the receiver of the packet carrying the SPI); thus an SPI is generally viewed as an opaque bit string. However, the creator of an SA may choose to interpret the bits in an SPI to facilitate local processing.

(Continued)

Table 6.4   Related Infrastructure (Continued)

Security Gateway	A security gateway is an intermediate system that acts as the communications interface between two networks. The set of hosts (and networks) on the external side of the security gateway is viewed as untrusted (or less trusted), while the networks and hosts on the internal side are viewed as trusted (or more trusted). The internal subnets and hosts served by a security gateway are presumed to be trusted by virtue of sharing a common, local, security administration. In the IPsec context, a security gateway is a point at which AH or ESP is implemented in order to serve a set of internal hosts, providing security services for these hosts when they communicate with external hosts also employing IPsec (either directly or via another security gateway).

- Security protocols (AH and ESP already described at a high level above),
- Security Associations (what they are, how they work, how they are managed, and associated processing),
- Key management (IPsec Key Exchange [IKEv1/IKEv2]) (this protocol provides a secure signaling mechanism for establishing, maintaining, and deleting an IPsec tunnel), and,
- Algorithms for authentication and encryption. The set of security services include access control service, connectionless data integrity service, data origin authentication service, protection against replays (detection of the arrival of duplicate datagrams, within a constrained window), data confidentiality service, and limited traffic flow confidentiality.

An SA is a one-way relationship between sender and receiver. The SA defines the type of security services for a connection. It usually contains the key needed for authentication or encryption, and the authentication or encryption algorithms to be used. The SA is uniquely identified by the Security Parameters Index (SPI) (a field in the AH/ESP header), destination IP address, and the security protocol (AH or ESP). The IPsec SA is a cooperative relationship formed by the sharing of cryptographic keying material and associated context. Security associations are simplex; consequently, two security associations are needed to protect bidirectional traffic between two nodes, one for each direction [HER200201], [RFC3775]. Typically, each IPv6 node manages a set of SAs, one for each secure communication currently active.

The SPI parameter (contained in both the AH and ESP headers) specifies which SA is to be used in decrypting or authenticating the packet [LIO199801]:

- In unicast transmissions, the SPI is normally chosen by the destination node and sent back to the sender when the communication is set up.

- In multicast transmissions, the SPI must be common to all the members of the multicast group. Each node must be able to identify the right SA correctly by combining the SPI with the multicast address.
- The negotiation of an SA (and the related SPI) is an integral part of the protocol for the exchange of security keys.

There are two ways to manage keys: manual and automatic. Manual key management may provide a higher level of security but entails high administrative costs and does not scale well because it requires the action of a security administrator on each network device taking part in the secure channel. Automatic key management makes use of appropriately designed protocols. Several proposals have been made for this over the years, but no general agreement has yet been reached on key management [LIO199801]. IKE is an IPsec protocol originally specified in RFC 2409 used to ensure security for VPN negotiation and remote host or network access. It describes the process used to negotiate parameters needed to establish a new SA (transfer of secret keys, cryptographic algorithm, etc.) IKE is a key-establishment protocol that is utilized to negotiate authenticated keying material for use with ISAKMP and for other security associations, such as in AH and ESP [RFC2409] [RFC2828]. IKE defines an automatic means of negotiation and authentication for IPsec SAs. As stated, SAs are security policies defined for communication between two or more entities; the relationship between the entities is represented by a key. The IKE protocol ensures security for SA communication without the preconfiguration that would otherwise be required. IKE implements two earlier security protocols, OAKLEY and Secure Key Exchange Mechanism for Internet (SKEME), within an ISAKMP Transmission Control Protocol/Internet Protocol (TCP/IP)-based framework.

IKE phase 1 negotiations are used to establish IKE SAs. These SAs protect the IKE phase 2 negotiations. IKE uses one of two modes for phase 1 negotiations: main mode or aggressive mode. The choice of main or aggressive mode is a matter of tradeoffs. Some of the characteristics of the two modes are as follows:

Main mode:

- Protects the identities of the peers during negotiations and is therefore more secure
- Allows greater proposal flexibility than aggressive mode
- Is more time consuming than aggressive mode because more messages are exchanged between peers (six messages are exchanged in main mode)

Aggressive mode:

- Exposes identities of the peers to eavesdropping, making it less secure than main mode

■ Is faster than main mode because fewer messages are exchanged between peers (three messages are exchanged in aggressive mode)
■ Enables support for fully qualified domain names (FQDNs) when the router uses preshared keys

ISAKMP protocol is used to negotiate, establish, modify, and delete SAs. Another aspect of ISAKMP is to exchange key generation and authentication data, independent of the details of any specific key generation technique, key establishment protocol, encryption algorithm, or authentication mechanism. ISAKMP supports negotiation of security associations for protocols at all TCP/IP layers. By centralizing management of security associations, ISAKMP reduces duplicated functionality within each protocol [RFC2408], [RFC2828].

OAKLEY is a key establishment protocol proposed for IPsec, but then superseded by IKE. OAKLEY is based on the Diffie-Hellman algorithm and designed to be a compatible component of ISAKMP. OAKLEY establishes a shared key with an assigned identifier and associated authenticated identities for parties; it is used to establish session keys on Internet hosts and routers. That is, OAKLEY provides an authentication service to ensure the entities of each other's identity, even if the Diffie-Hellman exchange is threatened by active wiretapping. Also, it provides public-key forward secrecy for the shared key and supports key updates, incorporation of keys distributed by out-of-band mechanisms, and user-defined abstract group structures for use with Diffie-Hellman [RFC2412], [RFC2828].

Unfortunately, planners cannot assume the existence of a global PKI or other global security infrastructure; the reality is that currently there is no authentication infrastructure that could be used for such global authentication between any two IPv6 nodes. As a consequence, using the conventional authentication mechanism limits route optimization to intraorganizational use where the required security services are in place [AUR200301].

In conclusion, IPsec is not a complete solution to IT security, particularly when the attack is application oriented (for example, against or via electronic mail systems, against a database system, against a host), rather than network oriented (for example, network tapping, packet redirection, or DoS).

6.6 Related Observations

Global Networks. Note that because of U.S. export laws related to the cryptographic strength of the encryption algorithms, a network planner may have to use less advanced algorithms in order to ensure global interoperability in a multinational intranet or an extranet environment.

Channel Overhead Due to Encryption. While physical-level encryption does not impact the message length and, consequently, the required channel bandwidth, network-layer encryption (e.g., IPsec) does impact the message length and required network bandwidth because of the overhead involved in the tunneling process (that is, the encapsulation of an IP datagram/packet inside another packet). This is particularly problematic for short packets (small payload) such as for Voice over IP (VoIP) applications.

Network Address Translation (NAT), Conflict with IPsec. The key management for IPsec can use either certificates or shared secrets. For all the obvious reasons, certificates are preferred; however, they may present more of a 'headache' for the system manager. There is strong potential for conflict between IPsec and NAT (RFC 2993). NAT does not easily coexist with any protocol containing embedded IP address; with IPsec, every packet, for every protocol, contains such addresses, if only in the headers. The conflict can sometimes be avoided by using tunnel mode, but that is not always an appropriate choice for other reasons. There is ongoing work to make IPsec pass through NAT more easily. Most current IPsec usage is for virtual private networks. Assuming that the other constraints are met, IPsec is the security protocol of choice for VPN-like situations, including the remote access scenario where a single machine tunnels back into its home network over the Internet using IPsec [RFC3631].

IPsec Limitations. IPsec's end-to-end protection model and its strict layering principle are unsuitable for an emerging class of new networking services and applications. Unlike in the traditional minimalistic Internet, intermediate routers begin to play more and more active roles. They often rely on some information about the IP datagram payload, such as certain upper-layer protocol header fields, to make intelligent routing decisions. In other words, routers can participate in a layer above IP [ZHA200401]. Some examples include "transport-aware link-layer mechanisms," Traffic Engineering, and Network-resident Application-Layer Proxies/Agents.

Multilayer IPsec (ML-IPsec). ML-IPsec is a *proposed* standard that uses a multilayer protection model to replace the single end-to-end model. Unlike IPsec where the scope of encryption and authentication apply to the entire IP datagram payload (sometimes IP header as well), ML-IPsec divides the IP datagram into zones. It applies different protection schemes to different zones. Each zone has its own sets of security associations, its own set of private keys (secrets) that are not shared with other zones, and its own sets of access control rules (defining which nodes in the network have access to the zone) [ZHA200401]. Multilayer IPsec applies separate encryption/authentication with different keys on different parts of an IP datagram. It allows intermediate routers to have limited and controllable access to part of IP datagram (usually headers) but not the user data, for applications such as flow classification, diffserv, transparent proxy, and so on (and those "intelligent routing" that need access to higher-layer protocol headers). The idea is to divide the IP datagram into several parts and apply different forms of protection to different parts. For example, the TCP payload part can be protected between two end points while the TCP/IP header part can be protected but accessible to two end points plus certain routers in the network. It allows TCP with Performance Enhancing Proxies (PEP) to coexist with IPsec, and provides both performance improvement and security protection to wireless and satellite networks. When ML-IPsec protects a traffic stream from its source to its destination, it will first rearrange the IP datagram into zones and apply cryptographic protections. When the ML-IPsec protected datagram flows through an authorized intermediate gateway, a certain part of the datagram may be decrypted or modified and re-encrypted, but the other parts will not be compromised. When the packet reaches its destination, ML-IPsec will be able to reconstruct the entire datagram. ML-IPsec defines a complex security relationship that involves both the sender and the receiver of a security service, but also selected intermediate nodes along the delivery path [ZHA200401].

References

[AUR200301] Aura, T. *Mobile IPv6 Security*. White paper, Microsoft Research Ltd., 2003. Roger Needham Building, 7 JJ Thomson Avenue, Cambridge, CB3 0FB, UK.

[CIS200601] Cisco Systems, VPN Services. *Managed VPN — Comparison of MPLS, IPsec, and SSL architectures*. http://www.cisco.com/en/US/netsol/ns341/ns121/ns193/networking_solutions_white_paper0900aecd801b1b0f.shtml.

[HER200201] Hermann-Seton, P. *Security Features in IPv6*, SANS Institute 2002, as part of the Information Security Reading Room.

[LIO199801] Lioy, A. Security features of IPv6, Chapter 8 of *Internetworking IPv6 with Cisco Routers*, Silvano Gai. New York: Mcgraw-Hill, 1998. Also available at www.ip6.com/us/book/Chap8.pdf.

[RFC1851] Karn, P., P. Metzger, and W. Simpson. Request for Comment: 1851, The ESP Triple DES Transform, RFC 1851, Sep. 1995.

[RFC2401] Kent, S. and R. Atkinson. Request for Comments: 2401, Security Architecture for the Internet Protocol, RFC 2401, Nov. 1998 (Obsoleted by RFC 4301).

[RFC2402] Kent, S. and R. Atkinson. Request for Comments: 2402, IP Authentication Header (AH), RFC 2402, Nov. 1998.

[RFC2406] Kent, S. and R. Atkinson. Request for Comments: 2406, IP Encapsulating Security Protocol (ESP), RFC 2406, Nov. 1998.

[RFC2408] Maughan, D., M. Schertler, M. Schneider, and J. Turner. Request for Comments: 2408, Internet Security Association and Key Management Protocol (ISAKMP), RFC 2408, Nov. 1998.

[RFC2409] Harkins, D. and D. Carrel. Request for Comments: 2409, The Internet Key Exchange (IKE), RFC 2409, Nov. 1998.

[RFC2412] Orman, H. Request for Comments: 2412, The OAKLEY Key Determination Protocol, RFC 2412, Nov. 1998.

[RFC2828] Shirey, R. Internet Security Glossary, RFC 2828, May 2000. Copyright (C) The Internet Society (2000). All Rights Reserved. This document and translations of it may be copied and furnished to others, and derivative works that comment on or otherwise explain it or assist in its implementation may be prepared, copied, published and distributed, in whole or in part, without restriction of any kind, provided that the above copyright notice and this paragraph are included on all such copies and derivative works.

[RFC3631] Bellovin, S., J. Schiller, and C. Kaufman, eds. Security Mechanisms for the Internet, RFC 3631, Dec. 2003. Copyright (C) The Internet Society (2003). All Rights Reserved. This document and translations of it may be copied and furnished to others, and derivative works that comment on or otherwise explain it or assist in its implementation may be prepared, copied, published and distributed, in whole or in part, without restriction of any kind, provided that the above copyright notice and this paragraph are included on all such copies and derivative works.

[RFC3775] Johnson, D., C. Perkins, and J. Arkko. Request for Comments: 3775, Mobility Support in IPv6, RFC 3775, June 2004.

[RFC3884] Touch, J., L. Eggert, and Y. Wang. Request for Comments: 3884, Use of IPsec Transport Mode for Dynamic Routing, RFC 3884, Sep. 2004.

[RFC3957] Perkins, C., and P. Calhoun. Request for Comments: 3957, Authentication, Authorization, and Accounting (AAA) Registration Keys for Mobile IPv4, RFC 3957, Mar. 2005.

[RFC4111] Fang, L., ed. Request for Comments: 4111, Security Framework for Provider-Provisioned Virtual Private Networks, RFC 4111, Dec. 2005.

[ZHA200401] Zhang, Y. A multilayer IP security protocol for TCP performance enhancement in wireless networks, *IEEE Journal On Selected Areas In Communications* 22, no. 4 (May 2004).

Chapter 7

Firewall Use in IPv6 Environments

Introduction

This chapter continues the discussion on IPv6 security that we started earlier in the text. The topic of perimeter firewalls in an IPv6 environment is covered here. As we saw in Chapter 4, firewalls are used to enforce a security policy that controls the types of traffic that may transit between public (external) networks and an organization's intranet. Firewalls are also employed to protect an enterprise from network-, transport-, and application-level exploitation and Denial of Service (DoS) (flooding) attacks. IPv6 firewall considerations that the planner needs to take into account include: firewall roles, packet filtering, extension headers, and use of IPsec Encapsulating Security Protocol (ESP), among others. Device performance may be an issue in IPv6 due to the impact of encryption processing (as in fact is also occasionally the case in IPv4).

Firewalls can run in a pure IPv6-only environment, or, more typically for the foreseeable future, can run in a mixed IPv4/IPv6 environment. In a mixed environment, IPv6-capable firewalls need to maintain state tables for both IPv4 and IPv6 (e.g., for TCP connections and for UDP sessions), and application-aware firewalls must track IPv4 and IPv6 transactions simultaneously. Additional computational burden arises from translation and tunneling (for example, IPv4 over IPv6 or IPv6 over IPv4*). These issues impact not only configuration complexity for the network/firewall engineer, but also impact the throughput performance of the firewall

---

* This topic is revisited in Chapter 8.

and the end-to-end session; performance could be a concern for Voice Over IP (VoIPv6), IPTV video applications (IPv6TV), and other real time applications.

7.1 Role of Firewalls for IPv6 Perimeters

Chapter 4 discussed the use of network-layer firewalls in a traditional IPv4 environment; their use is similar in IPv6. Firewalls, by design, enforce a uniform policy at the network edge perimeter and in so doing they are able to block traffic from external intruders, when properly configured. They provide a configurable control point; the basic approach of a firewall system is to undertake packet inspection and appropriate filtering. Three types of traffic inspection are used (in IPv4 environments): static packet filtering, stateful packet inspection, and application-layer inspection. The same kind of functionality is needed in IPv6 environments, plus the ability to deal with tunneled links. Typical issues with firewalls in general are that (i) they may have "too many holes" letting many protocols through; (ii) they may take a "superficial view of what is going through it," without "deep packet inspection"; or, (iii) they have no visibility to some of the data flowing through it, because the data may be encrypted. In these cases, reliable protection is difficult to accomplish. The same issues may be of concern in the pure or mixed IPv6 environment.

As of press time, some firewall support was available, but not with all the features of interest. For example, according to a 2007 ICANN study, at least 30% of 42 firewall vendors surveyed had IPv6 support (also see Appendix A at the end of the chapter). Table 7.1 (adapted from [ICA200701]) depicts the desirable features of IPv6 firewalls; as a minimum, firewalls should be capable of IPv6 traffic forwarding between internal and external interfaces, or able to accept IPv4 datagrams arriving from internal networks and hosts that are IPv4-only, encapsulating these as payloads in IPv6 datagrams, and forwarding these to IPv6 destinations, this in addition to having basic filtering capabilities. Table 7.2 summarizes traditional capabilities that should also be available in sophisticated IPv6 firewalls.

As implied above, IPsec tunneling and encryption may make classic policy enforcement difficult or even impossible: traffic cannot be checked at the firewall and attack vectors may penetrate the perimeter and impact desktop systems and other critical systems. As we saw in the previous chapter, IPsec establishes a secure channel between two points, but the tunneling problem in the context of firewalls has no easy solution. Basic IP filtering could be implemented by endpoints, however, it is impossible for a firewall to truly implement a security policy if it does not have visibility to the application or cannot parse the payload. Furthermore, IPsec places the burden on end systems rather than just at gateway points. If the designer makes use of (Transmission Control Protocol) TCP Port 80 for the IPsec tunnel, attack vectors may go through the firewall. One approach

Table 7.1 Desirable Firewall/Network and Security Features

(adapted from ICANN's Survey of IPv6 Support in Commercial Firewalls, October 2007)

Security Service or Feature	Description
IPv6 Transport	
– Forward IPv6 traffic	The product should be able to forward native IPv6 packets between internal and external (public) interfaces.
– IPv6 routing	The product should be able to participate in IPv6 neighbor discovery exchanges or act as a peer in IPv6 routing protocol exchanges.
Traffic Filtering	
– Static packet filtering	The product should be able to enforce a security policy by applying a filter on individual IPv6 packets.
– Stateful inspection	The product should be able to enforce a security policy by applying a filter on all IPv6 packets associated with a given connection or flow.
– Proxies or inspection engines run on top of IPv6 network protocol	The product should be able to enforce a security policy on protocols encapsulated in IPv6 packets (e.g., ICMP, TCP/UDP, and application protocols such as HTTP, SMTP, DNS...) using either application-layer gateway (proxy) or stateful inspection of application protocols and payloads.
IDS/IPS	The product should be able to provide intrusion detection and intrusion prevention measures on IPv6 traffic.
DDoS Protection	The product should be able to protect networks from IPv6, ICMP, and TCP flooding and malformed packet attacks.

(Continued)

Table 7.1   Desirable Firewall/Network and Security Features (Continued)

(adapted from ICANN's Survey of IPv6 Support in Commercial Firewalls, October 2007)

Security Service or Feature	Description
Network Address Translation and Tunneling	
– IP masquerading	The product should be able to map IP addresses assigned to endpoints on internal networks to a single IP address on the external (public) interface (and thus prevent the disclosure of the internal network addressing and topology information).
– 4to6	The product should be able to encapsulate (tunnel) IPv4 packets in IPv6 packets. This is useful when it is necessary to bridge two or more IPv4-only hosts or networks that do not use IPv6 and the only available transport between those hosts or networks is IPv6.
– 6to4	The product should be able to encapsulate (tunnel) IPv6 packets in IPv4 packets. This is useful when it is necessary to bridge two or more IPv6-only hosts or networks that do not use IPv4 and the only available transport between those hosts or networks is IPv4.
– Flow monitoring	The product should be able to monitor flows of traffic, detect and respond to known-to-be malicious or suspicious/anomalous traffic patterns.
– Log IPv6 traffic	The product should be able to record security events when the transport is IPv6.
– IPsec	The product should be able to support IP Security when the transport is IPv6.
– DHCPv6	The product should be able to support dynamic address assignment when the transport and addressing scheme is IPv6.
– RADIUS (Remote Authentication Dial in Use Service)	The product should be able to support authentication, accounting, and auditing (AAA) features in conjunction with a RADIUS-capable server when the transport is IPv6.

Table 7.2   Typical Firewall Types/Features

Static packet filtering	The most basic form of security policy enforcement performed by a firewall. Each packet is individually examined to establish if it complies with a stated policy. If the packet complies, it is allowed to transit through the firewall; otherwise it is blocked, logged, and discarded.
Stateful inspection of IP-layer packets	The inspection engine considers all IP datagram payloads associated with a given TCP connection, UDP stream, etc. and applies packet filtering policy to the complete traffic flows. It is a more effective form of security policy enforcement than just static packet filtering.
Application-level protection	Intruders seek out vulnerabilities of operating system (OS) and server applications, including Web-based applications (e.g., support of messaging services, streaming media, access to databases, and infrastructure servers such as DNS and e-mail). To address these vulnerabilities, this class of firewalls offers *application-layer inspection features* that protect Web, e-mail, DNS, and other Internet servers and clients from exploitation attacks. This is accomplished using application-layer gateways (proxies) or by extending stateful inspection to include application protocols (deep packet inspection).
Intrusion and DoS Protection	Firewalls that protect an organization from network, transport, and application-level exploitation and flooding attacks. These devices provide Intrusion Detection and Prevention Systems (IDS/IPS) and are designed to detect and block a variety of exploitation attacks.

is to make the router a true gateway that terminates and restarts IPsec sessions, as shown in Figure 7.1. The use of IPsec ESP does represent a challenge to perimeter security; few if any workable solutions to accessing encrypted content at the border have been identified, and a proposed approach to use the Flow Label bits has its own drawbacks. Therefore, the security planner may have to consider using host-based (this applies to a wide range on endpoints such as desktops, servers and mobile devices), but centrally administered (controlled) firewalls. As discussed in Chapter 8, IPv6 transition mechanisms use various tunneling stacks, hence security issues require particular attention.

Security planners have made heavy use of Network Address Translation (NAT) in recent years to support connectivity between other organizations and also to implement the concept of "security through obscurity." While most security professionals agree that security through obscurity (sometimes known as security by obscurity) does not provide true security, it is a reasonable part of the defense-in-depth strategy. While this concept is controversial, it has become commonplace for

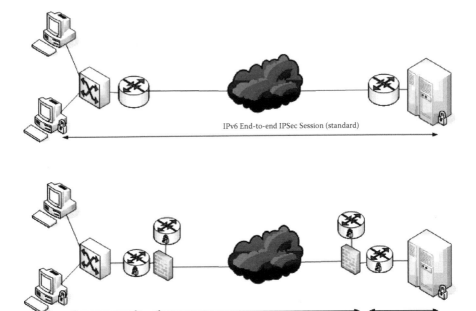

IPv6 End-to-end IPSec Session (standard)

IPv6 IPSec Session   IPv6 IPSec Session   IPv6 IPSec Session

Figure 7.1   End-to-end IPsec versus segmented IPsec.

NAT to be implemented to protect the internal IP addressing schemes of most orga-nizations. NATs* have also been utilized to extend the life of public IPv4 addresses, at the cost of global addressability and end-to-end connectivity. As we have seen, there is no obligatory need to use NAT in IPv6; yet, even without NATing, the same level of security with IPv6 is possible as with IPv4. Practitioners take the position that weaknesses of packet filtering cannot be hidden by NAT and that "IPv6 does not require end-to-end connectivity, but provides end-to-end address-ability" [MON200501]. In particular, IPv6 environments that do not use NAT make peer-to-peer networking more usable by making end-to-end connectivity easier to achieve.

In practical terms, firewalls will have to deal with dual-stack environments, as shown, for example, in Figure 7.2.

Some observers make the claim that the perimeter security model is changing at this time; for example, use of wireless LANs (Wi-Fi) or Bluetooth may impact the perimeter concept. Clear boundaries may not always exist in (some) contemporary networks and users are forced to secure computers, for example, by requiring pass-words on start-up and wake-up, routinely running virus protection, using personal

---

* NAT also refers to Network Address Translator, namely to devices that implement network address translation.

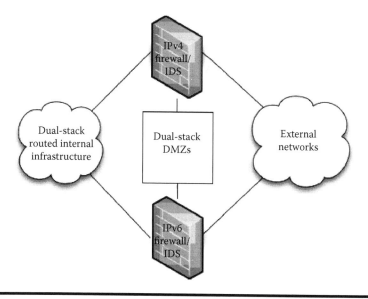

Figure 7.2 Dual-stack firewall environment.

firewalls, operating with encrypted e-mail (e.g., with PGP), and operating with encrypted files (this is known as data at rest). Firewall approaches are changing also in some instances: Location may move from the network to the end system (personal firewall), and some control may shift from the administrator to the end user [REN200701].

7.2 Packet Filtering

Typically, firewall packet filtering uses rules based on factors such as: source and destination addresses, protocol, source and destination ports, and other fields such as Traffic Class or Flow Label. Source and destination addresses filters are relatively easy to implement in principle, but IPv6 hosts may have several addresses. IPv6 makes it harder to apply ingress filtering consistently to prevent Denial of Service (DoS) attacks with spoofed source addresses. This is especially true when using randomized addresses (RFC 3041). Furthermore, there cannot be wholesale ICMPv6 filtering because a number of needed functions depend on ICMPv6.

What follows are some basic observations in reference to configuring IPv6 firewalls [KRA200601]:

■ The syntax on many of the available IPv6 firewalls is very similar to what one would have in IPv4 firewalls, and sometimes one can provide a simple and single line that covers both IPv4 and IPv6. It is important that security administrators pay close attention to IPv6 addresses as the opportunity for human error increases due to the complexity and additional length.

■ In IPv4, ARP handled some functionality that has moved into ND in IPv6; the implication is that one needs to allow (appropriate) ND packets.

■ Network administrators need to be mindful of the kind of IPv6 connection one has (for example: configured tunnel, automatic tunnel with 6to4)
  – For example, when one uses configured tunnels, the IPv6 packets are encapsulated in IPv4 packets with the protocol number 41. Therefore, one needs to allow the IPv6 in IPv4 packets with protocol 41.

One should keep in mind that IPv6 header parsing is more complex than IPv4 parsing. Encryption and authentication header sections must be parsed and filtered, hence they can affect routing and filtering decisions. In some instances, an integrated network security device may also need to perform encryption/decryption, or calculation of message authentication codes, in order to be able to filter application-layer headers and content. These additional processing requirements, compared to IPv4 environments, may impact firewall performance [AGI200801]. When multiple extension headers are used in an IPv6 packet, their order is as follows:

1. Basic IPv6 header
2. Hop-by-Hop Options
3. Destination Options (if the Routing header is used)
4. Routing
5. Fragment
6. Authentication
7. Encapsulating Security Payload
8. Upper-layer (TCP, UDP, ICMPv6, ...)

Packets including several extension headers must be processed by the destination firewall or nodes in the order they appear in the IPv6 packet.

There have been instances where IPv6 features in IPv4 networks (specifically in routers) have been used as points of vulnerability for such IPv4 networks. "Ghost" IPv6 (overlay) networks have been active and exploitable. To deal with this issue, tunneling protocols and transports should be blocked at all security perimeters (all tunneling protocols must be recognized by the organization's firewall), at routers and subnet boundaries, and across all VPNs. Intrusion Detection Systems/Intrusion Prevention Systems (IDS/IPS) systems should monitor for IPv6 link protocols such as Neighbor Discovery and Router Advertisements; Network Intrusion Detection Systems (NIDS) should be set to detect IPv6—native and tunneled. Furthermore, host systems should be monitored for IPv6 [REN200701].

Figure 7.3 shows three typical arrangements of perimeter firewalls in an IPv6 environment [MON200501]. The connection at top depicts an Internet router firewall. To be effective, the following needs must be met:

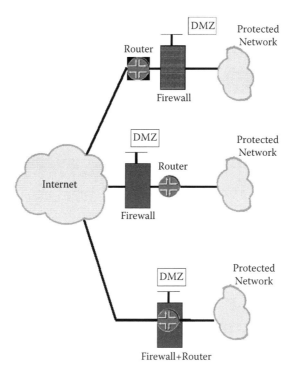

Echo request/reply			Debug
No route to destination			Debug
TTL exceeded			Error report
Parameter problem			Error report
	NS/NA		Required for normal operation– except static ND entry
IPv6 specific	RS/RA	required	Required for Stateless Address Autoconfiguration
	Packet too big		Required for Path MTU discovery
	MLD		Required for multicast

NS: Neighbor Solicitation RS: Router Solicitation
NS: Neighbor Advertisement RS: Router Advertisement

Figure 7.3 Typical firewall arrangements.

- Firewall must support/recognize Neighbor Discovery/Neighbor Advertisement (ND/NA) filtering
- Firewall must support Router Solicitation/Router Advertisement (RS/RA) if SLAAC (*stateless address autoconfiguration*) is used
- Firewall must support Multicast Listener Discovery (MLD) messages if multicast is required (MLD was mentioned in passing in Chapter 1)

For the connection at the center of the diagram in Figure 7.3, the following needs must be met:

- Firewall must support ND/NA
- Firewall should support filtering of dynamic routing protocols
- Firewall should have large variety of interface types

For the connection at the bottom of the diagram in Figure 7.3, the firewall:

- Offers one point for routing and security policy—this is fairly common in SOHO (DSL/cable) routers
- Must support router and firewall functions

It should be noted that there are a number of problems with some addresses in the IPv6 address range, and these addresses could be used to circumvent security. Some firewalls automatically null-route some bad address ranges in the network startup script; in other cases, one needs to manually null-route these or implement filtering on these addresses [KRA200601]. An example follows:

```
route -q add -inet6 ::224.0.0.0 -prefixlen 100 ::1 -reject > /
 dev/null
route -q add -inet6 ::127.0.0.0 -prefixlen 104 ::1 -reject > /
 dev/null
route -q add -inet6 ::0.0.0.0 -prefixlen 104 ::1 -reject > /
 dev/null
route -q add -inet6 ::255.0.0.0 -prefixlen 104 ::1 -reject > /
 dev/null
```

Some possible approaches in a tunneled environment include the following (see Figure 7.4):

- Allowing IPv6 tunnels pass through routers, firewalls and NAT
- Filtering IPv6 on servers
- Filtering IPv6 on clients

Doing filtering of IPv6 at a server level is generally straightforward. For example, with an OpenBSD PF (Packet Filter) one can have a command such as [KRA200601]:

```
pass in on $ext_if inet6 proto tcp to ($ext_if) port http
 keep state
pass in on $ext_if inet proto tcp to ($ext_if) port http
 keep state
pass out keep state
```

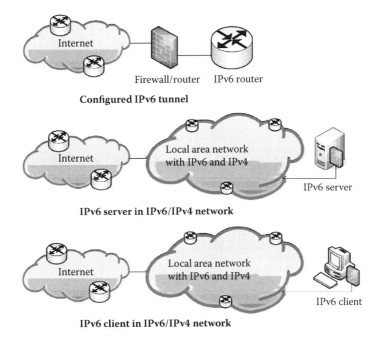

Figure 7.4   Examples of firewall usage in a tunneled environment.

For example:

```
pass in on sis2 inet proto tcp from any to 192.168.100.10 port
 = www keep state
pass in on sis2 inet6 proto tcp from any to
2001:1448:81:ff0f::10 port = www keep state
```

This is very similar to the IPv4 (inet) filtering done with OpenBSD PF. The syntax can also be (collapsing the two rules into one):

```
pass in on $ext_if proto tcp to ($ext_if) port http keep
 state
```

7.3 Extension Headers and Fragmentation

We have discussed extension headers in previous chapters. IPv6 headers and optional extensions need to be scanned to access the upper-layer protocols headers. The firewall may be required to search through several extensions headers. Processing IPv6 extension headers at the firewall requires more machine cycles. Given recent advancements in the area of deep-packet inspection, this should not always be seen as an issue, but it has some performance implications.

The IPv6 standard provides better fragmentation attack mitigation because [KAE200601]:

■ Fragmentation is prohibited by intermediary devices — this has a subtle advantage when it is definitively known between some communicating peers that no fragmented traffic will be used.
■ Overlapping fragments are not allowed — this is implied by specifying that only the source can actually create fragmented traffic.
■ Devices are required to drop reassembled packets that are less than the 1280-byte minimum Maximum Transmission Unit (MTU).

However, in IPv6, the firewall parsing engine must traverse the Next Headers before reaching the fragment header to extract the flags and offset. Thereafter it may need to traverse additional Next Head before reaching the upper-layer protocols (ULP) headers and then establish if enough of the ULP header is within the first fragment. This environment makes matching against the first fragment nondeterministic because the TCP/UDP/ICMP information may not be in the first fragment.

Authentication Header (AH) and ESP are well defined and the firewall should not require "special handling"; however, there may be a need in some situations to bypass headers to access transport or upper-layer protocols. Routing and fragmentation headers may trigger an access decision. There is a practical concern that the firewall engine may "get stuck on an unknown extension header" and be unable to make a proper decision (such as discard the packet). This is because the RFCs are somewhat unclear on firewall actions in these cases. Obviously, the administrator still needs to define a policy (e.g., "discard all") for unknown protocol/packet types. On the other hand, firewalls cannot filter out a priori all IP options (Extension Header) because these options have various applications as follows [MON200501]:

Hop-by-hop header	What to do with jumbograms or router alert option? — probably log and discard — what about multicast join messages?
Routing header	Source routing — in IPv4 it is considered harmful, but required for IPv6 mobility — log and discard one does not support MIPv6, otherwise enable only Type2 routing header for Home Agent of MIPv6
ESP header	Process according to the security policy
AH header	Process according to the security policy
Fragment header	All but last fragments should be bigger than 1280 octets

In IPv6, the Routing Header (RH) and the Home Address (HA) mechanism allow devices to rewrite IP addresses. This is a capability that is needed for Mobile IPv6 (MIPv6), which we covered briefly in Appendix B of Chapter 3. In effect, the RH and HA mechanism can turn any host behind a firewall into a router; however, this, unfortunately, may enable an unauthorized function, say a Web server, and may invalidate security controls (many IPv4 firewalls prohibit source routing). One needs to recognize legitimate MIPv6 addresses and route optimizations, but at the same time, there has to be network-level protection. Firewalls are required to characterize what RH and HA are doing. The recommendation for MIPv6 environments is to allow only one RH "segment left," only if policy and use correspond; the firewall should operate only with secure Binding Updates or an authenticated packet before accepting HA [REN200701].

7.4 Concurrent Processing

In addition to handling applications such as HTTP, FTP, POP3, and so forth, IPv6 firewalls *may* have to be able to support Voice over IPv6 (VoIPv6) signaling protocols, in order to dynamically open and close ports for the VoIP traffic, as well as track to assure that ports are open only for the duration of the call. VoIPv6 may be a key application in the near future [MIN200601]. IPsec encryption typically reduces the effective throughput of a channel (in the presence of small-payload packets.) IPv6-specific DoS attacks can severely disrupt VoIP and VoIPv6 services. Furthermore, IPv6 dual-stack operation adds complexity that may impact device call set-up rates. It follows that firewall policies must be rigorously tested on how effectively they protect exchanges between VoIP gateways (secured behind firewalls) and end devices. In some cases, firewalls can be used to separate voice and data traffic, to ensure appropriate policies are applied. VoIP traffic must not only be secured, but vendors must ensure that latency, jitter, and packet loss for VoIP traffic are not affected by firewall traversal.

7.5 Firewall Functionality

As noted, IPv6 firewalls can become a bottleneck. Several factors degrade device performance, including [AGI200801]:

- Longer IPv6 addresses — Firewalls need to filter and match on a much longer address field.
- Variable-length IPv6 headers — Optional encryption and authentication headers are more complex to parse.

- IPv6 and IPv4 concurrent processing — Dual-state tables and simultaneous operation sap performance.
- Application intelligence — Deep packet inspection requires decoding of IPv6 and tunneled packets.

Furthermore, the scalability and performance of network security devices can be difficult to predict because of the wide variety and expected mixture of IPv6 and IPv4 applications.

Some IPv6 firewalls available at press time include but are not limited to the following [DIL200701]:

- IPCop (based on Linux)
- m0n0wall (based on FreeBSD)
- pfSense (based on FreeBSD)
- FWBuilder (a management tool that builds filter setups for a number of firewalls)
- Checkpoint FW1 NGX R65 on SecurePlatform (supports IPv6)
- FortiGate (supports IPv6 in FortiOS 3.0 and higher)
- Juniper SSG (formerly Netscreen) (supports IPv6 in ScreenOS 6.0 and higher)
- Cisco ASA (formerly PIX) (supports IPv6 in version 7.0 and higher).

Table 7.3 provides a qualitative assessment of some firewalls on the market in the recent past, from the perspective of IPv6 [MON200501].

Network administrators have documented the need to be able to manage firewalls consistently for dual-stack IPv4/IPv6 nodes. These administrators report that as of press time there were as of yet no suitable commercial solutions for a unified IPv4/IPv6 environment. Early adopters have to make use of dual-stack DMZs, utilizing commercial IPv4 firewalls for the IPv4 traffic, and if the firewall does not have IPv6 support built in, something such as BSD Packet Filter for IPv6. Many IDS vendors (such as Snort, NFR owned by Check Point, and ISS owned by IBM) have products that can be used for both environments. Actual case studies of these dual-stack environments have shown (at least for the environments examined) that IPv6 firewall activity is light (relatively small number of cases where packets have to be blocked and logged) (but so is traffic level); IPv6 IDS do see IPv4-like attacks [CHO200701].

7.6 Related Tools

Table 7.4 shows a short list of IPv6-related network tools [REN200701]. At press time, reference [BIE200801] maintained an extensive online catalog of IPv6 capabilities and networking tools, which the reader may wish to consult.

Table 7.3 Overview of IPv6 Firewalls (Press Time Features)

	IP Filter 4.1	PF 3.6	IP6fw	Iptables	Cisco ACL	Cisco PIX 7.0	Juniper firewall	Juniper Net Screen	Windows XP SP2
Portability	Excellent	Good	Average	Weak	Weak	Weak	Weak	Weak	Weak
ICMPV6 support	Good	Good	Good	Good	Good	Good	Good	Good	Good
Neighbor Discovery	Excellent	Excellent	Good	Excellent	Excellent	Excellent	Good	Excellent	Weak
RS/RA support	Excellent	Excellent	Good	Excellent	Excellent	Excellent	Excellent	Excellent	Good
Extension header support	Good	Good	Good	Excellent	Good	Good	Good	Good	Weak
Fragmentation support	Weak	Complete block	Weak	Good	Weak	Average	Weak	Average	Weak
Stateful firewall	Yes	Yes	No	Csak USAGI	Reflexive firewall	Yes	ASP necessary	Yes	No
FTP proxy	No	Next version	No	No	since 12.3 (11)T	Yes	No	No	No
Other	QOS support	QoS support, checking packet validity	Predefined rules in *BSD	EUI-64 check,	Time based ACL		No TCP flag support today, HW based	IPsec VPN, routing support	Graphical and central configuration

Courtesy: J. Mohácsi, "IPv6 Security: Threats and Solutions".

Table 7.4   Partial List of Related IPv6 Security Tools

NMAP (http://www.insecure.org)	Open source port scanner with limited (TCP SYN) support
HalfScan6 (http://www.habets.pp.se/ synscan/programs. php?prog=halfscan6)	Open source port scanner
Strobe (http://www.tuxfinder.com/p ackages/?defaultname=strob e&nodesc=1)	Open source port scanner
Snort (http://www.snort.org)	Open source IDS with limited IPv6 support
ISS RealSecure 7.0 and Proventia (http://www.iss.net)	Commercial IDS with IPv6 support
NFR Sentivist 4.0 (http://www.nfr.com)	Commercial IDS with IPv6 support
Ethereal (http://www.ethereal.com)	Open source packet sniffer with full IPv6 support
NetCat6 (http://netcat6.sourceforge. net)	Simple Unix utility that reads and writes data across IPv6 or IPv4 network connections designed to be a reliable "back-end" tool
mPing (http://www.cdt.luth. se/~nord/progs/mPing)	Multicast monitoring tool; IPv6 support
TCPDump (http://www.tcpdump.org)	Open source program that dumps traffic on a network with full IPv6 support (Several other programs [COTS and F/OSS] with IPv6 support that have roughly the same functionality, including Solaris Snoop, COLD, Analyzer, WinDump, WinPCAP, NetPeek, and SnifferPro.)
SendIP (http://www.earth.li/ projectpurple/progs/sendip. html)	Open source command line tool for sending arbitrary IP packets with full IPv6 support

References

[AGI200801] Agilent Technologies. *IPv6 trends*. Santa Clara, CA. http://advanced.comms. agilent.com/networktester/technologies/ipv6/index.htm.

[BIE200801] Bieringer, P., F. Baraldi, et al. *Current status of IPv6 support for networking applications*. http://www.deepspace6.net/docs/ipv6_status_page_apps.html#security.

[CHO200701] Chown, T. *Observations on an enterprise IPv6 firewall and IDS*. IETF 68, Mar. 19 2007, Prague.

[DIL200701] Dillon, M. *IPv6 firewall support*. Merit Network, Oct. 26, 2007.

[ICA200701] ICANN Security and Stability Advisory Committee (SSAC). *Survey of IPv6 support in commercial firewalls*. Oct. 2007.

[KAE200601] Kaeo, M., D. Green, J. Bound, and Y. Pouffary. *IPv6 security technology paper, North American IPv6 Task Force (NAv6TF) Technology Report*, July 22, 2006.

[KRA200601] Kramshoej, H. *IPv6 firewall configuration* July 23, 2006. *inet6.dk — Internet Version 6 in Denmark*, http://www.inet6.dk/firewall.html.

[MIN200601] Minoli, D. *Voice over IPv6*. New York: Elsevier, 2006.

[MON200501] Mohácsi, J. *IPv6 security: Threats and solutions*. NIIF/HUNGARNET, May 11, 2005, National Information Infrastructure Development Institute (NIIF), 1132 Budapest, Victor Hugo u. 18-22. HUNGARY, net-admin@niif.hu.

[REN200701] Renard, K. *Security issues in IPv6*. San Diego, CA: WareOnEarth Communications Inc., 2007.

[TRH200401] Trhulj, Z. IPv6 network security—A practical approach. *6Sense Magazine*, Sep. 6, 2004. Agilent Technologies.

Appendix A: Market Status

In late 2007 the ICANN Security and Stability Advisory Committee (SSAC) undertook a survey of IPv6 support in commercial firewalls [ICA200701]. Because of the importance of the results, we include herewith their results, verbatim:

1. *How broadly is IPv6 transport supported by commercial firewalls?*

   IPv6 transport is not broadly supported by commercial firewalls. On average, less than one in three products support IPv6 transport and security features. Support among the firewall market share leaders improves this figure somewhat.

2. *Is support for IPv6 transport and security services available from commercial firewalls available for all market segments—home and small office, small-to-medium business, large enterprise and service provider networks—or is availability lagging for certain segments?*

Support for IPv6 transport and security services is available from commercial firewalls for all market segments, however, availability of advanced security features is lagging in SOHO and SMB segments and strongest in the LE/SP segment.

3. *Among the security services most commonly used at Internet firewalls to enforce an organization's security policy, which are available when IPv6 transport is used?*

Overall, relatively little support for IPv6 transport and security features exists. However, some form of traffic inspection, event logging, and IPsec are commonly available among products that support IPv6 transport and security services.

4. *Can an organization that uses IPv6 transport enforce a security policy at a firewall that is commensurate to a policy currently supported when IPv4 transport is used?*

Internet firewalls are the most widely employed infrastructure security technology today. With nearly two decades of deployment and evolution, firewalls are also the most mature security technology used in the Internet. They are, however, one of many security technologies commonly used by Internet-enabled and security-aware organizations to mitigate Internet attacks and threats. This survey cannot definitively answer the question, "Can an organization that uses IPv6 transport enforce a security policy at a firewall that is commensurate to a policy currently supported when IPv4 transport is used?" The survey results do suggest that an organization that adopts IPv6 today may not be able duplicate IPv4 security feature and policy support.

Chapter 8

Security Considerations for Migrations/Mixed IPv4-IPv6 Networks

Introduction

This chapter continues and concludes the discussion on IPv6 security that we started in Chapter 4 and takes a look at some of the practical security aspects. Of late the issue of how to affect a "secure transition" is receiving industry attention and preparation is critical for any organization prior to implemented IPv6. Issues related to IPv6 transition security include transition strategies, tunneling approaches, and considerations on the potential abuse of transition mechanisms. There are indications that attackers have been exploiting IPv6 for a number of years; therefore, it is important for network administrators to be aware of these issues. The transition mechanisms generally include:

■ IPv6 over IPv4 tunneling approaches. Encapsulating IPv6 packets within IPv4 headers to carry them over IPv4 routing infrastructures. Two types of tunneling are employed: configured and automatic.
■ Dual IP layer approaches. Providing complete support for both IPv4 and IPv6 in hosts and routers.

8.1 Transition Basics

The current expectations are that IPv6 deployment will be incremental: WAN/Internet services may not be upgraded to support IPv6 on a broad scale until the

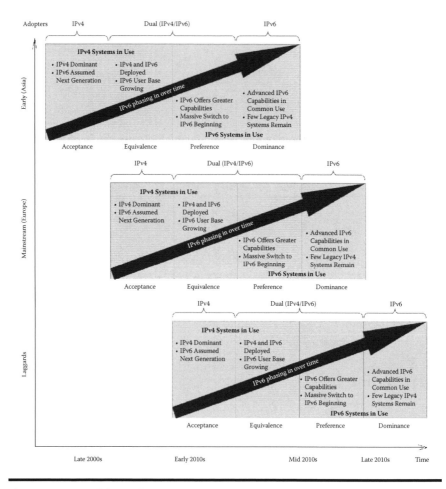

Figure 8.1   Possible evolution scenarios.

early part of the 2010 decade, particularly in North America. Figure 8.1 (inspired by [JUN200801]) depicts a possible description of the environment. This means that IPv4 transport implementations will coexist in various "islands" and organizations will require routers and firewalls that encapsulate (tunnel) packets. Specifically, intranets that use IPv6 transport locally may be unable to connect to other IPv6-enabled networks without traversing an IPv4 network, in an encapsulated fashion. Organizations that adopt IPv6 transport require routers that tunnel IPv6 packets in IPv4 packets to connect to IPV6-enabled destinations when the only available transport is IPv4. On the other hand, if the only available transport between hosts (or networks) is IPv6, then IPv4 packets need to be encapsulated in IPv6 packets to interconnect two or more IPv4-only hosts or networks.

Considerable work documented in a number of RFCs has been undertaken in recent years to develop IPv6 transition strategies and mechanisms to facilitate the migration from IPv4 to IPv6. Examples of proposed approaches include, but are not limited to: SIT/6over4 ("Simple Internet Transition" or "Six In Tunnel"), 6to4 automatic SIT tunnels, and Teredo (IPv6 over UDP). The basic transition approaches include (i) the use of dual stacks in appropriate Network Elements including possibly end systems; (ii) the use of tunneling; and (iii) the use of protocol conversion (translation). There are a number of variants with these basic techniques, but in general, the three categories capture the various approaches. Table 8.1 provides a basic migration glossary [RFC1933]. The security issues are similar for all

Table 8.1   Basic Migration Glossary

IPv4-only node	A host or router that implements only IPv4. An IPv4-only node does not understand IPv6. The installed base of IPv4 hosts and routers existing before the transition begins are IPv4-only nodes.
IPv6/IPv4 node	A host or router that implements both IPv4 and IPv6.
IPv6-only node	A host or router that implements IPv6, and does not implement IPv4. The operation of IPv6-only nodes is not addressed here.
IPv6 node	Any host or router that implements IPv6. IPv6/IPv4 and IPv6-only nodes are both IPv6 nodes.
IPv4 node	Any host or router that implements IPv4. IPv6/IPv4 and IPv4-only nodes are both IPv4 nodes.
IPv4-compatible IPv6 address	An IPv6 address, assigned to an IPv6/IPv4 node, which bears the high-order 96-bit prefix 0:0:0:0:0:0, and an IPv4 address in the low-order 32 bits. IPv4-compatible addresses are used by the automatic tunneling mechanism.
IPv6-only address	The remainder of the IPv6 address space. An IPv6 address that bears a prefix other than 0:0:0:0:0:0.
IPv6-over-IPv4 tunneling	The technique of encapsulating IPv6 packets within IPv4 so that they can be carried across IPv4 routing infrastructures.
IPv6-in-IPv4 encapsulation	IPv6-over-IPv4 tunneling.
Configured tunneling	IPv6-over-IPv4 tunneling where the IPv4 tunnel endpoint address is determined by configuration information on the encapsulating node.
Automatic tunneling	IPv6-over-IPv4 tunneling where the IPv4 tunnel endpoint address is determined from the IPv4 address embedded in the IPv4-compatible destination address of the IPv6 packet.

the transition scenarios, although there are some differences in the specifics. The key objectives in developing a secure transition strategy are:

- Allow IPv6 and IPv4 hosts to interoperate
- Allow IPv6 hosts and routers to be deployed on the Internet in a diffuse and incremental fashion, with few interdependencies
- Make the transition as transparent as possible for end users, applications, and system and network administrators

As already discussed, the following transition strategies have been widely discussed in the industry:

- Encapsulation (tunneling)
  - The Simple Internet Transition (SIT) (RFC 1933)
  - 6over4 (RFC 2529)
  - 6to4 (RFC 3056)
  - Teredo (UDP port 3544). Teredo allows IPv6 connectivity between IPv6/IPv4 nodes that are separated by one or more NATs [For example, on Microsoft systems Teredo is available for Windows Vista, Windows XP with SP2 and later, and Windows Server 2008, among others].
- Dual-Stack Transition Strategy
  - Intra-Site Automatic Tunnel Addressing Protocol (ISATAP) (RFC 4214). Dual-stack nodes use the ISATAP protocol to automatically discover IPv6 routers and tunnel IPv6 packets over an IPv4 infrastructure. ISATAP is a simple mechanism for automatic deployment of IPv6 in enterprise, cellular, and Internet Service Provider (ISP) networks that are IPv4 based.

A network tunnel supports encapsulated connectivity over existing infrastructure to a new infrastructure. Figure 8.2 depicts the general concept of an overlay tunnel. In a tunneling environment, a network protocol (the payload protocol) is encapsulated within a different delivery protocol. Typical motivations for using tunneling include (i) the desire to provide a secure path through an untrusted network (for example a VPN over the Internet), or (ii) the desire to carry a payload (for example IPv6) over an incompatible delivery network (for example IPv4.) Overlay tunneling encapsulates IPv6 packets in IPv4 packets for delivery across an IPv4 infrastructure (a core network or the Internet). A number of the transition strategies identified above can be implemented by using a tunnel broker; a tunnel broker is a service that provides a network tunnel.

By using overlay tunnels, one can communicate with isolated IPv6 networks without upgrading the IPv4 infrastructure between them. Overlay tunnels can be configured between border routers or between a border router and a host; however, both tunnel endpoints must support both the IPv4 and IPv6 protocol stacks. For example, Cisco IOS IPv6 supports the following types of overlay tunneling mechanisms on routers [CIS200601]:

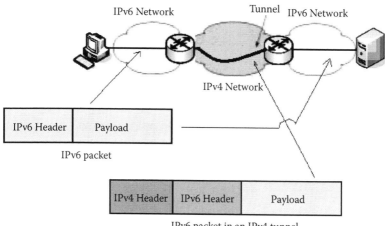

Figure 8.2 Generic concept of tunnel.

- Manual
- Generic routing encapsulation (GRE)
- IPv4-compatible
- 6 to 4
- Intra-Site Automatic Tunnel Addressing Protocol (ISATAP)

More specifically, there are two types of tunnels of interest:

1. Configured tunnels
2. Automatic tunnels

Configured tunnels include *Router-to-router* tunnels and *Host-to-router* tunnels, as shown in the first two diagrams in Figure 8.3. Router-to-router tunnels occur when IPv6/IPv4 routers interconnected via an IPv4 infrastructure are able to tunnel (encapsulate) IPv6 packets across the IPv4 infrastructure. Host-to-router tunnels occur when IPv6/IPv4 hosts can tunnel (encapsulate) IPv6 packets to an intermediary IPv6/IPv4 router interconnected via an IPv4 infrastructure. In both of these cases, the IPv6 packet is tunneled to a router. The termination point of this type of tunnel is a router that must be able to process the IPv6 packet and forward it to its final destination. No relationship exists between the router address and the final destination address, and the router address that is the tunnel's termination must be manually configured. A manually configured tunnel provides a pseudopermanent link between two IPv6 domains over an IPv4 backbone. The primary use is for stable connections that require regular secure communication between two edge routers or between an end system and an edge router, or for connection to remote IPv6 networks. An IPv6 address is manually configured on a tunnel interface, and

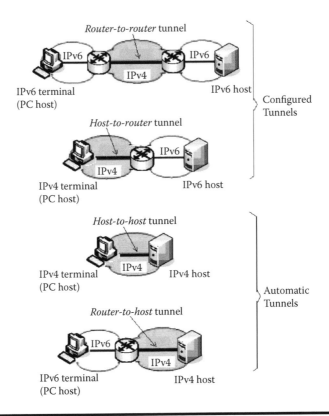

Figure 8.3 **Various types of tunnels.**

manually configured IPv4 addresses are assigned to the tunnel source and the tunnel destination. The host or router at each end of a configured tunnel must support both the IPv4 and IPv6 protocol stacks. Manually configured tunnels can be configured between border routers or between a border router and a host [CIS200601].

Automatic tunnels include *Host-to-host* tunnels and *Router-to-host* tunnels, as shown in the lower two diagrams in Figure 8.3. Host-to-host tunnels occur when IPv6/IPv4 hosts that are interconnected by an IPv4 infrastructure can tunnel (encapsulate) IPv6 packets between themselves. Router-to-host tunnels occur when IPv6/IPv4 routers can use tunnels (encapsulation) to reach an IPv6/IPv4 host via an IPv4 infrastructure. In this case the IPv6/IPv4 packet is tunneled from a host or router to its destination host. Note that the tunnel endpoint address and the destination host address are the same. If the IPv6 address used for the destination node is an IPv4-compatible address, the tunnel endpoint IPv4 address can be automatically derived from the IPv6 address, making manual configurations unnecessary. The automatic tunneling mechanism uses a special type of IPv6 address, termed an "IPv4-compatible" address. An IPv4-compatible address is identified by an all-zeros 96-bit prefix, and holds an IPv4 address in the low-order

```
|              96-bits              |    32-bits   |
+----------------------------------+--------------+
|      0 : 0 : 0 : 0 : 0 : 0       | IPv4 Address |
+----------------------------------+--------------+
```

Figure 8.4   IPv4-compatible IPv6 address format.

32 bits. IPv4-compatible addresses are structured as shown in Figure 8.4. IPv4-compatible addresses are assigned to IPv6/IPv4 nodes that support automatic tunneling. Nodes that are configured with IPv4-compatible addresses may use the complete address as their IPv6 address, and use the embedded IPv4 address as their IPv4 address. The remainder of the IPv6 address space (that is, all addresses with 96-bit prefixes other than 0:0:0:0:0:0) are termed "IPv6-only Addresses" [RFC1933]. Figure 8.5 (courtesy Cisco Systems) summarizes some key information about IPv6 tunnels.

Tunneling approaches can be supported over private infrastructures as well as over public infrastructures. Transition mechanisms can make use of tunnel brokers, thereby making IPv6 immediately available to users. A tunnel broker is a service provider. The term tunnel broker is typically used to refer to an IPv6 tunnel broker, as defined in RFC 3053 (RFC 3053 describes an arrangement where a user can request the establishment of an IPv6 tunnel from a host—called a Point of Presence—which, using the tunnel, then provides the user with IPv6 connectivity.) Tunnel brokers provide IPv6 tunnels to clients across an intervening IPv4 network. These tunnel brokers provide IPv6 tunnels to endusers/endsites using either manual, scripted, or automatic configuration. In most instances, tunnel brokers offer so called protocol 41 tunnels where IPv6 is tunneled directly inside IPv4 by having the protocol field set to 41 (IPv6) in the IPv4 packet. Table 8.2 lists some of the tunnel brokers available at press time. Table 8.3 depicts one example of a tunnel broker. Several tunnel brokers provide tunnel services free of charge to promote the propagation and deployment of IPv6. Tunnel brokers typically provide prefixes for Internet6 (address prefix 2001::/16) (and also for the earlier 6Bone system (address prefix 3ffe::/16)). Some tunnel brokers support single address routing while others provide /64 subnets; some provide entire /48 networks (65,536 subnets) (some brokers require changes to tunnel endpoints performed via their Web interface and do not adapt easily to dynamic address changes of the tunnel endpoints) [WAR200401].

8.2 Security Issues Associated with Transition

Some of the transitioning mechanisms designed to allow for seamless interaction between IPv6 and IPv4 networks can be misused by attackers. Transitioning tools create a way for IPv4 applications to connect to IPv6 services, and IPv6 applications

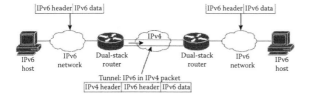

Tunneling Type	Suggested Usage	Usage Notes
Manual	Simple point-to-point tunnels that can be used within a site or between sites	Can carry IPv6 packets only.
GRE- and IPv4-compatible	Simple point-to-point tunnels that can be used within a site or between sites	Can carry IPv6, Connectionless Network Service (CLNS), and many other types of packets.
IPv4-compatible	Point-to-multipoint tunnels	Uses the ::/96 prefix. We do not now recommend using this tunnel type.
6to4	Point-to-multipoint tunnels that can be used to connect isolated IPv6 sites	Sites use addresses from the 2002::/16 prefix.
ISATAP	Point-to-multipoint tunnels that can be used to connect systems within a site	Sites can use any IPv6 unicast addresses.

Tunneling Type	Tunnel Configuration Parameter			
	Tunnel Mode	Tunnel Source	Tunnel Destination	Interface Prefix or Address
Manual	ipv6ip	An IPv4 address, or a reference to an interface on which IPv4 is configured.	An IPv4 address.	An IPv6 address.
GRE/IPv4	gre ip		An IPv4 address.	An IPv6 address.
IPv4-compatible	ipv6ip auto-tunnel		Not required. These are all point-to-multipoint tunneling types. The IPv4 destination address is calculated, on a per-packet basis, from the IPv6 destination.	Not required. The interface address is generated as :tunnel-source/96.
6to4	ipv6ip 6to4			An IPv6 address. The prefix must embed the tunnel source IPv4 address
ISATAP	ipv6ip isatap			An IPv6 prefix in modified eui-64 format. The IPv6 address is generated from the prefix and the tunnel source IPv4 address.

Figure 8.5   Key tunnel concepts. Courtesy of Cisco Systems.

to connect to IPv4 services. With transitioning methods, such as 6to4, SIT tunnels, and IPv6 over UDP (such as Teredo and Shipworm), IPv6 traffic may be coming into networks without their administrators being aware of the fact (and thus, without them being aware that they are vulnerable to IPv6 exploits). For example, since many firewalls allow UDP traffic, IPv6 over UDP can get through those firewalls without administrators realizing what is happening. Attackers can use 6over4 tunnels to evade Intrusion Detection software. It is also important to note that the

Table 8.2   Partial List of Tunnel Brokers Available at Press Time

Provider	Scope	Subnet
Aarnet	Australia	
Hexago/Go6	Canada	/48 subnet
Hurricane Electric	United States, Europe (Germany, UK)	/64 and /48 subnet
IIJ	Japan	
Mytbs	Malaysia	/64 subnet
NECTEC	Thailand	
Singnet	Singapore	
SixXS	United States, Europe (13 countries), New Zealand	/64 tunnel + /48 subnet
SSC IPv6	Norway	/124 subnet
UKERNA	UK	/56 or /64 subnet
XS26	Europe (6 countries)	/48 subnet

Internet Connection Firewall (ICF) that is included with Window Server 2003 was only capable recently of filtering IPv4 traffic, hence it cannot block IPv6 traffic. Attackers can exploit this and get into a firm's network with IPv6 packets if the administrator does not implement other firewall software that has this capability [BRO200801].

Keep in mind that 6to4 tunnels are automatically configured tunnels based on the IPv4 address of the host. This option imposes trivial support from the underlying IPv4 network, specifically simple forwarding of IPv4 datagrams, and no blockage of IP protocol 41 (IPv6 on IPv4, as defined in the SIT protocol). Anyone with an IPv4 address can immediately be on IPv6 using 6to4 auto tunnels with an entire /48 size IPv6 network at their disposal [WAR200401].

Transition mechanisms can be exploited by potential intruders in a number of ways. Enabling IPv6 may open routers to instabilities or inefficiencies. We mentioned earlier in the text that IPv4-compatible addresses used to signal automatic tunneling (::192.168.0.1) can be problematic. IPv4-mapped addresses used to specify IPv4 transport (::FFFF:192.168.0.1) can also be problematic. These are both internal address representations and should never be propagated or found "on the wire." There is a need to filter before translation is done. There are issues associated with tunneling. As we have seen, tunneling makes perimeter defense difficult to enforce. Automatic tunneling accepts packets from "everywhere," therefore

Table 8.3   Illustration of a Tunnel Broker (Web page)

Hurricane Electric Free IPv6 Tunnel Broker

Welcome to the Hurricane Electric IPv6 Tunnel Broker! Our free tunnel broker service enables you to reach the IPv6 Internet by tunneling over existing IPv4 connections from your IPv6 enabled host or router to one of our IPv6 routers. To use this service you need to have an IPv6 capable host (IPv6 support is available for most platforms) or router which also has IPv4 (existing Internet) connectivity. Our tunnel service is oriented towards developers and experimenters that want a stable tunnel platform.
Advantages of using our tunnel service over others include:

■ Run by a Business ISP with 24 x 7 staff at multiple locations and an International backbone
■ Ability to get your own /48 prefix once your tunnel is up
■ Ability to get a full view of the IPv6 BGP4+ routing table
■ Ability to use your tunnel now after a simple registration process. (It takes less than a minute.)
■ Ability to create your tunnel on geographically diverse tunnel-servers (Fremont, CA; New York, NY; London, UK; Frankfurt, Germany)

If you are a new user please register by clicking on Register below. After registering your password will be mailed to you and you can return here to activate your tunnel.
Upon tunnel activation configuration commands for a variety of platforms will be automatically generated. Once you configure your side you will be able to reach the IPv6 Internet.

the network/security administrator should use some access control or firewall functionality.

The following are some recommendations related to security issues associated with transition offered by practitioners [REN200701]:

■ Do not mistakenly configure a back door around firewall (e.g., tunneling)
■ Make sure that VPN policies are not violated
■ Do not let the IPv6 network open attacks on the IPv4 network
    – After decapsulating, enforce address-interface consistency (antispoofing) and firewall rules
    – Requires careful configuration

- Do not provide a hiding place for DoS attacks
  - Including broadcast and reflection varieties
- Do not violate address legitimacy assumptions
  - For example, ingress filtering, use of special addresses, broadcast, multicast

The IPv6 Operations (v6ops) working group in IETF has selected (manually configured) IPv6-in-IPv4 tunneling (as described in RFC 4213) as one of the IPv6 transition mechanisms for IPv6 deployment. When running IPv6-in-IPv4 tunnels (unsecured) over the Internet, it is possible to "inject" packets into the tunnel by spoofing the source address (data plane security), or if the tunnel is signaled somehow (e.g., using authentication protocol and obtaining a static v6 prefix), someone might be able to spoof the signaling (control plane security). The recommended solution is to use IPsec to protect IPv6-in-IPv4 tunneling. The IPsec framework plays an important role in adding security to both the protocol for tunnel setup and data traffic. (Note that RFC 4891 does not address the use of IPsec for tunnels that are not manually configured, for example, 6to4 tunnels defined in RFC 3056; presumably, some form of opportunistic encryption or "better-than-nothing security" might or might not be applicable) [RFC4891].

Transitional IPv6 tunnels should be terminated at or outside the network security perimeter and firewalls, and routed natively through the firewall where appropriate rules and tests can be applied. As we have hinted elsewhere in this text, tunneling protocols represent a significant hole through firewalls lacking rules that can be applied directly against the tunneled payload traffic, and should be blocked from forwarding across security perimeters and across firewalls [WAR200401].

There are indications that "black hats" often have deeper expertise and better tools for the IPv6 space than many "white hats" and security professionals; this fosters a dangerous situation in which IPv6 knowledge becomes increasingly critical over time. The material that follows, taken verbatim from a key paper by M. H. Warfield [WAR200401], provides an excellent recent assessment of the IPv6 situation.

Underground sites now offer IPv6-enabled and IPv6-specific tools such as relay6, 6tunnel, nt6tunnel, asybo, and 6to4DDoS. Relay6, 6tunnel, nt6tunnel, and asybo are protocol bouncers which accept connections on IPv4 or IPv6 and redirect those connections to IPv6 or IPv4. This ability allows IPv4-only applications to connect to IPv6 services and vice versa. While these tools are legitimate, they are easily abused by the underground to create tunnels and redirects for backdoors and trojans. By comparison, 6to4DDoS is a Distributed Denial of Service attack tool specifically designed to attack IPv6 sites and to attack IPv4 sites by using 6to4 tunneling.

Even mainstream sites such as Freshmeat.net offer IPv6 tools such as halfscan6 and netcat6 which are useful to the underground community. These IPv6-enabled versions of established open source security tools are frequently used by defenders and attackers alike. IPv6 patches have been released for many favorite underground trojans, backdoors, and zombies. IRC "bots" or "robots" such as Eggdrop have been adapted to utilized IPv6 IRC sites for command channels. Even without IPv6 patches, protocol bouncers enable IPv6 access to many older tools and exploits.

Backdoor programs can lurk on an IPv6 6to4 interface hidden on a system that otherwise has no IPv6 facility. An IPv6-based backdoor simply configures 6to4 on the compromised system and picks an SLA (Site Local Aggregation — the 16 bit IPv6 sub-net number) and an EUI (End Unit Identifier — the lower 64 bits of the IPv6 6to4 address) and then listens on that specific backdoor address and port. This port does not show up in IPv4 security scans. Even if the host is scanned for IPv6 6to4 access, the scan-ner must determine the exact SLA and EUI in order to begin a scan for the port on that device. To do so successfully is quite an achievement — analogous to guessing an 80-bit key just to get started. This information can be detected by properly configured intrusion detection systems (IDS) monitoring for backdoor traffic. In other words, if administra-tors know to look and know where to look, these backdoors can be detected.

Some operating systems allow applications to listen for IPv6-only traffic and do not require the application to listen to specific addresses to avoid detection through the IPv4 interfaces. Others, such as Linux, deliver IPv4 traffic to IPv6 applications as IPv6 traffic, utilizing IPv6 compatibility addresses (IPv6 addresses which logically equate to IPv4 addresses). On platforms such as Linux, backdoors and trojans attempting to hide from detection by IPv4-based scanners must take the additional measure of only listening on specific IPv6 addresses and not the IPv6 "receive-any" address of "::". This modification is not difficult to do and works equally well on platforms with even stricter isolation between the two protocol stacks.

IPv6 addresses hidden behind an IPv4 interface create a form of stealth barrier to detection by many scanner technologies currently in use. Some forms may be detectable only by sophisticated host-based security scanners or IPv6-aware network IDS. The inherent difficulties in scanning address spaces as large as a /48 IPv6 network with 80 bits of host addressing, make the detection of stealth backdoors via scanning from the external network almost impossible. A fusion of IPv6-aware network scanning and IPv6-aware intrusion detection can alleviate the threat.

The same holds true for "reverse backdoors" — backdoors and trojans that connect outwards from a compromised host. These attack tools do not hide server ports behind 6to4 stealth interfaces but instead hide traffic in SIT tunnels or in UDP-based IPv6 tunnels. Compromised hosts may advertise IPv6 routes and forward IPv6 traffic back through them-selves for an entire network behind firewalls and NAT devices. Even devices on a private address space may become globally visible and routable over IPv6 through Shipworm or Teredo type IPv6 over UDP tunneling, bypassing the NAT devices and firewalls. Evidence already exists that intruders use IPv6 as a screen to avoid detection. Break-ins against "honeypots" reflect clear evidence that the attacker enabled IPv6 over IPv4 to create com-munications tunnels that evade security scanning and IDS detection. Malicious code often contains IPv6-capable components such as 6to4DDoS and other DDoS flood tools.

IPv6 backdoors, Trojan horse programs and assorted malicious code easily evade most IPv6- unaware security or vulnerability scanning programs. These attacks also easily evade most IDS systems that are not IPv6-aware. If an IDS only examines IPv4 traffic and does not support IPv6, either natively or over various tunneling and encapsulation schemes, then an intruder can easily deliver exploits through unsupported tunneling mechanisms.

An IDS must be able to decode IPv6 and IPv4 equally well to detect these exploits and backdoors. The IDS must dig deeper into the packet and analyze a deeper level of the encapsulated traffic to handle either static SIT or 6to4 auto SIT. To handle something like Teredo, the IDS must dig even deeper into UDP than the current practice of un-encapsulating the IPv6 traffic.

SIT

SIT (also know[sic] as 6over4 in IETF RFCs) is the standard for tunneling or encapsulating IPv6 over IPv4. SIT is also supported under GIF (General IP Forwarding) in the BSD operating systems. SIT is listed as IP protocol 41 (ipv6) for assigned IPv4 protocols. If IPv6 is not provided or supported, any form of SIT traffic would be abnormal and indicative of possible malicious traffic. If IPv6 is being provided and supported, SIT traffic and tunnels to and from infrastructure routers and gateways are normal.

6to4

The 2002::/16 prefix was allocated for use by 6to4 automatic SIT tunnels on IPv4 hosts with no external IPv6 support and no static-configured SIT tunnels. 6to4 can be readily configured on supporting systems and used to establish IPv6 based connections between individual IPv4 hosts with no actual IPv6 network present at either end, or anywhere in between. This special category of SIT tunnels uses the SIT protocol with a special purpose IPv6 prefix to autoconfigure the tunnel endpoints.

For 6to4 to communicate with the other two global prefixes, a gateway is required. Standards have defined certain "anycast" addresses on the core IPv4 Internet to provide gateways between 6to4 and the 6bone and Internet6. All three of the global top-level prefixes interoperate and communicate with each other regardless of differences in allocation schemes, management schemes, and routing.

Because the source gateways do not require static configuration of the endpoints, it is possible to direct 6to4 packets at a destination gateway that does not support IPv6 or SIT. This ability opens up the possibility of DDoS attacks against IPv4 hosts from IPv6 networks even where no IPv6 or SIT support exists on the target systems.

Addresses with 2002 in the high order word of the IPv6 address and with a non-local IPv4 address in the next 32 bits are often normal traffic when communicating with remote 6to4 nodes. They do not necessarily indicate malicious activity.

IPv6 and Broadcast Addresses

It is worth noting that IPv6 has no broadcast addresses. The broadcast address functionality has been subsumed into the multicast address groups. Standards prohibit the transmittion[sic] of IPv6 datagrams with multicast addresses in the source address and most multicast addresses are limited in scope. Consequently, security problems created by broadcast address such as directed-broadcast probes and "smurf amplifiers" are eliminated on IPv6.

All of this reinforces the need for network/security administrators to become IPv6 security savvy. In the context of tunneling, practitioners offer the following advice: do not operate completely automated tunnels and avoid "translation" mechanisms between IPv4 and IPv6, use dual stack instead; only authorized systems should be allowed as tunnel endpoints [BER200701]. The goal of this text is to frame some of the issues and to start the thinking process. Because security threats are constantly mutating, the security professional is well aware of the need to daily seek up-to-the-minute information on threats, vulnerabilities, patches, remedies, and so forth. This cannot be done by a textbook, but the text serves as a point of departure of the conversation.

8.3 Threats and the Use of IPsec

This section, based on RFC 4891 [RFC4891], describes security approaches that can be used in transition environments that make use of IPv6-in-IPv4 tunnels. There are security concerns related to address spoofing threats:

1. The IPv4 source address of the encapsulating ("outer") packet can be spoofed. The reason that this threat exists is the lack of universal deployment of IPv4 ingress filtering.
2. The IPv6 source address of the encapsulated ("inner") packet can be spoofed. The reason that threat exists is that the IPv6 packet is encapsulated in IPv4 and hence may escape IPv6 ingress filtering.

RFC 4213 specifies the following strict address checks as mitigating measures:

■ To mitigate threat (1), the decapsulator verifies that the IPv4 source address of the packet is the same as the address of the configured tunnel endpoint. The decapsulator may also implement IPv4 ingress filtering, that is, check whether the packet is received on a legitimate interface.
■ To mitigate threat (2), the decapsulator verifies whether the inner IPv6 address is a valid IPv6 address and also applies IPv6 ingress filtering before accepting the IPv6 packet.

RFC 4891 proposes using IPsec for providing stronger security in preventing these threats and additionally providing integrity, confidentiality, replay protection, and origin protection between tunnel endpoints. IPsec can be used in two ways, in transport and tunnel mode.

IPsec in Transport Mode

In Transport Mode, the IPsec Encapsulating Security Payload (ESP) or Authentication Header (AH) Security Association (SA) is established to protect the traffic defined by (IPv4-source, IPv4-destination, protocol = 41). On receiving such an IPsec packet, the receiver first applies the IPsec transform (e.g., ESP) and then matches the packet against the Security Parameter Index (SPI) and the inbound selectors associated with the SA to verify that the packet is appropriate for the SA via which it was received. A successful verification implies that the packet came from the right IPv4 endpoint, because the SA is bound to the IPv4 source address.

This prevents threat (1) but not threat (2). IPsec in transport mode does not verify the contents of the payload itself where the IPv6 addresses are carried. That is, two nodes using IPsec transport mode to secure the tunnel can spoof the inner payload. The packet will be decapsulated successfully and accepted. This shortcoming can be partially mitigated by IPv6 ingress filtering, that is, check that the packet is arriving from the interface in the direction of the route towards the tunnel endpoint. In most implementations, a transport mode SA is applied to a normal IPv6-in-IPv4 tunnel. Therefore, ingress filtering can be applied in the tunnel interface.

IPsec in Tunnel Mode

In Tunnel Mode, the IPsec SA is established to protect the traffic defined by (IPv6-source, IPv6-destination). On receiving such an IPsec packet, the receiver first applies the IPsec transform (e.g., ESP) and then matches the packet against the SPI and the inbound selectors associated with the SA to verify that the packet is appropriate for the SA via which it was received. The successful verification implies that the packet came from the right endpoint.

The outer IPv4 addresses may be spoofed, and IPsec cannot detect this in tunnel mode; the packets will be demultiplexed based on the SPI and possibly the IPv6 address bound to the SA. Thus, the outer address spoofing is irrelevant as long as the decryption succeeds and the inner IPv6 packet can be verified to have come from the right tunnel endpoint.

Using tunnel mode is more difficult than applying transport mode to a tunnel interface, and as a result RFC 4891 recommends transport mode. Note that even though transport rather than tunnel mode is recommended, an IPv6-in-IPv4 tunnel specified by protocol 41 still exists.

There are three general scenarios:

1. (Generic) router-to-router tunnels.
2. Site-to-router or router-to-site tunnels. These refer to tunnels between a site's IPv6 (border) device and an IPv6 upstream provider's router. A degenerate case of a site is a single host.
3. Host-to-host tunnels.

Router-to-Router Tunnels

IPv6/IPv4 hosts and routers can tunnel IPv6 datagrams over regions of IPv4 forwarding topology by encapsulating them within IPv4 packets. Tunneling can be used in a variety of ways. IPv6/IPv4 routers interconnected by an IPv4 infrastructure can tunnel IPv6 packets between themselves. See Figure 8.6. In this case, the tunnel spans one segment of the end-to-end path that the IPv6 packet takes. The source and destination addresses of the IPv6 packets traversing the tunnel could come from a wide range of IPv6 prefixes, so binding IPv6 addresses to be used to

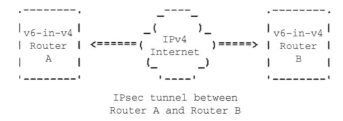

IPsec tunnel between
Router A and Router B

Figure 8.6 Router-to-router scenario.

the SA is not generally feasible. IPv6 ingress filtering must be performed to mitigate the IPv6 address spoofing threat.

Site-to-Router/Router-to-Site Tunnels

This is a generalization of host-to-router and router-to-host tunneling, because the issues when connecting a whole site (using a router) and connecting a single host are roughly equal. See Figure 8.7 and Figure 8.8.

IPv6/IPv4 routers can tunnel IPv6 packets to their final destination IPv6/IPv4 site. This tunnel spans only the last segment of the end-to-end path. In the other direction, IPv6/IPv4 hosts can tunnel IPv6 packets to an intermediary IPv6/IPv4 router that is reachable via an IPv4 infrastructure. This type of tunnel spans the first segment of the packet's end-to-end path. The hosts in the site originate the packets with IPv6 source addresses coming from a well-known prefix, whereas the destination addresses could be any nodes on the Internet.

In this case, an IPsec tunnel mode SA could be bound to the prefix that was allocated to the router at Site B, and Router A could verify that the source address of the packet matches the prefix. Site B will not be able to do a similar verification for the packets it receives. This may be quite reasonable for most of the deployment cases; for example, an ISP allocating a /48 to a customer. The Customer Premises Equipment (CPE) where the tunnel is terminated "trusts" (in a weak sense) the ISP's router, and the ISP's router can verify that Site B is the only one that can originate packets within the /48.

IPv6 spoofing must be prevented, and setting up ingress filtering may require some amount of manual configuration.

Host-to-Host Tunnels

IPv6/IPv4 hosts interconnected by an IPv4 infrastructure can tunnel IPv6 packets between themselves (see Figure 8.9). In this case, the tunnel spans the entire end-to-end path. In this case, the source and the destination IPv6 addresses are known a priori. A tunnel mode SA could be bound to these specific addresses. Address verification prevents IPv6 source address spoofing completely.

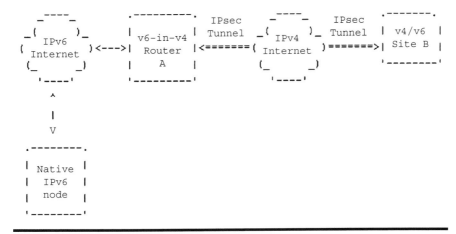

Figure 8.7   Router-to-site scenario.

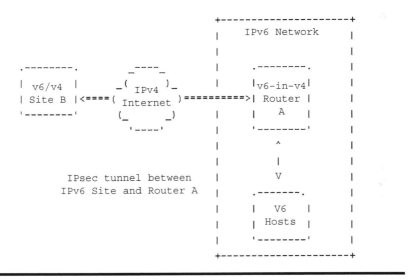

Figure 8.8   Site-to-router scenario.

Figure 8.9   Host-to-host scenario.

8.4 NATs, Packet Filtering, and Teredo

As we have seen earlier,* NAT allows multiple computers that use private IPv4 addresses on a private network (e.g., "10," "192.168," or "172.16" through "172.31") to share a single public IPv4 address and to communicate with the Internet. NATs are typically implemented in routers. NATs translate addresses and ports for the traffic that they forward. See Figure 8.10. At the same time, NATs provide simple packet filtering for private network hosts: the NAT will discard all incoming traffic from the Internet that is not locally destined and does not correspond to a NAT translation table entry. NAT translation table entries are created dynamically when private network hosts initiate traffic; one can also manually configure static NAT translation table entries to allow unsolicited incoming traffic (for example, when one wants to allow traffic to a Web server that is located on the private network). Typical NATs only allow configuration based on opening a port, allowing all traffic addressed to that port to be forwarded to the private network. Static NAT translation table entries do not time out. Table 8.4 depicts typical Cisco System commands for NAT functionality on a router.

Teredo enables connectivity for IPv6-based applications by providing globally unique IPv6 addressing and by allowing IPv6 traffic to traverse NATs. With Teredo, IPv6-enabled applications that require unsolicited incoming traffic and global addressing, such as peer-to-peer applications, will work over a NAT (these same types of applications, if they used IPv4 traffic, either would require manual configuration

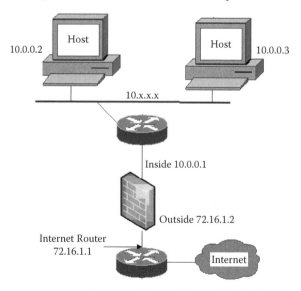

Figure 8.10   Simple example of NATing.

---

* This subsection is based on reference [MIC200801].

Table 8.4   Typical Cisco System NAT Functionality/Commands

Command	Action
ip nat inside source	■ Translates the source of IP packets that are traveling inside to outside. ■ Translates the destination of the IP packets that are traveling outside to inside.
ip nat outside source	■ Translates the source of the IP packets that are traveling outside to inside. ■ Translates the destination of the IP packets that are traveling inside to outside.

of the NAT or would not work at all without modifying the network application protocol). Teredo works across NATs because Teredo clients create dynamic NAT translation table entries for their own Teredo traffic. Once these entries are created, the NAT forwards incoming Teredo traffic to the host that created the matching NAT translation table entry. The NAT will not forward Teredo traffic to computers on the private network that are not Teredo clients. Therefore, if only one computer on a private network is a Teredo client, the NAT will only forward Teredo traffic from the Internet that is for that Teredo client. Teredo does not change the behavior of NATs. All types of IPv6-enabled applications can work with Teredo and require no additional modification for Teredo support.

To restore end-to-end connectivity for IPv6 traffic, Teredo traffic treats the NAT as a simple IP router that is not providing a packet-filtering function. To provide protection against unwanted, unsolicited, incoming IPv6 traffic, private network hosts must use a host-based stateful firewall that supports IPv6 traffic, such as Windows Firewall on XP SP2, that drops all unwanted, unsolicited, incoming IPv6 traffic. It is important to note that most organizations have yet to implement host-based firewalls on all desktop systems and servers, based on the increased complexity and overhead. The combination of IPv6, Teredo, and a host-based stateful IPv6 firewall does not affect the packet-filtering function of the NAT for IPv4-based traffic and does not make a Windows-based computer more susceptible to attacks by malicious users and programs that use IPv6 traffic, rather than IPv4 traffic. During start-up a Windows-based computer using Teredo sends some Teredo traffic to automatically configure a global Teredo IPv6 address; however, no unsolicited, incoming, IPv6 traffic is allowed unless it matches a configured host-based firewall exception.

Treating the NAT as a simple IP router makes configuration of wanted, unsolicited, incoming traffic easier. Without IPv6 and Teredo, one would have to configure the following:

■ An exception for the host-based firewall
■ A static NAT translation table entry

With IPv6 and Teredo, one no longer has to configure the static NAT translation table entry. If the IPv6-enabled application can create dynamic port or program exceptions with Windows Firewall, a user does not have to perform any configuration to allow their traffic to be forwarded by the NAT. Because most NATs only allow configuration of unsolicited incoming traffic for a port number (rather than configuring the incoming traffic for a specific port and IPv4 address), the combination of IPv6, Teredo, and the Windows Firewall with program or port-based exceptions is more secure because it only allows traffic to a specific port and IPv6 address on the Teredo-enabled computer.

8.5 Use of Host-Based Firewalls

Host-Based Firewalls (also referred to as personal firewalls) have much of the same functionality as discussed previously with network firewalls. The major difference is that host-based firewalls are not aimed at implementing a security policy at the perimeter, but are intended for a host or endpoint. As a result, it is only possible for a host-based firewall to provide protection for the endpoint where it is installed.

Even though it was widely agreed that most attacks (roughly 70%–80%) originate from the inside of an organization, firewalls continued to be deployed only at perimeter points for a number of years in the recent past. More recently firewalls have been implemented, as discussed previously, only inside corporate intranets but they still only provided segmentation and security at a subnet level. If an attacker could gain access past an organization's perimeter firewall, there would be numerous attack vectors because most assets, and specifically desktops, were wide open. Personal firewalls made their way into the mainstream market in the late 1990s, and even though companies such as Check Point Software Technologies Ltd targeted organizations for deployment [FRA199901], host-based firewalls did not immediately take off as expected, but rather became popular with home users that had always-on Internet connections. During the 1990s and early 2000s most organizations relied on the security that was provided at the perimeter and did not see the need for endpoint security as it increased complexity and cost.

In October 2001, Windows XP shipped with a personal firewall called the Internet Connection Wizard built into the operating system; however, it was not enabled by default. It provided rudimentary filtering of incoming packets and was initially aimed just to cloak a machine from attackers. The firewall was designed so that it would prompt a user to launch the firewall in situations where there might be risk. It was a step in the right direction of implementing endpoint security but compared to other personal firewall products such as ZoneAlarm (now a Check Point company) and Norton Personal Firewall, Microsoft's built in firewall lacked sufficient functionality and failed to block suspicious outbound traffic [SAL200101].

At press time, a list of personal firewall products on the market was extensive, and included the following:

■ ZoneAlarm Pro
■ Kaspersky Internet Security
■ Norton Internet Security 2008
■ AVG Internet Security

Just as with the perimeter firewall products, host-based firewalls have evolved to protect an endpoint against numerous threats including:

■ AntiSpyware
■ Anti-virus protection
■ Network filtering (firewall capabilities)
■ Intrusion Detection and Prevention
■ Logging and monitoring

Many organizations still have not implemented host-based firewalls at this point due to a false sense of security with their perimeter firewalls. In addition, organizations are also reluctant due to the potential for increased complexity of the network and cost of management. However, with IPv6, much of the perimeter-based security that organizations have implemented and rely on may not be in the proper position to provide adequate security. It will be critical that organizations evaluate the use of host-based firewalls to provide controls prior to the transition to IPv6.

Organizations should look to implement more of a distributed security model through the use of host-based firewalls. In order to provide maximum security while embracing the new capabilities provided by IPv6, security administrators will need to create security policies based on assets for specific applications rather than having a single perimeter point of control with a generic security policy. Taking advantage of IPv6, an organization will be able to identify and define specific levels of trust and implement appropriate levels of security based on the end-to-end model. This granularity will provide much greater levels of security but will only be successfully implemented with a properly managed host-based firewall architecture that is distributed through the organization but able to be controlled by security administrators from a central point [ABI200701].

Host-based firewalling on all private hosts (desktops, servers, etc.) is highly recommended to prevent the spread of viruses and other malware. A virus or worm that relies on unsolicited incoming traffic typically cannot penetrate a NAT or edge firewall to attack the hosts of a private network; therefore, virus and worm creators package their malware in the form of Trojan horses that are transmitted through file downloads, e-mail attachments, or Web pages. In all of these cases, the Trojan horse bypasses the edge device because it is solicited traffic. After a private host is infected, the virus or worm will then attempt to infect the other computers on the private network. Therefore, it is recommended that administrators enable host-based stateful firewalls on all the firm's private intranet hosts. As an example, Windows Vista, Windows XP with SP2 and later, Windows Server 2008, and Windows Server 2003 with SP1 and later include Windows Firewall, a host-based stateful firewall that supports both IPv4 and IPv6 traffic. Windows Firewall is enabled by default for Windows Vista, Windows XP with SP2 and later, and Windows Server 2008 [MIC200801].

8.6 Use of Distributed Firewalls

The concept of distributed firewalls has been advanced of late to implement hybrid security models. The distributed firewall model consists of managed host-based firewalls in conjunction with conventional perimeter firewalls. The addition of managed host-based firewall security adds "defense in depth" to an enterprise's security architecture and reduces reliance on a single "chokepoint" perimeter security network design. The concept of distributed firewalls is well suited to an IPv6 environment, and there is some expectation that this approach may become reasonably well deployed in the future in IPv6 intranets.

Classical firewall systems typically perform all security screening through a common checkpoint. The performance of a single checkpoint approach is increasingly degraded as broadband traffic increases over time, new network protocols are added, and as end-to-end networking and encrypted tunneling become more common. With most netcentric enterprises investing in enhanced IT performance, a network-based firewall model may have drawbacks. In emerging security architectures, more coordination will be established between network and host-based firewalls. Distributed security endpoints consisting of host-resident firewalls, intrusion detection, security patching, and security status monitoring can be accomplished by kernel-mode processes within an operating system. These host-based security checkpoints would be managed by a central system used to distribute and monitor security policies and updates. A managed, distributed, host-based firewall system utilizing end-to-end IPsec can implement separate multilevel security policies with fine granularity. Using this end-to-end model, it is possible to divide users and servers into various trust groups and interest communities to implement separate security rules. Applications and services that are used exclusively in one community may be blocked in other communities. This simplifies the screening rules (and exceptions) at a perimeter firewall and may prevent a breach in one network area from spilling into other network segments. If and when a breach occurs, containment of that breach is more easily managed. An additional benefit is that an incorrectly implemented security policy in one area (or at the perimeter) does not necessarily compromise the entire system [KAE200601].

References

[ABI200701] Abidah Hj Mat Taib. *IPv6 transition: Why a new security mechanisms model is necessary?* Aug. 2007. Asia Pacific Advanced (APAN).

[BER200701] Bereski, P., S. Muyal, and B. Tuy. *IPv6 security*. Mar. 28–30, 2007, 6DISS Project. www.6diss.org.

[BRO200801] BroadbandReports.com, dslreports.com. *Does IPv6 introduce new security vulnerabilities?* New York: Silver Matrix LLC, Feb. 15, 2008. http://www.broadban dreports.com/faq/ipvsix/4.0_IPv6_Security.

[CIS200601] Cisco Systems. Implementing Tunneling for IPv6, *IOS IPv6 Configuration Guide, Release 12.4*, San Jose, CA: Cisco Systems, May 1, 2006.

[FRA199901] Frank, Diane. *Check point secures net from within*. August 1999. http://www.fcw.com/print/5_166/news/68343-1.html.

[JUN200801] Juniper Networks. An IPv6 security guide for U.S. government agencies: Executive summary, *The IPv6 World Report Series* 4, Feb. 2008, Sunnyvale, CA. www.juniper.net.

[KAE200601] Kaeo, M., D. Green, J. Bound and Y. Pouffary. IPv6 security technology paper, *North American IPv6 Task Force (NAv6TF) Technology Report*, July 22, 2006.

[MAR200801] Marsan, C. D. Carriers quietly developing IPv6 services, *NetworkWorld*, Apr. 2, 2008.

[MAU200801] matousec.com. *Firewall challenge*. Apr. 4, 2008. http://www.matousec.com/projects/firewall-challenge/results.php#firewalls-ratings, http://www.matousec.com/projects/firewall-challenge/product-list.php

[MIC200801] Microsoft. *Using IPv6 and Teredo*. Microsoft TechNet. http://www.microsoft.com/technet/network/ipv6/ipv6_teredo.mspx.

[REN200701] Renard, K. *Security issues in IPv6*. San Diego, CA: WareOnEarth Communications Inc., 2007.

[RFC1933] Gilligan, R., and E. Nordmark. Request for Comments: 1933, Transition Mechanisms for IPv6 Hosts and Routers, RFC 1933, Apr. 1996.

[RFC4891] Graveman, R., M. Parthasarathy, P. Savola, and H. Tschofenig Request for Comments: 4891, Using IPsec to Secure IPv6-in-IPv4 Tunnels, RFC 4891, May 2007.

[SAL200101] Salkever, Alex. Windows XP: A firewall for all, *Business Week*, June, 2001. http://www.businessweek.com/bwdaily/dnflash/jun2001/nf20010612_227.htm.

[WAR200401] Warfield, M. H. *Security implications of IPv6*. X-Force, Internet Security Systems, Inc. (ISS), 16th Annual FIRST Conference on Computer Security Incident Handling, June 13–18, 2004, Budapest, Hungary. www.iss.net, http://www.first.org/conference/2004/papers/c06.pdf.

Index

Printed and bound by CPI Group (UK) Ltd, Croydon, CR0 4YY

23/10/2024

01777670-0010